1 MONTH OF
FREE
READING

at
www.ForgottenBooks.com

By purchasing this book you are eligible for one month membership to ForgottenBooks.com, giving you unlimited access to our entire collection of over 1,000,000 titles via our web site and mobile apps.

To claim your free month visit:
www.forgottenbooks.com/free559240

ISBN 978-0-331-77470-2
PIBN 10559240

This book is a reproduction of an important historical work. Forgotten Books uses
state-of-the-art technology to digitally reconstruct the work, preserving the original format
whilst repairing imperfections present in the aged copy. In rare cases, an imperfection in
the original, such as a blemish or missing page, may be replicated in our edition. We do,
however, repair the vast majority of imperfections successfully; any imperfections that
remain are intentionally left to preserve the state of such historical works.

FAITH WORK

UNDER DR. CULLIS,

IN BOSTON.

CONSUMPTIVES' HOME.
CHILDREN'S HOME.
DEACONESSES' HOME.
GROVE HALL CHAPEL.
WILLARD TRACT REPOSITORY.

TIMES OF REFRESHING. A MONTHLY PAPER FOR CHRISTIANS.

LOVING WORDS. A MONTHLY PAPER FOR CHILDREN.

THE WORD OF LIFE. A MONTHLY PAPER FOR THE PEOPLE.

Also soon to be commenced, toward each of which considerable contributions have been received,

A CANCER HOME,

AND

A CHAPEL AND TRAINING–COLLEGE

FOR CHRISTIAN WORKERS.

CONSUMPTIVES' HOME, GROVE HALL, BOSTON HIGHLANDS.

AITH WORK

UNDER DR. CULLIS,

BOSTON.

BY

REV. W. E. BOARDMAN,

DNESS IN JESUS," "THE HIGHER CHRISTIAN LIFE," "IN THE POWER
OF THE SPIRIT," "HE THAT OVERCOMETH," ETC., ETC.

ORPHELINES' HOME, GROTE EYL.

FAITH WORK

UNDER DR. CULLIS,

IN BOSTON.

BY
REV. W. E. BOARDMAN,

AUTHOR OF "GLADNESS IN JESUS," "THE HIGHER CHRISTIAN LIFE," "IN THE POWER
OF THE SPIRIT," "HE THAT OVERCOMETH," ETC., ETC.

BOSTON:
WILLARD TRACT REPOSITORY.
1874.

Ascription.

———◆———

Unto Him
who hath wrought
all our works in us ; who
is able to ·do exceeding abundantly
above all we can ask or think, according to
the power that worketh in us ; unto
Him be glory by the Church,
throughout all ages, world
without end.
Amen.

CONTENTS.

HISTORY OF THE FAITH WORK.

I.

FACTS.

1. ALL means for the work have been freely given.

2. Not a dollar has been solicited of any one but the Lord.

3. No debts have been made for current expenses.

4. Daily supplies have been asked of the Lord and received.

5. Doctor Cullis first gave himself to the Lord in the work.

6. His lucrative practice as a physician he gave with himself.

7. All the proceeds of his professional services, over and above expenses, he has devoted to the work, and has asked of the Lord whatever further supplies have been required.

8. The real estate necessary for the work has been purchased, in part on time, secured by mortgage.

9. The value of the property has greatly increased.

10. All is secured to the work in case of the death of Doctor Cullis, conveyed in trust to a legal corporate body consisting of seven substantial citizens.

11. The most perfect liberty is secured to Doctor

Cullis in the work, in sole dependence on the Lord for guidance during his life-time, by a life lease of all the property given back to him by the trustees.

12. During the year 1871 the work was removed from Willard Street.

13. The Tract Repository has been opened at 12 West Street, in a business centre of the city, where also are published " The Times of Refreshing," " Loving Words," and " The Word of Life."

14. The Homes for Consumptives, for Children, and for Deaconesses, are now established on Boston Highlands, on the Grove Hall estate purchased for the purpose, including eleven acres of ground.

15. A Chapel has been nicely fitted up in the Consumptives' Home, specially for the patients, yet open to all.

16. Another Chapel has been opened outside on the grounds for the benefit of the public generally.

17. It is intended to erect a suitable building, also on the grounds, for the Cancer Home, as soon as the Lord wills.

18. Also other Cottage Homes for children — the first being full and many turned away for want of room.

19. It is in contemplation to buy or build a chapel and house in the city — contributions to a considerable amount having been received for the purpose — as a Faith Chapel and Training-College for Christian Workers.

20. The Lord graciously and wonderfully supplied, during the seventh and eighth years of the work, considerably more than had been received in all the six years before, thus meeting the necessities of the work growing out of its removal to new and enlarged quarters.

21. Each Annual Report has contained, immediately after the title-page, the following, which still remains true.

STATEMENT.

In reply to frequent questions, the fact, which is well known to those most intimately acquainted with the " Home," ought perhaps to be publicly stated, that

There is no fund, endowment, or known pecuniary provision whatever existing for the support of the Home; no human friend of it who has ever made any promise, express or implied, to preserve it or relieve its necessities; and no person in any way connected with Doctor Cullis, who has the control of means sufficient to do more than render small contributions towards its maintenance.

22. It is necessary to add that the report, believed by many to be true, that Mrs. Cullis has a fortune of her own, out of which she supports their family, and is able to relieve her husband in any emergency in the work, is entirely without foundation.

Mrs. Cullis has no fortune. She has a small income enabling her to clothe herself and to give something to the cause of the Lord; this is all, she has nothing more. This fact is given lest the report should detract from the glory of the Lord in his faithfulness to faith in his promises.

II.

GREETING AT THE HOME.

FEW, comparatively, of those who will read this account of the work under Doctor Cullis, have seen it for themselves. A visit in imagination may be better than none at all. For this reason those who choose to follow, are invited to put themselves under such guidance as I can give them for such a visit.

We meet then, beloved, you and I, as reader and editor of this marvelous history, in one of the most wonderful places of modern times. It is one of the two, soon to be three, centres of the work we are about to trace from its little beginnings onward to its present development. A good look at it, with all its appointments, may enable us to carry the picture of it with us as we go, and help us to appreciate the work from its starting point in the purpose of him to whom it and the glory of it all belongs.

As the choice of the place, the plan of the buildings and grounds, and everything about it, has been the Lord's own, for the benefit of his own loved poor, we should expect it to be beautiful, right, and good, and so it is.

The position is elevated, commanding, and convenient. Although as the crow flies, it is about five miles south from Beacon Hill and Boston Common, it is yet within the lines of Boston, and under its municipal protection. Two lines of horse-cars connect it with

the centre, either of which takes one up at the open
gateway of the grounds to be set down for a few
pennies on Tremont Street, not far from the famous
Old Park Street Church, or wherever one chooses
along the line.

THE VIEW,

taken all in all, is magnificent. The blue hills of
Milton beyond Dorchester, which is near at hand, are
seen on the south. Jamaica Plains and Brookline
on the west, are hidden by intervening woodlands.
Stretching away northward lies the city with its
countless buildings and numerous spires; the State
House in the centre, Cambridge beyond, Bunker Hill
and the Harbor at the right. Eastward roll the
tides of Massachusetts Bay, studded with islands, and
dotted with the white wings and whiter breath of
commerce. A rare expanse is embraced in the view,
especially from the tower of the Home, and it catches
healthful breezes for the sufferers, to feed in them the
flame of the smoking flax.

Ample room is afforded on the grounds for buildings, lawns, gardens, roadways, and walks. By com-
pass and chain the measurement is eleven acres, form-
ing an unequal sided triangle. The apex, pointing
northward, wedges open the principal thoroughfare,
south from State Street to Dorchester, and separates
it into two, one of which skirts the western side of
the grounds, and the other the eastern. Not far from
the north point of the triangle on the east side, is the
gateway of a drive, over-arched by grand old elms
planted by a generation that had not the remotest
idea of the hallowed use for which the Lord intended
the way and the place. This drive forms a crescent
with its centre under the porch of the Home, and its

other terminus near the south end of the eastern line
of the grounds.

Standing on the lawn within the half-moon encircled
by the carriage-way, facing westward, we have before
us in the centre foreground, the Consumptives' Home.
At the left, a little receding, the assistant's cottage.
Beyond that the house which shelters the handsome
and commodious semi-omnibus like coach, a gift of
one in whose heart it was conceived for the benefit of
those in the Home strong enough to ride, and under
the same roof the stable which is to cover the horse,
when it comes, for the coach. Farther away in the
same direction stands the Children's Cottage Home ;
the first and only one yet erected, of a cluster which
faith is on the out-look to see built in the future. At
the right stands Grove Hall Chapel, fronting the street
which skirts the west side of the lot, with its front
entrance inviting all comers from without, and its side
entrance open to all within the grounds.

THE CONSUMPTIVES' HOME,

which for the time being is also the Deaconesses'
Home, immediately before us in the centre, is im-
posing, symmetrical, beautiful : four stories high, with
a tower and wings ; modern in style and cheerful in
aspect. The one thing of all others which rivets attention is the inscription in letters of gold upon the
marble tablet over the porch,

" HAVE FAITH IN GOD."

Well may it be in letters of gold, large and distinct,
for it tells us the secret of the story in its beginnings,
and in every stage of its progress to which we are
coming. As upon Hannah's noble son, so here, the

name of Samuel — asked of God — might be truthfully put upon every one of this remarkable set of buildings, in their existence and in the plan and structure of every room and every appointment, and upon the ground upon which they stand, and upon every one of the seven houses in the old Willard Street tenting-place of the work, and on every good thing about them, and upon the burial places of the dead, and upon the living souls in glory of the departed. Faith, faith, faith, — by faith the thing was conceived; by faith it has been realized in every particular; by faith the poor, homeless, hopeless ones, have been sheltered, fed, comforted, instructed; by faith they have been saved; some to glorify God on earth, and others in heaven. All has come as the gift of God's grace, and each thing by itself has been asked of God and received. Buildings and grounds are a perpetual monument of God's loving faithfulness to his exceeding great and precious promises, and are a perpetual proclamation, in their very existence, to every one who passes by, and to all who read about them, of our Saviour's words inscribed on the front of the Home, " Have Faith in God."

The picture outside is lovely; let us enter within. Passing under the porch, we are ushered through the front door into a reception-room, octagon-shaped, large, airy, light, and cheery. On the right, opens out a door into the office. On the left a corresponding door opens into the library and reading-room, so comfortable that it must add a charm to the pastime and profit of those who frequent it, free to all. Back of this, adjoining it on the south side, is a delightful parlor, neat and cozy as one could wish. From the rear of the reception-room, opposite the front door, opens out a broad passageway through the building, separated into sections by a number of folding doors, each having an oval glass panel. These occupy the first floor in front, whilst in rear are the dining-room, kitchen, laundry, and other rooms for domestic purposes, all wonderfully complete and convenient in place and appointments. In rear of all and underground, essential to all, is the boiler-room from whence the rooms of the Home are kept, by means of steam apparatus, delightful in temperature, day and night, in the coldest of weather; and from which also Grove Hall Chapel at a distance on one side, and the assistant's residence on the other, are warmed in like manner, by means of steam conveyed underground through pipes.

This completes our imperfect survey of the first floor. Come with me now to where the central and side passageways intersect, and ascend with me the broad central staircase. At the top we land near the door of the chapel. Passing through the rooms, we find them neatly and comfortably furnished, though free from all extravagance, well lighted and ventilated, and all having bath-rooms and every convenience in abundance, easily accessible. We cannot fail, as we pass, to observe the cheeriness of the invalids, and the kindliness of tone and manner, and freedom from peevishness and murmuring, and fret and worry, in all. Returning now and entering

THE HOME CHAPEL,

do you notice its singular structure? The floor, you see, is that of the second story, and the gallery is on a level with the third story. All the rooms on each side on both floors open directly into the chapel, so

that those who are able to walk have only a few
steps to take to the comfortable settees in the chapel,
while through the doors left open, the voice of worship,
whether in reading or speaking, prayer or song, pene-
trates and is heard by those too weak to leave their
beds. And happily there is in the worship so much
of faith and love, peace and joy, that it is sought
by all in the house and serves to cheer and sustain,
instead of crushing and depressing them. Precious
place! Blessed room! O how many burdens have
here been laid off on the great Burden-bearer! O
how many blind ones have had sight given them!
How many have been set free in this sweet Home
Chapel and that in the Willard Street Home, its
forerunner! Do you observe the windows? Perhaps
you wonder that splendid stained glass windows,
beautiful in design and in colors, should be found
here, and ask why was not the money they cost
put to other use? They cost nothing. Each one
was a gift unsolicited. Do you see how appropriate the several designs? They cost no thought.
They were designed as they were given, freely.
Plainly we see that the Lord loves to give his loved
ones, his suffering poor, confined within walls, not
only the comforts of a blessed Christian home, but
the beauties of rare things to enjoy. He sends them
flowers and fruits which would not be bought with
money given for general purposes, *the rarest in their
season.* So also he has provided this lovely place
of his worship for them. And what is more, he
makes this place of his feet, glorious. If the cloud
of his glory shines through all the house, here is the
shekinah of his presence. Here are the evident tokens of his overshadowing wings. Here is the secret

place of his pavilion. Here he breathes peace in power. Here he writes love in the heart, and fills the soul with glory, and with God. Such scenes as here often occur have their record on high, and though unpublished, they live in the hearts and lives of those who are privileged to be in them. For example : in this place, one precious Sabbath morning, it was in the usual

FELLOWSHIP MEETING,

when all are free to speak, first one, then another, testified of the wonders of grace recently shown them while in attendance at the Sea Cliff Grove national meeting. Doctor Cullis leading, heard them with delight, and in heart said, " O that all could have been there and received like precious blessings!'" Then instantly reflecting, he said in heart again, " All may be blessed here as truly and deeply as there. Why not?" So he told them what had passed in his mind, and in few warm and encouraging words put the question to all present, whether they would like to be so filled with the Spirit, and asked them if so to express it by raising the hand. He thought all raised their hands. To make sure he asked all who desired it to rise, and instantly every one in the room rose, Catholics and Protestants side by side, those who had, and those who never before had confessed Christ, and when they were seated, the Doctor proposed prayer in faith, for the fulfillment of this universally expressed desire. They all bowed together. Several short prayers went up, one after another, in the fervor and confidence which asks *and* receives, and they arose and dispersed. Many testified to signal blessings upon them in that precious scene, amongst others an Irish Catholic boy who said the Lord had forgiven him and saved him. And who would dare to say that the blessing was not, like the expressed desire, all embracing?

And now beloved, from this hallowed place we will go forth and trace together the history of the work here represented, as the Lord may guide us, from its hidden implantation in germ from the mind of God into the mind of his servant; yes, and before that, in the preparations for it before ever it entered the heart of his servant, down to its present status.

From time to time, in snatches as opportunity served, sometimes in this beautiful and hallowed chapel of the Home, and sometimes in his own family home, but still more frequently as we have utilized the moments while riding together from one to the other, and from house to house as he went on his professional visits, Doctor Cullis has related to me the principal events in his life, in preparation for the work, a preparation which he understood not, for a work he never dreamed of, until the Lord's own time came for unfolding it to him. To withhold this remarkable chain of events would be to rob God of the glory of his wisdom and goodness in it all, and suppress much of the instruction which should be derived from the history as a whole. I shall therefore give it as well as I can. Of course the language of the Doctor could not be exactly remembered. I shall feel free to put such words and illustrations into his mouth as will convey the truth as he has given it; and to insure the essential faithfulness of the narrative, it will be submitted to him for correction before it goes to the public.

This verbal account as given by the Doctor, will embrace several distinct stages of preparation for the work, which will be embodied in as many different chapters.

III.

EARLY DISCIPLINE.

"Now no chastening for the present seemeth to be joyous, but grievous: nevertheless, afterward it yieldeth the peaceable fruit of righteousness to them which are exercised thereby." — HEBREWS xii. 11.

THE concluding words of Doctor Cullis in one of our conversations, impressed me profoundly. He had been telling me of sickness and suffering through all his years from infancy up to manhood, and of crosses and disappointments, bereavement and loneliness, heart-heaviness and of death to all the world has to offer, whether in pleasure, gain, or fame, while as yet he knew almost absolutely nothing of the joy, the delight, the glory of living by faith in the living present Saviour, insomuch that the settled and constant desire of his soul for many, many weary months, was to die and go away from the earth ; and then in tones of deepest sincerity he added : —

" By the grace of God I am what I am, and I praise the Lord for every step of the way in which he has led me ; for every loss and cross, sorrow and trial; for every circumstance of my life, because by it all, he has brought me where I can trust him, obey him, and be used by him."

How in this instance the fact stated by the Apostle Paul in the eighth of Romans, that " all things work together for good to them that love God, called according to his purpose," is confirmed ! Whether we shall see it or not, as step by step we follow the

Doctor in his recollections of early life, he sees and accepts it as blessedly true.

His account is this : —

"I was born in Boston on the 7th day of March, 1833.

"The only recollections of childhood are those of being carried up and down stairs, in the arms of one and another, and doctored and cared for as a sick child.

"During my boyhood, I was sent to school, but was too miserable in health to enjoy play, much less study, and finally I broke down completely and was taken out of school and put to business in the hope that my health would be benefited by the change.

"I was sent also to Sunday-school, and then the task work of committing to memory things I did not understand and had no relish for, disgusted me and made me determine to leave and have done with it as soon as I should be free to do so. And I did so.

"Once while bathing with a school-fellow I was drowned — so far as to lose consciousness. O what a moment was that ! In that breath of time every event of my life passed in review before me, then all things turned green and I was gone.

"At sixteen I entered a dry goods store in Boston to learn the business and continued in it three years, not having the slightest thought that the Lord had anything to do with it, never dreaming that it was my apprenticeship in the knowledge of men and affairs for another sort of business altogether. And when at nineteen my health gave way again and compelled me to abandon my situation, I was equally unaware that this was the Lord's way of leading me to accept another opening of a totally different kind, yet just as necessary to the training required for the work designed for me. The knowledge of business and of men gained in those three years is now of the greatest advantage to the work.

"My health failed. I lost my voice entirely and could speak only in a whisper. I was thrown out of place by this, but I had no thought of giving up forever mercantile life. I expected simply to rest and grow strong and then return and live and die a business man, but God had another life for me and therefore though I rested I did not grow strong, nor did I recover my voice, so I could not return to business. During the days of my rest I read many books. Those which pleased me most were not trashy but improving, not sensational but instructive. The British poets were my delight. I knew nothing of religious books then. Doctor Johnson I devoured. Boswell's " Life of Johnson" was a feast to me.

" One day a physician of my acquaintance kindly invited me to ride with him in his rounds to see his patients, from day to day, for the benefit of my health, and offered me the freedom of his office and books. I accepted and was greatly profited. Soon he proposed to me the study of medicine. I declined. The profession had no attractions for me, neither had I money to carry me through the course of study. Finally he proposed to supply me and see me through. I reflected that I had nothing else to do, and thought I might as well read for improvement, at least until I could return to business; so I began reading under his guidance. Here, again, was the hidden hand of a gracious leadership opening the way to knowledge and a profession indispensable to my preparation for that of which I was then wholly ignorant, but in which I am now joyously engaged.

" The days wore on; study advanced ; the time came when money was requisite to complete my course, but the promised supply failed me. Here I might have stopped, but the same invisible hand which led me, supplied, in a way I love to remember, all I needed. A young man, who had been a fellow clerk of mine, had been drawn to me like Jonathan to David, and I loved him also dearly. He cheerfully advanced all. I insured my life to secure him, and went forward. In due time I received my diploma, and then was completed another step in the pathway of preparation, along which I was led as a blind man. Meanwhile two things of heart history transpired which had an important bearing upon what was to follow.

" During the time these events were transpiring, I began to feel that I ought to be a Christian, that is, that I ought to read the Bible, pray, be confirmed, receive the communion, and conform to the requirements of the Episcopal Church, in which I was bred. After considering the matter, I made up my mind, went forward, and thought myself all right. Singularly enough, while I was thinking over this matter, the friend, who afterwards came to my help in the hour of need, to enable me to go on with medical study, was thinking, too, upon the same subject, and reached the determination to be a Christian indeed. Wiser than I, however, he became a true child of God, I only a son of the Church. Strangely enough, though our souls were as one, and we were in closest confidence in all other matters, nothing passed between us upon this most momentous of all things, until our minds were both made up, and then not enough to have it of any special advantage to me. O how marvelous it is! O how much would be gained if the false restraints in such instances were broken through! One day he said to me, 'I am to be baptized next Sunday, at such a Baptist church; come and see.' 'Yes,' I answered, 'I will, and I am to be confirmed at such a time in such an Episcopal church; come and see.' 'Yes,' he replied, 'I will.' And that is all that passed between us on the subject. He was baptized, I was confirmed. We saw each the ceremony in the other's case as we had promised. Nothing more. This was but a poor beginning of a religious life for me, yet such as it was, it was a beginning and that is much. And in so far it was the beginning of another line of preparation indispensable to the work in store for me.

"During the days of study, the physician, in whose office I was reading, had in his family a sister-in-law with whom I became acquainted. Imperceptibly a mutual affection took possession of our hearts. When this became known and read of others besides ourselves, violent opposition was shown which only increased our ardor. I was poor, slender in health, slim in prospects, a wretched oak for an ivy to twine around, and very naturally friends thought and said so. The storm only made the clinging the closer, and finally we settled the matter satisfactorily at least to ourselves, and told our friends what we intended to do. They wisely submitted to it, and we went to the altar and were wedded. We all remained together. Our marriage and the subsequent death of my dear wife had a wonderful influence upon me in preparation for the then unknown future. I loved my wife with all my heart; she was dearer to me than life itself; a perfect idol; I would gladly have died with her. I had gone on into practice, and on my wife's account still remained in the office of her brother-in-law, until after her death. Now I come to one of the most momentous points in the story of God's marvelous dealings with me in reference to his plan of my life."

As this was the beginning of the second period, we will let it open a new chapter in the history.

How wonderful is God in counsel, and how excellent in working! O the depth of the riches both of the wisdom and knowledge of God! how unsearchable his judgments, and his ways past finding out!

2

IV.

THE WORLD ABANDONED.

BEFORE resuming the story as related by Doctor Cullis, let me say concerning him, that the common order of life seems in his case reversed. As a rule, childhood is the butterfly period, when one flits from flower to flower, and from pool to pool, in perfect freedom from care, but his earliest days were weighed down with pain and dread. Boyhood is usually made bright with castle-building, but with him it was filled up with forebodings. Manhood generally opens one's eyes to see that the castles of boyhood stand, like the pictures of the Chinese, upon nothing, and tumble to pieces at the touch of actual life, and from thirty to forty the real affairs of the world with many begin to be crushingly felt, and their hearts turn fondly toward the time when a satisfactory competence shall enable them to retire and lay off the wearying load; but with him in these later years the freedom from care and the playfulness of childhood have come to his heart, and he is looking forward with exultation to see the Lord's work in his hands become, if he will, a hundred fold greater, and never cease growing while he lives. It is founded on the Rock and built up in the promises by the Lord himself. Why should it not grow?

He says : —

"My first uplifting out of sorrow, suffering, and dread was

transitory, a dream which soon passed away. It came with the attachment formed between me and my departed wife. When this ripened into matrimony, and our lives like our names were merged into one, my happiness was complete. Then when dis-ease fastened upon her, the hectic flush came out also upon the face of all my joys. And when she was laid low in the grave, it was the funeral of the new life I had begun to live in her. The separation between her soul and body was not more real than that which it caused between my soul and the world. I died in that hour to the main object of my life, and was buried with my wife to the new life I had just begun to live. But alas for me, I did not die to self and sin, nor did I rise to God in Christ Jesus. Shall I explain? It was like this. During the bright months of our wedded life, the future for the first time loomed up before me like a panorama, each changing step in our prog-ress unfolding a picture of beauty. An independent practice; a delightful office and home rented; a name; a lucrative career; a home of our own with every luxury and convenience; and finally retirement amid the laurels of success and the pleasures of abundance. In each of these pictures the central group was two figures entwined in one, and when one of these figures came to be blotted out it blotted out the whole; every picture became simply hideous. Thus again, and more than ever before, the future became to me a dread and life a burden. I would have hailed death as the king of delights, but it would not come. I was alive and could not die. What must be done with my life? Success, too, seemed assured to me. There was a pang in the thought of that now when all was gone which had given it a charm. Yet all the more I felt confident that money would flow in upon me. What should I do with it? During the dark hours while the lifeless form of my wife was still above ground, I was much in the room where we had laid it, and there these reflections ripened into purpose and the purpose took the form of a vow, like, and yet, O how unlike the vow of Jacob at Bethel. O how widely different my circumstances and sur-roundings from his! In one respect there was indeed similarity between him and me. He had died to the hope of being heir to his father's princely possessions, as I had died to the hope of a life of happiness with my wife. He had been, up to the night before, since the late unhappy scenes in his father's tents, as I was there in that room, thoroughly miserable. But with him the night was over and gone : the morning had come. The vision of the night in answer to his cry unto God when he was about to lay himself down upon his bed of earth and pillow of stone, had brought new light into his soul and brighter sunshine upon his pathway than he had ever before known, whilst I was yet in darkness. That morning, there alone in the wilds at Bethel, he set up his pillow of stone for a memorial, poured his thank-offering of oil upon it, and by its side vowed his vow. There in that room, alone with the cold form of her I had loved, I bowed at her side and gave utterance to my vow. Jacob vowed in view of the wonderful assurance of the Lord's continued presence and keeping power given in the vision of the night. I vowed without any vision of the presence of the Lord and without the sweet assurance that he would be with me and would keep me. Jacob put an *if* in his vow, 'if the Lord will be with me and will keep me, and will give me bread to eat and raiment to put on, and will bring me in safety again to my father's house, then he shall be my God, and of all that thou givest me behold I will give a tenth unto thee.' I put no *if* in my vow, nor did I reserve nine tenths for myself and promise one tenth only unto the Lord, but vowed to give all, saying, 'Lord, my wife is dead and I have no one now to make money for. I will give all I receive over expenses for thy cause.' This may seem on its face a sweeping vow, and so it was in a sense. Yet after all it was a sort of a slave's vow to a distant master, with little in it with reference to the personal relations which ought to have been accepted between God and myself. A cold vow of money to the cause of a distant Lord, that was all. All imperfect as was this covenant with the Lord, it was however the seal of my own vow to the death of my soul to the world. And as such it was a great step toward the unseen goal before me of complete self-abandonment to Christ in preparation for his work."

V.

CHRIST FULLY ACCEPTED.

" WE laid away the body of my wife to await the archangel's call. My mind had been made up to a separation from the physician with whom I had been associated ; and as soon as it could be done without impropriety, I took an office and set up for an independent practice. Marvelously soon for a young man in an old city, my hands were full, a horse and carriage were required and purchased, and a surplus of money began to flow in. My vow was kept. I scattered tracts by thousands. As trees in autumn do their ripened leaves, I flung them into every stream around me. And I bestowed money right and left to every Christian cause, without letting my right hand know what my left hand gave. Yet I was not happy ; indeed I was miserable, and every day of my life I wished myself dead. This was not strange. As I said, my vow was that of a slave, and it was a slave's life that it led to. Selfishness was not dead ; pride was not dead ; vanity was not dead ; envy and malice, and the whole brood of vipers which are born of self, still lived. And as for the love of Christ which passeth knowledge, I did not comprehend it, nor had responsive love been yet awakened in my heart for Christ in any considerable degree. A slave might give all his earnings to his master without love on either side. He might have liberty to go where he pleased, and do what he liked, and earn what he could and send it all to his master, and yet look with coldness upon him, as high and far away above him. O how wide the difference between this and the relation between a loving bride and bridegroom ! She gives herself to him in response to his gift of himself to her. And they live to each other and in each other as one. This is the true symbol of the relation between the Christian and Christ ; but, alas, I knew very little of it, indeed almost nothing at all. Dissatisfaction with my state of mind gradually and insensibly came upon me like

hunger while one sleeps, and desire for deliverance sprang up
and grew, I scarcely knew how. My bondage was Egyptian,
and grew heavier every day. Another thing at the same time
came up before me to destroy all complacency in the life I was
leading. My eyes began to be opened to the fact that of all I
gave to the cause of Christ a large percentage was used to keep
open the receiving and disbursing channels. This might be indispensable in the present state of things, but it was anything
but satisfactory to me. I was bound to give by my vow, and I
did not want to withhold; but I did long for some channel purely
Christian which would not absorb in itself what was poured into
it to save the perishing. I was in fact thoroughly dissatisfied with
the way my earnings were used, and perfectly disgusted with myself. By and by I will tell you how the Lord led me into his own
plan for me in the employment of my money, but now let me first
recount to you the way in which he led me to the only true source
of satisfaction for my own personal spiritual wants. The two
desires, one for purity of heart, and the other for an unwasting
channel for my gifts, sprang up and grew together simultane-
ously, and ripened into realization not far apart; yet it will be
better for me to tell how it came about with each by itself. All
along I had been reading the Bible and saying prayers from a
sense of duty. In fact, my religion consisted mainly in these
two things, together with the scattering of tracts and giving
money, which were impelled also by conscience. I was under
law, not under grace, and it was a hard, dry kind of religion.
When, however, I began to be hard-bestead and hungry for the
two things, a better heart and a better channel for my earnings;
then I began really to pray. Then the Lord began to open my
eyes to the Scriptures as something more than a great field to be
gone over piecemeal day by day, as the slave hoes a field of corn
so much daily as his task. First of all he caused them to increase my sense of want, and to intensify my dissatisfaction with
myself, and to sharpen my hunger and thirst for something better. Then, as I read the Bible with eyes just beginning to open
to its teachings of duty and privilege, the question came up as
to its being true in every part, Old and New, but the Lord led
me to what has proved to be an end of all controversy in my
soul on the subject, as I believe it would be in every other soul if
really adopted. I took the Bible in my two hands, closed it, held

.t up thus, and said, 'I do and will forever, by God's grace, believe every word between these two lids, whether I understand it or not.' I have had no trouble about it from that day to this.

"Another thing has helped me amazingly. I was somewhat perplexed with the question whether I might appropriate the promises to myself; whether they were not many of them limited to the persons to whom they were given. Here again the Lord led me in the dark to adopt a principle, the solid foundation of which I now see, but which at the time I did not understand, that has brought me into great light. I said, 'I will take every precept and promise in the Bible as my own, just as if my own name, Charles Cullis, was written in every one of them.'

"One day — it was the 19th of August, 1862 — I was reading in the morning the second chapter of Second Thessalonians, and came, in the 13th verse, to the words 'through sanctification of the Spirit,' and they arrested my attention and held me for some time, while I read and reread it again and again, and prayed God to sanctify me wholly by the Spirit, and destroy all selfishness and unbelief in my heart. The longing to work for Jesus grew apace, and the yearning for purity kept even pace with it. After the Lord began to open my ears to his teachings, he led me sweetly into many things a step at a time Two great things must be specially mentioned. First, he unfolded clearly and fully to me the fact that he himself is my righteousness; that in him, not in myself, I am justified; and that in him, not in myself, I have eternal life. He caused me to see that he who believes in the Son of God hath life, — hath life already, — whilst he that believeth not in him hath not life, and maketh God a liar because he believeth not the record God hath given of his Son. This gave me full assurance of faith for present acceptance and eternal salvation, and it was a wonderful advance, a great and glorious step out from under law into grace for salvation. For this I shall praise God forever and ever.

"After this I found, however, that I was not saved from fret and worry and impatience. Often a hasty word would escape me, which I would willingly have given my right hand to recall. The fact is, I had not learned yet that Christ must keep me or I could not be kept. The keeping power of Christ was the second great lesson of the two taught me by the Lord. I knew my need of being kept, but thought at first that it could only be met

by a greater vigilance in self-keeping, and a greater firmness of
self-reliance and determination; but this failed me. Then I
tried prayer for help in self-keeping, but my failures were just
as frequent and 'grievous as ever. Finally, one day, whilst re-
peating the Lord's Prayer, the petition, 'Keep us from evil,'
seemed instinct with a significance I had never before appre-
hended. The evil it refers to I had always until then supposed
to be that which is external to us, and which comes upon us
without our choice, — accidents, diseases, losses, and the like, —
but then I saw it to refer to evil in the heart, evil in the dispo-
sitiou, evil in the spirit. I saw that, like the petition 'Let thy
kingdom come,' it related primarily to our inner life, not to our
outward circumstances. Then this new light was sealed home
to me by the Spirit, in the words 'For thine is the kingdom, and
the power, and the glory, forever and ever. Amen.' I saw that
the kingdom within is the Lord's, and the power to set it up and
keep it up forever and ever is his also. Not the helping power
to self-keeping, but the keeping power altogether; and when I
saw this I said with all my heart, 'Yea, Lord. Amen, so it is.
Hallelujah! Praise God, from whom all blessings flow.'

"Before this great and blessed lesson had been taught me,
I thought I knew what it would be worth if I could be kept.
There was no price, which could have been commanded by me,
that I should have thought too great for it. Yet I must say that
I knew comparatively nothing at all of its value. The power
that keeps is a power that illuminates, subdues, teaches, strength-
ens, upholds, guides, sweetens, enlivens, gives peace and everything else that pertains to God's kingdom within. I do not see
how I ever lived without it, and I am sure that but for this I
should have been poorly prepared for the dear work which the
Lord has called me to do. O, I bless him for it every day.

> "'Bless the Lord, O my soul,
> And all that is within me bless his holy name.
> Bless the Lord, O my soul,
> And forget not all his benefits.'

From that day to this I have had daily proof of the truthfulness
of the name of Jesus, for he does save his people from their
sins. And I have found the prophet Isaiah's assurance verified, —

> "'Thou wilt keep him in perfect peace
> Whose mind is stayed on thee,
> Because he trusteth in thee.'"

˙VI.

THE WORK DESIGNATED.

" THE Lord, wonderful in counsel and excellent in working, taught me in a single hour the economy of his kingdom in regard to work as I had never before understood it. My desire for a special work had been a blind one, except in so far as I saw that it would afford me an unwasting channel for my earnings, until at a certain time the words of the Bible as I read them,

TO EVERY MAN HIS WORK,

stood out boldly from the sacred page, and spoke to me as distinctly as if in a voice they had suddenly been uttered in my ear from the Book. The truth instantly flashed through my soul that God appoints every man his work if he will take it, and that the miscellaneous way in which men choose their own work for the Lord, instead of looking to him and having him designate it for them, is all wrong. Is he a King? Then shall he not appoint to each servant his work. Is he a Captain? And shall he not assign to every officer and soldier his post? Is he a husbandman? And shall he not designate to each of his laborers his field? Yet we, as servants, as soldiers, as laborers, each choose our own work and post and field, as if it were our prerogative to do so, and go on in our own will and way, calling it serving the Lord, and are often terribly disappointed because he does not own and bless our work. We rob God and reap defeat, and blame the Lord for it all. I resolved not to do so, but to look to the Lord for my work, and then go forward in it, trusting wholly to him for guidance.

" One day, whilst the daily cry of my soul to God was for the twofold boon, a pure heart and a special work, a stranger called upon me in behalf of a poor man in consumption who had no home, and had been refused admission into the public hospitals because he was incurable. It gave me a pang deep and keen to be compelled, as I was, to send the stranger away without being able to point him to a home for the poor, homeless, hopeless one. Instantly, however, a voice within said, as plainly as words could speak, 'There, that is your work.' My soul replied, ' Yes, Lord, that is my work.'

"From that hour, this part of 'my twofold cry was modified. The daily prayer was no longer ' What, O Lord, is my special work ? ' but, like Manoah, I wanted to know how it should be ordered. If I had been left to my own impulse I should have followed the usual plan, secured a board of managers, adopted the many customary devices for raising money, and gone forward in this way to found and sustain a hospital for those toward whom my heart was moved, but the Lord would not let me do that. He showed me first that in such a hospital, under the rule of a number of men, unrestricted freedom to teach the truth as it is in Jesus would be almost if not quite impossible, and that it would assuredly come short of being purely and gloriously a place wholly given up to the Lord Jesus Christ. He made me also to see that, as a channel for my earnings and those of others, it would be just what my heart had become tired of, absorbing in its collecting processes and administrative agencies a large proportion of all received. So the Lord smashed up that idea.

"Another plan, a device of my own, came to a like end. I felt confident that by appealing to my personal friends I could secure help to found and sustain such a hospital, without a board of managers, and with entire liberty to make it and keep it purely Christian in all its appointments and influences. And I was strongly inclined to undertake it in that way. The Lord quickly put a stop to it by leading me to perceive that instead of opening in this way an unwasting channel for my earnings, it would absorb all my time and keep me from earning anything at all, and would make of me a perpetual beggar, dreaded and shunned by every one who had an aversion to being asked for money. So the Lord smashed up that idea.

"Now I was at the end of my wits. The only ways I could devise as really feasible were entirely and forever abandoned as utterly unsuitable for me. What should be done? The Lord now began to teach me his way. Franke's great Orphanage in Germany, established and sustained wholly by the unsolicited contributions of the people in answer to prayer to God alone, came to my knowledge. Then just at the opportune moment Muller's 'Life of Trust,' fell into my hands. This fairly opened my eyes to see the principle of faith as applied to the Lord's own work, and as wonderfully suited to the anticipated work to which I felt called. If the Lord would supply all the money in answer to prayer, none of it would be absorbed in collecting. If he would furnish all the helpers as volunteers out of love to the Lord and his work, little would be used in the daily administration, beyond the actual expenses for food. If he would send all the invalids, no time would be required in that matter more than just to see that they were not imposters. My time almost unbroken would be left to earn money in aid of the work, and in seeing to the welfare of those in the Home. I should not be dreaded and shunned as a beggar, and the Lord would be honored by every gift received, every helper who should volunteer, and every invalid who should come. And perfect freedom would be enjoyed to do everything for the comfort of the sufferers, and to tell them all the Lord should put upon our hearts for their salvation. Everything was in favor of the trust principle, nothing against it. Evidently it was from the Lord. Thus the dear work in the first of its branches was clearly designated to me by the Lord, and its principle defined, and I gave to it the fullest assent of my understanding and heart. Yet the actual acceptance of it, and the practical entrance upon it, was quite another thing, and much more than I saw at the time remained for the Lord to teach me before he could say to me as he did to Israel at the Red Sea, ' Go forward.'"

VII.

FINAL LESSONS.

"Two full years rolled away after the work was designated and defined in principle to me, before the Lord permitted me to begin seeking a place for the Home. Waiting was all against my nature. I am quick to decide, impulsive in action, and impatient of delay; yet during the entire twelve-month twice told, the Lord held me still with constantly increasing confidence and joy in the faith that my most sanguine hopes would be fulfilled. As the heifers drawing the cart bore the Ark of the Lord up out of its Philistine captivity toward its resting-place in Israel against all that we call instinct, so I went forward in all this two years' journey, in a peacefulness and patience, in perfect contrariety to my native disposition. The heifers left their young calves behind, and of their own accord went right away from them lowing as they went. In like manner my pathway was pursued cheerfully through all those months, yet made vocal every day by my cries unto God. And of all the cries of these two years the one most constant and earnest was for faith to enter upon the work. 'Lord increase my faith,' was my daily prayer.

PATIENT WAITING,

however, was only one of the lessons instilled into me in this in-terval. The practical method of faith's working was most effect ually taught me. Probably most of those who learn finally to walk by faith, fall at some time or other into the false notion, for a time longer or shorter, that as we are to receive all by a sim-ple trust in Christ there is no necessity for making our requests unto God. He knows, they say, all our wants and exactly what it is wise and best to give, and how and when to bestow his gifts, and we see this so clearly that we unwittingly settle down for a time into what seems to be the true way of honoring and pleasing the Lord, trusting without asking; but this is in fact counter to his will and way, and against all his instructions. And he lets us go on, until like Peter on the housetop, we become very hungry and are compelled to slay and eat against our foolish prejudgment, and so have our eyes opened to God's own way for us, which is to

ASK AND RECEIVE.

To ask that we may receive, and to receive as well as to ask, and to keep on asking till we receive.

" Early in the year of our Lord 1862, the work and its plan were unfolded to me, and I began asking the Lord from time to time, with growing earnestness, for faith and means to open it. The Lord had fairly put upon me his yoke of discipleship in the school of prayer, as well as of faith, and I began to be a learner of this great secret of power in his kingdom.

" About the middle of that same year I began to pray regularly every day and many times in the day, that the Lord would supply the means. Still the answer came not in money but in constant accessions to the flame. One day, instead of having money sent to me, I was sent to visit a poor girl in the last stages of consumption, in the most pressing need of such a home as my heart yearned to open. I was deeply moved, and my confidence was strengthened that the Lord would at some time give me my heart's desire. Still I could do nothing but pray on until I should receive, and this I did with ever-growing importunity, and so while the Lord taught me to ask and ask on until the answer should come, he taught me the great fact also, that ' he that believeth shall not make haste.'

" Another of the blessed lessons of those waiting days was that of

THE WAY TO PROVE GOD'S WILL.

" This, as one sees at a glance, is of vital importance. The Lord suggests to us his will for us. Satan has his devices for us in the name of the Lord. We may originate schemes for ourselves, and our friends will be sure to have any number of devices for us. How shall we know which is from the Lord and which is not? Must we go on and test them in practice and obtain proof by success or failure? That would be to waste our lives largely in fruitless experiments ending in disappointment, and keep us perpetually in the uncertainties of a lottery, with many chances against us. Thank God, there is no necessity for this. We may prove the will of the Lord in regard to every practical step in life.

" Others may have been led into other ways of doing this. *Alternative prayer* has been the Lord's own Urim and Thummim for indicating his will to me, in two ways. First I have asked him concerning any given plan suggested to me, that if not from him he would overthrow it in my mind, and if from him that he would establish and strengthen it.

" In the case of both my first and second plans for founding and sustaining the Home, he broke them to pieces effectually, and when it came to the third he caused it to grow upon me every time I put this test, and I did put it over and over again.

" The second form of alternative prayer to which I have been led is that of asking the Lord in respect to a given object, that if from him he would show it by a given sign, as in the case of Gideon's fleece, and said to him that if he did not give the sign I would take it as conclusive that it was not from him.

" The first contribution I received for the work was a token of this kind given in answer to my earnest prayer to know *certainly* whether it was the Lord's will to found such a Home. It was on the 19th day of January, in the year of our Lord 1864. Nearly two years I had been asking, a year and a half I had asked daily many times a day, for means to commence the Home. On the morning of that day I asked again and put my prayer in the alternative, 'If it is thy will to have a Home, begin to bestow the means, but if not, I will willingly give it up, as my sole desire is to have thy will done.' That very evening my dear friend and brother in Christ, C., who knew about my idea of a Home, gave me for it, *of his own accord*, one dollar. This was the first contribution, and small in amount yet great in its influence as a turning-point of my faith and a test of God's will, and I felt as rich as if it had been a thousand. My faith was greatly confirmed, and I said with the Psalmist, ' I love the Lord because he hath heard my voice and my supplication ! '

" At another time the question came up whether the Home should be exclusively for consumptives ? There were reasons which had satisfied me before that it should be so, especially as the suggestion of it came in connection with an application in behalf of a poor man in consumption ; but I was not solidly settled in the knowledge that this was God's will. The case of another poor man suffering from another disease started the question anew. I inquired of the Lord about it, and put a test which was met as distinctly as that of the fleece, settling the fact that the Home must be for consumptives only.

" Contributions did not begin to come in ; even that first dollar was not received until after the Lord had so far strengthened my faith that I was willing to speak of what he had put in my heart. When he had secured my confidence in himself, and in the fact that it was his will that I should found such a Home, in so far that I was ready to open my mouth and confess my faith to near and dear friends, he began very soon to open the hands of one and another to encourage me to still greater boldness. The first person to whom I mentioned my thoughts was my sister, and she promised me her prayers ; the next one was a friend and brother, who gave me the impression that he thought I was moved by undue enthusiasm which would soon subside.

" The second contribution was also a small one, and came from a lady to whom I confided my thoughts. She promised to pray for me at the time, and shortly after gave me two dollars and sixty cents in aid of the anticipated work.

" At last the Lord added to my faith for the work, the quality of virtue as our translators render it, boldness or courage, as Peter gave it in the original, insomuch that I was as free to speak of it as of my faith for salvation, and thus wrought in me another practical lesson indispensable to the conduct of trust work for Jesus,

BOLDNESS IN THE FAITH.

" All along I was well aware that I could not look to the Lord to furnish the means for the work from others if there should be any holding back on my own part ; therefore I stood ready to put in the little I had in hand to begin with, and to devote to the work every dollar I should receive not required for expenses. Indeed the first thought of a special work had sprung from desire for a better channel for my own earnings, vowed to the cause of Christ, and from that time forward my only desire in asking the Lord for means from others was to have enough, including all I could supply myself, to justify me in entering on the work. And when finally I did enter upon it the amount received from

others was so insignificant that my boldness in making the start
would have been temerity and presumption, had not the Lord's
will been previously so fully and satisfactorily ascertained. As
it was, the first step was much the same as that of the children
of Israel when at the Red Sea, and also at the Jordan; by command of the Lord, Go forward! they set foot in the waters while
yet they had not been separated. The result has gloriously
justified this step, as it did those of the Israelites, and as it ever
has and ever must justify every step of true faith in God."

This closes the account, gathered as at different
times it has fallen from the lips of Doctor Cullis, of all
the way in which the Lord has led him in preparation
for the work given him to do. Before commencing to
trace the work itself through the various stages of its
history, an understanding of the acknowledged position
of Doctor Cullis in it, and of the spirit of the work
itself, seems necessary to a clear comprehension of the
work we are to trace. To this two short chapters
will be devoted.

VIII.

ACKNOWLEDGED POSITION OF DOCTOR CULLIS.

AN intelligent friend of mine, who was familiar with the faith work under Doctor Cullis in its original tenting-place in Willard Street, was kindly shown by him through its new quarters in West Street and on Boston Highlands. This was some time ago, shortly after the new Home on the Highlands was opened, and before the later and new branch of the work in the city, the Faith Chapel and Training-college for Christian Workers had been thought of. What she would have thought and said in view of this proposed enlargement if she had known about it, I do not know; as it was, four things impressed her greatly: the extent of the work at the time, the rapid expansion of the work in the past, the accelerated progress indicated for the future, and the perfect freedom of Doctor Cullis from all appearance of the burden of care under his great and growing responsibilities.

Within six years the mustard-seed had become a great tree with its various branches, yielding their different manner of fruits perennially, and scattering their healing leaves near and far.

The seventh year nearly as much had been received for its enlargement and support as in all the six years before; and as if its first form had been but like the chrysalis, it had burst forth and come out in new and enlarged forms in two new localities, instead of one:

the *publication work* in a business centre of the city
with enlarged lines of tracts and books, and an increased circulation of its two monthly papers, " Times
of Refreshing," to promote full salvation, and " Loving Words," to win children to Jesus ; and the *several
Homes* in a lovely place on Boston Highlands, having out-o'-door room enough — eleven acres of ground,
with broad avenues on two sides, pure air, and magnificent views, as well as greatly enhanced indoor
room and comfort.

Everything too, pointed, as it appeared to her, to
possibilities, probabilities, certainties under God, in
the future which amazed her. Willard Tract Repository she could not but see as having for itself a
distinct mission, bounded in time to come only by the
hunger of souls and the supplies of God's hand.

And the Homes, — standing as she did in the beautiful Chapel of the Consumptives' Home, so central and
easy of access for the inmates from all parts of the
building, the thought came in upon her of the invitation to increased comforts and benefits of this Home
for double the number of sufferers accommodated in
Willard Street ; and then of the new Chapel out on
the grounds in process of completion for a work of
its own, and of the new Cottage Home for children,
and the room on the grounds for a score more like it,
and then of the site for a Cancer Home, for which
contributions are coming in, and then of the room also
for the Deaconesses' Home with its hands and hearts,
multiplied to meet all the wants of the work by an
ample supply of helpers, — she could not but wonder-
ingly ask in her heart whereunto shall this thing grow ?

Doctor Cullis stood there in the Chapel with her.
She saw that he, like Jacob in his youth starting

from his father's tents in Mamre, had set out with only his staff in his hand, and now already in less than half the time taken by the patriarch, he had become two bands. What a work upon his shoulders! thought she ; what a responsibility! A hundred people or so entirely dependent upon him every day for everything, soon to be seven hundred, for the next Sabbath of years gives promise of sevenfold increase, and then who can tell how many more! So turning to the Doctor, she said, "Doctor, your responsibilities are great, and are growing greater very fast; do not you begin to feel them becoming heavy?" His answer was, "Heavy! No, not at all. The work is not mine, but the Lord's. I am not my own, but his. The responsibility is not on me, but on him. I have only to look for and accept daily orders and supplies, obey my orders and dispense my supplies, and leave all with the Lord. A clerk in a large house has no more responsibility than a clerk in a small one. If the business is a million a year, its weight is no more upon a clerk than if it was only a hundred thousand a year."

This is the true and only position in a trust work, and since Doctor Cullis was brought into this position for the work, he has been led also into the same position for salvation from sin, as he has told us in the account already given, and rests in the Lord for the power that keeps in perfect peace him whose mind is stayed on him, and finds his promise made good. Yea more, for with the perfect peace comes also perfect rest, and with perfect rest perfect love which casts out fear ; and with this comes patience, too, and forbearance and hope and power to prevail; and so he has found himself in an atmosphere in which it is

sweet to live and move and breathe, sweet to work
and sweet to rest, sweet to lie down and sweet to
rise up, sweet to go out and sweet to come in — an
atmosphere which diffuses itself through every day of
the year and over every scene of life.

IX.

SPIRIT OF THE WORK.

THE cheeriness of the atmosphere attending the chief worker naturally enough is carried into and pervades the work in both departments in all their branches. In the tracts, books, and papers it is seen on their face, in their names, in such words as Life, Faith, Rest, Victory, Blessing, Refreshing, Gladness, Deliverance, Keeping, Loving Words, and the like.

The chapel services and work are pervaded with the same sweet words and restful thoughts, and full of the power of that unity in the bond of love which convinces that Jesus is the Christ, and that God loves us even as he loves his Son, and so wins wanderers to the Lord ; full of the power which lifts Christians into perfect light and liberty, and drives away fogs and clouds and lets the sunshine into their hearts.

The Children's Home is made, by this loving atmosphere, a home indeed for the children. The absence of instinctive maternal affection which, alas, too often dwells in the same breast with impatience, temper, violence, and unrest, is more than compensated for by the love of Christ in the hearts of those in charge.

The Deaconesses' Home is at once a home where abides the Son of Peace, and a school in which daily lessons are learned under the Great Teacher, the meek and lowly One.

All this might be expected in these various branches of the work, and being found, might give joy indeed, but not surprise.   But when the same blessed atmosphere is seen also in the Consumptives' Home, surprise can hardly fail to fill the mind.   What! a place where scores of men and women, old and young, are coughing, expectorating, wasting, suffering, dying, — cheery! Yes, cheery and delightful.   Love reigns there.   Hope is born there in many a soul.   Kindness makes home there, and speaks and acts in every word and tone and deed.   A glory — God's glory, love — rests upon it.   The bitterest prejudices are taken away, and the greatest darkness is dispelled ; and it is marvelous how quickly and easily it is done. There is no talking at people, no heaping up burdens of responsibility upon them, no working up any religious excitement or feeling, no straining at anything.   The gospel of grace and love and gladness is simply lived out and talked out freely and fully ; and for the rest, asking and receiving of God, and instructing those who inquire the way of salvation, is the sum of it all.

One morning I stopped at the bedside of a poor Irish girl, who was evidently dipping her feet in the brim of the waters of death, but just as evidently about to make the passage in triumph by an open pathway through the river, and said to her, assured by the joy in her face that it was true, " You are trusting in Jesus."   She responded, " O yes, I am ! I learned to trust him since I came here."   " How long have you been here ? "   " About two weeks. But O they are all so kind here ! "   Kindness was the Lord's hand knocking at the door, in obedience to which she opened it wide and let the Lord come in and sup with her and she with him.

At another time I stopped at the bedside of one who died about two days afterwards. She too was from Ireland, a waif, who had never known a home, as she told me, until she was welcomed here a short time before; and as she spoke of it, tears of joy and gratitude streamed from her eyes. " O ! " she said, " the Doctor, he's been a father to me; he's been a real father to me. Why, I came here to find out what was the matter of me, and when I asked the Doctor, he just said, ' You'd better go up-stairs.' And I said, ' Doctor, you don't think I've got the consumption, do you ? ' And he said, ' Yes, my child, I am afraid you have indeed.' And I began to cry, and said, ' O, what shall I do? What shall I do ? I've no father or mother or home, nowhere in the world to go to, and nobody in the world to take care of me ; and now they won't let me in at the hospital 'cause I've got the consumption;' and then the Doctor he just said, so kindly, ' Why, my child, *this* shall be your home as long as you live. *I'll* be a father to you. Just go up-stairs to the matron and she'll give you a bed, and we'll take care of you.' O, how his kindness did go to my heart! And *they're all* so kind here ! Why, I never had a home before. And the Doctor, he's the first father I ever had. He's been a real father to me." When she had told her story through, I said something about the blessed Jesus to her. She responded gladly, saying, " I never heard much about the blessed Jesus till I came here. I heard a great deal about saying prayers to the blessed Virgin, but I never heard say much about the blessed Jesus. But now tell me, what do you think of this ? Yesterday I heard through the open door. I couldn't go into the chapel; I'm too far gone now for that ;

but I heard the sweet singing about Jesus, and I
heard you talk about being like a little child in the
arms of Jesus, and I wished I was a little child in
his dear arms. And last night I was in such pain I
couldn't sleep, and I prayed to Jesus to take away
my pain and it went all away, and I fell asleep, and
I dreamed that I was a little child in the arms of
Jesus, and that he loved me and told me I should
always be with him. When I woke up in the morning my heart was glad, and I wondered whether it
was true that the blessed Jesus did love me and that
I should be always with him ; so when nurse came I
told her about my prayer and my dream, and asked
her, ' What does it mean ? ' And she said, ' Why, it
means that Jesus *does* love you and you *are* his little
child.' And then O how happy I was." So she
talked as if joy did make her talk, and the hope of
glory new-born into her soul beamed in her face.
Two days later she passed peacefully away.

In one of the Chapel services a young man rose,
and in a hoarse whisper said in substance, " I was
born in Canada, my parents are French. I was
brought up a Roman Catholic. I never knew anything of salvation till I came here. My prejudices
were very strong. I hated the Protestants. I was
awfully wicked ; my sins have been the death of me.
I shall soon die. This may be the last time I shall
be able to be in the Chapel, but I am happy in Jesus.
My sins are all forgiven. I am trusting fully in the
Lord. He saves me from sin, and keeps me in perfect peace. ' O the joy of knowing Jesus ! ' I learned
to know Jesus here. And now I have learned to
trust him to save me wholly, and he does it, O, so
sweetly. I wanted to say this for fear I should never

have another opportunity to do it. My soul is at rest. I shall soon be in glory."

Side by side in the Chapel with this young French Canadian sat another young man, a New Englander, a representative of another hard class, the so-called gospel-hardened, but I should call them law-hardened, rather. His testimony was to this effect: " I was strictly brought up. My parents are Orthodox. They live in ——. Religion was forced upon me everywhere, and it was all must, must, must. There was nothing to win me, and I learned to hate everything religious. When I got old enough I came here to Boston, and went into a store as a clerk. My money went pretty fast, but I laid up some. After a while the house failed, and I was out of place. Falling into the company of some pretty fast fellows, I was out late nights. One night at a theatre I took cold and it settled on my lungs. Then I spent all the money I had on the doctors, and grew worse all the time. At last I heard of Doctor Cullis as a good doctor for such cases as mine, and was directed here to the Home to find him, not knowing that it was a Home. I came to ask him whether I really had consumption. He met me and kindly asked of me the object of my call. I answered, ' To find out whether my lungs really are diseased.' He examined me and said, ' I fear they are.' My heart sank within me. I was two hundred miles from home. Home had no welcome for me if I could get there, and my last dollar was gone. I exclaimed, ' What shall I do!' The Doctor asked me if I loved Jesus. I answered ' Well — I — can't say — that — as you mean — exactly I do. No, in fact — as you think about it — I suppose I do not.' I thought of course that this would shut up his heart against me, but he said as kindly as ever, ' Would you like a home? You are welcome here if you would.' O, what a relief to my poor burdened heart that was! He sent me up-stairs. The matron gave me a bed, and now I am so far recovered that the Doctor says it will be safe for me to go out and begin work again, and this very morning a good place has been offered me. But the best of all is that I am going out an entirely changed man. I hadn't been long here until the love and peace and joy I saw in others oppressed me, and I asked the Doctor what I must do, and he pointed me to Jesus, and I am saved."

These facts are given in illustration of the power there is in the constantly recognized presence of Jesus, and the sweetness of spirit begotten by it, to pull down the strongholds of false education, bitter prejudice, and hardness of heart. They are simply such as have fallen under my own notice, a few of many, and are mentioned because they show how the so-called hopeless classes are affected in the atmosphere of the work.

The concurrent testimony of those engaged in the work is that of all who have come into the Consumptives' Home unconverted, one only has left it unsaved, all the rest have either *died in hope, or* gone out improved in health or cured, *trusting in Jesus.*

X.

THE BEGINNING.

THE time came at last for commencing the work Considerably more than two years had passed aftei the Lord said to his servant, concerning the care of poor, homeless, hopeless consumptives, " this is your work," before he said to him, " the time has now come to begin." All this time was taken to teach his servant the true principles of the work and to strengthen his faith for it. At last, however, the pillar of cloud and of fire lifted, and led forth to the first tenting place of the work. Even after it lifted, more than two months passed away before it settled upon the house intended for the Home.

HOW THE LORD SHOWED THE TIME FOR BEGINNING.

Doctor Cullis began to feel that the time was at hand, and, like Daniel, when convinced that the time drew near for the return of his people from captivity, he began asking the Lord about it. His question assumed definite form : " Is it time to begin ? " The answer to this question was sought in a form as definite as the question. There remained one only obstacle, as it seemed to Dr. Cullis, to his taking a house and opening the Home. There was one dependent upon him for support, and he felt that it would not be right to commence under this weight, so he asked the Lord, saying, " If it be thy will that I now take measures to open the Home, be pleased to make it known by relieving me from this last weight, before the end of this present week." This was on Monday, May 9th, 1864. On Thursday, the 12th, the weight was removed. This was done without any word from Doctor Cullis himself to any one but the Lord, or any step whatever to secure its removal. He would not take the lot into his own hand and cast it, because he wanted to be sure that the disposal thereof was from the Lord. Then when the answer came he could say, as his journal gives the record, " Thanks be unto the Lord that he has answered my prayer, and removed the last obstacle which prevented me from the immediate prosecution of the work which has so long lain near my heart. I am now ready to go to work. I feel that I am right about the matter, but am still leaning on the Lord. I desire to take the first step only as he shall lead me."

HOW THE LORD DIRECTED THE PURCHASE OF THE HOUSE.

It was all against the prejudgment of Dr. Cullis; his mind was made up beforehand, upon the matter-of-course principle, without submitting the question to the Lord, that he was to rent a moderate sized house and not purchase at all until the Lord should supply the money for that purpose. He could not run in debt, and he had of his own earnings very little in hand, "never less at any time, with one or two exceptions," as he says in his Journal, and next to nothing as yet given him in contributions; therefore he settled it that *of course* he must not think of purchasing. What had he to buy with? And of course he must rent, if he should begin at all. This was Doctor Cullis's plan in accordance with his own prejudgment of the matter. The Lord's plan was that he should not rent but purchase a suitable house, and the way he took to overrule and supplant the Doctor's idea and bring him to make the purchase is very instructive. It was done effectively, but in doing it nearly three months' time was consumed.

Immediately after the Lord said to his servant " Go forward," he commenced seeking a house. On Thursday the last obstacle was removed, and the following entry was made in his Journal the Monday after : " I have looked for a house, but have not found a suitable one. *I propose merely to hire a dwelling-house at as moderate a rent as possible. I look for thousands and know in whom I trust.* My prayer even now is, that if I am too fast the Lord will hold me back, and if it is not his will that the hospital shall be started now, he will put obstacles in my way, that I may not be able to find a house, or in some manner reveal to me his will."

Day after day passed in fruitless search for a house until a fortnight had been consumed ; then, on the 27th of May, he resolved upon a further step in the same direction. He says : " As yet I have not been successful, although I have spent much time in the pursuit. To-morrow I shall advertise."

The advertisement like the search, however, proved fruitless. This he states in his Journal, June 3d, and adds, " I am looking wholly to the Lord." On that day the Lord gave — not a house — but a new and gentle spur to his faith for the work. Some one told him of a poor consumptive needing such a home. This was the second time his faith had been stimulated in this way, so he says, " His will be done, and

all shall be to his glory." Two months more passed
away in fruitless search, when suddenly success seemed
to crown his efforts, but disappointment followed. He
found a house suitable in size and location at a moderate rent, and took it at once. It was on Vernon,
afterwards changed in name to Willard Street. The
rent was $500 a year. The agreement was made and
the affair settled. The very next day, however, the
owner came to him saying that some one opposite
objected to having a hospital so near, and that the
agreement must be given up. The Doctor refused to
give it up. The owner insisted, but finally said,
" Why don't you buy the house ? I will sell it to
you." The Doctor declined, saying, " I have no
money to buy with." The owner said, " You don't
need any money. The house is mortgaged for so
much to such an institution ; give a second mortgage
to me for the balance ; take your own time for payment, and the house shall be yours to do what you
like with it."

This brought the Doctor to a pause. The matter-
of-course conclusion upon which he had so far acted
was shaken. The question came up before him, " Is
it the Lord's will, after all, that I should purchase ? "
He answered saying, " Let me have twenty-four
hours and I will pray over it." The owner assented.

Left to himself, he waited on the Lord for an answer to the question. The alternative was presented
in prayer, and the scale put entirely into the hands of
the Lord. In the one scale was the question " Shall
I purchase ? " in the other, " Shall I rent ? Show
me, dear Lord."

Very soon he saw that if he should purchase, the
interest and taxes both together, would not amount to

as much by more than $100 a year, as he had agreed to pay for the rent of the house, and that the purchase would not contravene the principle "owe no man anything" adopted by him. It would not be the contraction of a personal debt at all, as the seller would look to the property itself, and not to him, the purchaser, as his security for payment; whereas a debt for expenses would be a personal obligation binding upon him. He saw also that he would not only save to the Lord and his work more than $100 a year by the purchase, but would be at liberty to alter the house in any way to make it more suitable to his purpose. This showing he believed to be from the Lord, because he had laid the question before him and asked him in faith to let him see and know what his will was. Moreover he saw that the seller of the property would run no risk, as the property itself would amply secure him. This showing was conclusive, and the very next day he completed the purchase.

An entry in his Journal on the evening of the day in which the purchase was made, shows how perfectly he was satisfied that he was in the will of the Lord: —

"*August* 3. I never felt so calm as this evening since the matter is settled."

The Lord abundantly justified the transaction, and the principle upon which it was done, for he gave his servant the money to pay the whole price of the property within less than one tenth part of the time agreed upon, and enabled him, by the wise use of the money in paying off the second mortgage so long before it matured, to get a reduction of $500 from its face.

All this taken together settled also the principle of future purchases of the real estate necessary for the work, by means of which the prosperity of the work itself has been greatly aided.

XI.

CHEER FROM THE LORD AFTER THE PURCHASE.

THE idea of a house instead of a large edifice, and of a home instead of a hospital, came evidently from the Lord, and the plan of purchasing was also the Lord's own, accepted by his servant only when made so evident that he could not help seeing it. The plan of renting was not the Lord's, and was therefore obstructed from day to day until abandoned. The purchase was the first solid step of faith before God and the world in the work, and from that moment the Lord began to cheer the heart of his servant in various ways, and strengthen him for the next step.

Already, before the purchase, he believed " with his heart," and was right in the main, but now " confession was made with his mouth " in the voice of his act. Condemn it who might, he stood out a believer in the Lord in regard to his work, stepping — yea, already having stepped — out on the promises, and going forward trusting in the Lord to open the way before him and supply all the needs of " the dear work," as he calls it with evident delight.

Behold the result! Two years and more he had been praying for means, and next to nothing had been received. Two little gifts, indeed; nothing for supply, though great as tokens of God's love and of God's will. Each one had been a scintillation of light from the precious Urim and Thummim in the breast-plate of our Great High Priest, answering a question and confirming his servant in the knowledge of his holy will. Yet nothing for supply. No, not exactly so; they were as much as the two little loaves in the hands of the lad in the wilderness, and, put into the hands of the blessed Jesus, they could be multiplied to feed the hungry thousands. Yet what were they — $1.00 and $2.62 — toward the great work? But now the instant the purchase is made the Lord pours his own peace into the heart of his servant, so that he can record with truth the fact, saying, " I never have felt so calm as this evening since the matter is settled."

Two days later his friend comes from New York to visit him — his friend C., the very one who was the Lord's hand before to confirm his faith by the gift of the first dollar for the work. Now he comes again, the Lord's chosen one to be the first to cheer him on. They go to view the house together, and C. expresses much love and sympathy, and the next day gives ten dollars for the work. This is not a large amount, though ten times as large as the first gift, but it is wonderfully timely and cheering. The gladness thus put into the heart can better be imagined than expressed. If he was calm before, he is joyous now; his peace wells up and goes out into the sweet melody of thanksgiving. He records it in his Journal in this way: " May the Lord bless him. I thank the Lord for this his love to me. How can I doubt? I do not. It is the Lord's work, and he will bless it." Articles for household use began to come in, as well as money. Work of various kinds on the house, such as painting, whitewashing, and the like, was freely given, and everything came freighted with a double fullness of love and good-will. Each separate thing told of the loving invisible hand of the Lord moving the hearts of the people, and of the perfect good-will of the donors in their free, willing offerings unsolicited by man.

About eight weeks from the first of August were occupied in alterations and preparations before the house could be opened to receive the Lord's guests and make them comfortable. And each week brought its glad surprises from the Lord and the people.

In the report of the first year's history of the dear work there is found tucked away in a corner just in the last end a dry list, which only needs in this connection to be hauled out and read over, dry as it is, to give us some idea of how much there was in those days of cheer from the Lord. The little short list of the first four weeks will suffice. This is it: " Six chairs;" "a carpet;" "a barrel of flour;" "window curtains *for the whole house!*" "two cot beds;" "an extension table;" "chairs and tables;" "twelve husk pillows;" "a stair carpet;" "glass ware;" "cotton cloth;" "mattresses and boxes;" "two floors painted and lettering done out of good will;" "two *contribution boxes lettered;*" "a clock *loaned.*"

This, with a cord of wood worth $12 given, and the free offer of coal for the Home at $11 a ton, — the price being $14, — makes the catalogue complete of that first four weeks. That of the next four weeks, while the repairing and furnishing were in progress, is four or five times longer and not less significant; but this will enable us to catch some glimpse of the successive surprises of those weeks of preparation, and we shall therefore expect just what we find in the Journal of those weeks. The heart of Dr. Cullis, full of thanksgiving before, now breaks forth into singing.

August 18th, in the beginning of the third week, his song is, "'Have faith in God!' I can sing now the song of David:

'Blessed is the man that maketh the Lord his trust.'

He is bountifully supplying all my needs. O, how faithful!"

During those two months, as well as at other times, but especially then while the dear work was yet all in the untried future, there were those who, like Sanballat and Tobias of old, were ready to ask, "What doth this feeble Christian build?" And to say, "Though only a fox go up against it, he shall break down that which he builds." One and another — better meaning, no doubt, than those old enemies of the Lord's work — said to Doctor Cullis, "I doubt your ability to carry on such a work." The Lord enabled him to give the true answer, saying, "I, too, doubt *my* ability, but I do not doubt the Lord. My trust is in him. He will not let me be confounded."

The exact amount received in cash during the first four weeks was not large, only one hundred and fifty-one dollars and thirty-one cents; and the cash value of the contributions in household articles and work, though somewhat larger, was yet small in comparison with the magnitude of the work as it is now unfolding, only two hundred and sixty-nine dollars and fifteen cents; making, in all, not much over four hundred dollars. Yet the value is poorly told — nay, not told at all — in the dollars and cents. To know that, we must be able to compute the cheer from the Lord that came in it and with it from day to day, and the courage it gave for the dear work in the days then yet to come.

All through those eight weeks the Lord was saying to Doctor Cullis, and making it ring in his heart again and again, in substance, as he did to Joshua when with the children of Israel he was about to go into the land of promise : " Be strong and of a good courage ; only be strong and very courageous ; turn not to the right hand nor to the left, that thou mayest prosper whithersoever thou goest. Have I not commanded thee ? Be strong and of a good courage ; be not afraid, neither be thou dismayed ; for *I the Lord thy God am with thee* whithersover thou goest."

XII.

COMING BEFORE THE PUBLIC.

WE come now to one of the most critical stages of the work, that of its unfolding to the people. Was this to be God's work or man's ?

As a work of faith in God, the people must not be appealed to in its behalf either directly or indirectly. God alone must be asked for the means to found and sustain the Home. Appeals to the people would be to trust them instead of the Lord. Yet at every step God must be openly acknowledged and glorified before the people as the author and giver of every gift received. Any withholding, any shrinking, any failure to declare what God had done, and was doing, would be disloyalty to him through fear of man.

Any indirect appeal to the people by engineering to bring the work into public notice, and so to move the people to bestow upon it their gifts, would be worse than a direct one. An indirection is a deception, and would therefore be doubly offensive to God.

Faith in the Lord would say, let him take care of the matter of unfolding the work to the people. Let me take care only to acknowledge the Lord openly, and give him glory for all he does and all he gives.

Human reason would say, that although all the means come from the Lord, yet he bestows his gifts through the hands of the people, and their hearts must first be touched before their hands will be opened, and their ears must be reached to touch their hearts, so you must use the means to bring the work before them if you would receive their benefactions.

To this process of reasoning there would surely come the support of human counsel. Wise men, good men, those venerated by the people, would surely advise and urge prudent but effectual measures for making the work known.

At a glance we see that nothing but a faith in God superior to human reasoning, strong enough to resist the counsel of the best men, could hold a young man like Doctor Cullis in such a crisis. Here was the work in its infantile stage little and unknown, without funds or patrons, with a wide field before it, yet without a dollar in its treasury, dependent upon free gifts from the people, but not placed before them so that they could know about it and supply its wants, and here were wise and good men advising measures to make it known. How could he resist? What did he do?

Two months passed by after the purchase of the house before it was dedicated. During this time not a dollar, not a cent was expended in bringing out the work before the world. The purchase itself, and the process of fitting up and furnishing the Home to receive its expected guests arrested the attention of many and gave rise to much inquiry about it, which was always answered frankly and fully, giving glory to God. While this was going on, gifts of money and household articles of various kinds, from sources far and near, came in, and all were duly acknowledged. In the nature of the case this work could not be done in a corner; its object could not fail to interest the people, and the novelty of the principle upon which it was undertaken, could not but cause it to be much spoken of. This was the Lord's own enginery for making it known and opening the hearts and hands of the people in its behalf.

Meanwhile there were no advertisements or paid-for puffs, nor solicited articles about the Home in the public journals, nor any collecting agencies or organized auxiliaries, nor any machinery whatever brought into requisition, nor any attempt at securing publicity in any way.

When the house had been fitted up and furnished, and the time had come for opening it to receive the Lord's suffering children for whom it was designed, it was publicly dedicated to God. In the service a number of prominent clergymen and laymen assisted, and said many kindly things of the work, and the newspapers reported their sayings and doings. Editors and writers in the daily and weekly periodicals freely commended the work to their readers, and by these things thousands heard of the Home who before had not known of its existence. Of course, Doctor Cullis knew very well that a public dedication of the Home, assisted by those well known and highly esteemed by the people, would be reported in the papers and would elicit much comment, and would result in wide-spread knowledge of the work. And he knew another thing, that it would give rise to criticisms in all probability, or questionings at least, in many minds as to whether it was not done *for the purpose of making the work known and of inducing gifts to it from the people.* Yet he went forward with it. Why? Was it as a means of making the work known and getting money?

No, not at all. The thought of that was all against the dedication. The one reason impelling him was that it was the Lord's will. He was bound to glorify

God by acknowledging his gifts in every suitable way. God had given the house for the Home and everything necessary to put it in readiness to receive the sufferers, and he was bound to acknowledge the gift and glorify God for it, and also by a public dedication to devote it to the Lord for the purpose for which it had been bestowed. This was his to do, whatever any one might say or think about the motives for doing it, and it was the Lord's means, not his, for making his own work known. So the Lord pressed him to this his first public step in the work, and he did not shrink from the duty.

One other thing in this connection demands passing notice. A circular was issued about this time bearing the signatures of the Reverend Doctors Huntington, Kirk, Hague, Lothrop, and Miner, and of the Honorable Messrs. Alexander H. Rice, Jacob Sleeper, and E. S. Tobey. In this, they announce the fact that " The Home for Indigent and Incurable Consumptives " has lately been opened; and state further, that its design is for the help and comfort of a class of sufferers not before provided for, and so for the honor of Christ; that it has no funds or patrons to trust in but God only ; that so far it has been prospered; that to sustain it gifts must be constantly coming in ; that various things are needed ; that they have confidence in the economical use of all that shall be given ; and that everything possible will be done to soothe the pain and sustain the spirits of the sufferers and to console the last hours of those appointed to die.

This circular, if it had borne the signature of Doctor Cullis, would, against the uniform tenor of his course before and afterwards, have given indubitable evidence of a swerve from the principle of the work. It looks much like one of the customary means used by those who trust in God's blessing on the use of means devised by men, rather than in the Lord alone. But as it does not bear his signature and stands alone, the only thing of its kind in the record, we may safely assure ourselves that it was not his measure at all, but a kindly thing offered by good and wise men, which he did not feel at liberty to refuse.

Franke, the celebrated German, whose faith-work in Halle and in his parish of Glauca, just out of Halle, stands as the first great modern example of work upon this principle, was at one time offered by the King of Prussia a general collection in all the churches of the kingdom in aid of his work, a thing he never would have asked or thought of seeking, but which, offered unasked as it was, he could not and did not refuse, lest he should be found rejecting a gift from the Lord. So Doctor Cullis could not and did not refuse the aid of these noble and good men, proffered as it was in the form of a circular of commendation and appeal.

In the matter of coming before the public, however, as in everything else, Doctor Cullis has taken only a step at a time. In the opening of the Home, he asked and received light enough for guidance in the practical steps then to be taken and took them, and went peacefully and prosperously forward. A year later the matter came up again in the form of a question about reporting formally and fully the work of the year. This question tried him severely. He shrunk back at the thought of the step, lest it should be misunderstood as an appeal to the people on the one hand, and on the other as an egotistic parading of himself and his faith before the public. And it was settled only after much prayer that the report should be made, but not by himself ; that he should put his Journal into the hands of a beloved Christian friend in whose judgment and ability he could place im-plicit confidence, and let this friend select from it at discretion, and report whatever was deemed necessary to glorify God.

This was done, and as the subsequent history shows, it met the approbation of God and was signally owned and blessed by him.   Thus was settled finally the principle, that although *nothing must be published as an appeal to the people, yet everything must be publicly acknowledged to glorify God.*

THE FIRST YEAR.

XIII.

DEDICATION OF THE FIRST HOUSE.

September 27th, 1864.

THE twenty-seventh day of September has become a day of mark in the annals of the work as quite the dedication day. · There have been no less than eight dedications within the eight years, including that of the first house, and all but one have been on the twenty-seventh day of September. The simple reason for choosing that day in the first instance, was the excellent one that all things were ready. This is the record : —

" *Tuesday, September* 27, 1864. The evening of the dedication has closed. And such a feast of the soul! Many said it was a heavenly place. The house was crowded ; the services were excellent; and all seemed to enjoy it.

" Dr. Huntington introduced the exercises by explaining the object, and giving God the glory. A hymn was then sung, after which Dr. Kirk read selections from the Holy Book. Dr. Huntington then offered prayer, dedicating the house, the founder, and all connected with the Institution to the service of the Lord, to be wholly his. Singing followed, and the benediction.

" All were then invited to partake of ample refreshments, generously bestowed and prepared in the room below. After this feast of the body, the soul was again fed. The company having reassembled up-stairs, Dr. Kirk made some remarks, followed by Rev. J. D. Fulton, of the Tremont Temple, Rev. G. W. Gardiner, of Charlestown, Rev. O. T. Walker, of Bowdoin Square, Rev. N. G. Allen, and Dr. Hague, of Charles St. Church. Then Dr. Eames, of Concord, N. H., who came to Boston especially to attend the dedication, stepped forward, and taking me by the hand, said 'God bless you, and God keep you.' From all hearts and lips an Amen echoed throughout the room. This produced as deep a sensation as an eloquent speech. The exercises were interspersed with singing, and closed by all present uniting in prayer and a doxology.

"An aged widow lady gave, as she said, and which really was, the 'widow's mite,' consisting of a towel, a pillow-case, and a sheet.

"But the most touching incident of the whole day was at noon. While at dinner, little Mary called and brought five dollars from her mother, and then said, handing me a two and a half dollar gold piece, '*I* want to give this to your Institution. I have had it ever since I was a little bit of a girl, and I cannot spend it because it was given to me; so I want to give it to you.' I asked her if she had thought of it seriously, and if she would not be sorry if she gave it. But she was decided. So I took it for the Lord. More than eighty dollars were given during the day and evening. O, Lord, this is for thy glory. Bless it for Jesus' sake."

B. P. Shillaber, Esq., read a poem written by him specially for the occasion, commending the Love Divine shown in the object for which the work was undertaken, and admiration for the unostentatious manner in which it was displayed.

XIV.

THE FIRST HOUSE FILLED.

DOCTOR CULLIS looked to the Lord alone to send his poor sufferers to become his own guests in his own house prepared for them. In his Journal he says, three days after the dedication, " I have been praying for patients and hope to see the house filled. That same day a gentleman called about getting a man into the Home, and it was arranged that the Doctor should go and see him the next day. One week later, on the 7th day of October, the first guest of the Lord was received, and the Journal in recording the fact breathes the prayer, " May the Lord be with him while in the Home, and take him to himself when his days on earth shall close."

The second one was received three days later — with the prayer, " May the Lord be with her and make all her bed in her sickness." At the end of the month there were five, and before the close of the second month eight, and early in the third month the Journal speaks of the Home as full and also of the fact that Doctor Cullis had begun praying for a second house.

One of the beautiful things connected with this reception of the Lord's poor suffering children, is the pleasure it gave. This is all and alone to the glory of God, for none other than the Lord ever could have inspired any man with delight in receiving as guests, poor, hopeless, homeless consumptives, to whom he must give his time and attention, and for whom he must first expend his own earnings and then take all the risk of not having supplied to him what would be required over and above all he could earn. There could not be the pride of professional skill, or the hope of a name on account of extraordinary operations as in the case of curable patients, and of those requiring critical performances in surgery for their restoration. The money pleasure was all on the side of the greater blessedness of giving than of receiving, connected with the lesser blessedness of receiving as well as of earning in order to give. There could be no hope of requital in this life, through the gratitude and generosity of those who were received as guests, because they were not expected to recover, but to die. It was not as it would have been if those received had been hopeful children instead of hopeless consumptives. Surely nothing could have made it a delight to provide a home for these poor hopeless children of our Father but the Father's love in the heart of his child.

Another of the remarkable things connected with the filling up of the Home is the faith which looked and longed for, and expected and accepted the salvation of all who were received. There were none refused because of belonging to hopeless classes. The one question asked was, Are they homeless and hopeless? no question was asked as to their creed. The atheist, the deist, the bigot, the gospel-hardened, alike with the true follower of Christ, were taken if sent of . God, and given a home with every comfort possible, with the implicit confidence that the Lord who sent them would hear prayer in their behalf and save them.

Therefore, as they came in one by one, they were

accepted and sent to their quarters with benediction and the breathing of such a prayer as that recorded for the first one received, " May the Lord be with him while in the Home and take him to himself when his days on earth shall close."

And the thing of all others most extraordinary in this whole history is the fact that, although a very large proportion of those received, not only in the first house, but in all the houses added, and from first to last, have been from the ranks of those who are scarcely thought to be accessible at all by Christians, yet nearly all of the hundreds who have entered the Home have given good evidence before leaving it that the Lord had saved them.

5

XV.

PROVIDENCES DURING THE FIRST WEEKS.

FIRST acts become precedents. First gifts are often prophetic. On the 6th of October, within ten days from the dedication, a donation, accompanied by a good letter, came

FROM ACROSS THE ATLANTIC.

This was indeed prophetic of the many precious gifts and letters which have since come from totally unexpected quarters and from distant lands. When this gift came with the cheering words of the donor, the Doctor wrote in his Journal, " My heart did rejoice, and ascended to him who giveth all these good gifts. What a blessing that we have a Father who knoweth all our doings and can plan and order for us better than we can think."

Two days after this

A TEST OF FAITH

came also by letter. " A worthy clergyman," the Doctor says, " wrote advising me to have an organization, a board of trustees appointed, and an act of incorporation procured, *that thereby funds might be obtained more readily.* To this I replied that then the plan of this being a work of faith, would thus be lost sight of, — that the work is the Lord's, and to him I am looking, and on him I am leaning."

. Two days later the Journal records

HOME GIFTS,

which evidently came like sunshine after rain.

"*October* 10. Yesterday several donations in money were received, besides a variety of useful articles. May the Lord remember all who are so kindly interested in the work that they may be rich in Christ. It was a peaceful day to me. My heart seemed filled with love to the Lord, and he was near me all day. O, what gratitude I owe to him for his great goodness to me because he hath kept me in perfect peace, with all the care of the hospital work, with no funds only as he giveth. Yet I have not a fear nor an anxious moment about it. How faithful is the promise, ' Thou wilt keep him in perfect peace whose mind is stayed on thee, because he trusteth in thee.' One more patient entered this afternoon."

HELPERS,

like other good gifts, were amongst the early providuces and prophecies of the work. The Journal records, under date

"*October* 17. Miss K. called on me to offer her services gratuitously as nurse in the Home for the winter. I had been asking the Lord about nurses. She will enter upon her work in a day or two. Another offered her services one or two days in the week. The Lord supplies all our wants."

The Lord has supplied helpers from the beginning, like everything else, in answer to prayer. If, at any time, the want has been felt, it has simply caused a call on the name of the Lord, and he has supplied all that was needed, and his name has been glorified for the answer. And the best of it is that the helpers of his choice have been the best in the world. They have been greatly blessed in the work, and the work has been wonderfully blessed in them. Personal acquaintance with both work and workers en-

ables me to say this most heartily.   Another of the
noticeable first things of the opening weeks is

THE GIFT OF THINGS PRECIOUS TO THE GIVERS

for the work.   As a measure of appreciation this is
invaluable.   When the Tabernacle was in course of
construction in the wilderness, the children of Israel
took off their jewelry, the gift of their personal
friends in Egypt, and freely gave it for the service.
To the Home and its kindred branches of the work,
as we shall see from time to time, things most precious, because of endearing associations, have been
given freely, and the words accompanying them have
been such as to show that it has been " the expulsive
power of a new affection," the constraining sense of
the wonderful preciousness of the work as peculiarly
the Lord's, that has caused the gifts.   It was a month
after the opening of the Home, on the first day of
November, that the first gift of this kind came.   This
is its record : —

" *November* 1.   To-day has been one of many blessings.   This
morning a widow sent a valuable gold chain, once the property
of her late husband.   She had kept it for many years, and now
the Lord put it into her heart to give it to this cause.   How
many ways the Lord has of sending donations.   Each day some
rich experience proves that he is dealing with me in the work."

It is not strange that, much as he valued this token
of appreciation, and greatly as he desired all the Lord
would give him for the Home, the Doctor should have
hesitated about appropriating this gift until he should
ascertain whether the giver would not regret her generosity afterward.   Nor is it more wonderful that this
hesitation on his part should call forth from her an
expression of faith more precious than all the golden

ornaments in the world. The Journal says, under date three days later, that is, —

"*November* 3. To-day I received a note from the person who gave the chain. I had sent her word that I would retain it a while, that she might have further time to think of it, so that if she should alter her mind it could be returned to her. To which she replied that the chain was not given without thought and prayer, but she wished it kept secret for the present, as there were those among her friends who did not believe in trusting fully for *everything*, and who might think it ought to be sold for her use. 'I have lived the life of faith,' she adds, 'the last two years, and have had all my wants supplied. It is a blessed life.' May her faith ever be as strong in the Lord. To-day a bill was paid of thirty-one dollars, which I had given up as good for nothing. A long time ago I gave it to the Lord in prayer, and promised him, if it was ever canceled, that it should be his. This certainly is the Lord's donation to the work. I thank him with all my heart for his mercies. May I be more and more grateful."

There was no need of a death in the Home to foretell that death must come ; but there were two things connected with the first that occurred there worthy of note. It occasioned prayer, which was soon signally answered, for a burial place for the bodies of these children of the Lord, and it gave rise to a record which was prophetic of what might be written of all who have since died in the Home save one,

SHE DIED HOPING IN CHRIST.

"*November* 13. This morning the first death occurred. A German woman from Dorchester. She died hoping in Christ.

"*November* 14. To-day the first funeral rites were solemnized at the Hospital. The body was placed in the receiving tomb at Mount Hope, until a lot can be obtained. I have been praying for a place in some cemetery where all can be buried together and am daily looking for an answer."

We shall soon see how this prayer was answered.

The next gift received was valued, as from his friend, by the Doctor, and it was followed by one from a stranger through other parties, showing the gratitude felt by him — a representative of many — for the Home as a home for those whose condition had been so pitiless, yet so pitiful. The double record is this : —

"*November* 16. This morning a good Christian letter from my friend C. brought with it five dollars. Afterwards Dr. Kirk called and handed me a note containing ten dollars. This note was directed to Rev. F. D. Huntington or E. N. Kirk. It reached Dr. K., who brought it to me. It read as follows : —

"'I thank God that there is at last a place provided for the poor incurable, besides the almshouse. I inclose ten dollars, and pray God bless you.   Your Bro.   E. M. P. W.'

"To thee, O Lord, belongeth the praise for the bounties of this day. O, that my pen could tell even the half my heart feels of thanksgiving to God for his blessings upon the work. May I prove my gratitude by daily striving to live nearer to Jesus."

No gifts to any work of the Lord are more precious to him or his servants in the work than those

OF THE CHILDREN.

And from the beginning to the present time there have been many precious gifts to this work in its various branches from them. The perfection of praise in the form of gifts is from the children. Here is the account of the first : —

"*November* 25. This afternoon the following note was received, giving me the first account of a fair, undertaken by children who were unknown to me. May the Lord take these little ones in his arms and bless them.

"'Dr. CULLIS : —

"'*Dear Sir*, — Please find inclosed the sum of fifteen dollars, thirty cents, which is the proceeds of a children's fair, held in my house in Roxbury, for the benefit of the Consumptives' Home. After reading your circular, my little daughter, wishing to do something for the object, with the assistance of two school-mates, made up and procured in various ways, many small articles, which were sold with the above result. The little girls are delighted, and think it is a large fund. The sum, although small compared with the enormous receipts of the charitable fairs of the present time, will, I trust, like the widow's mite, prove an acceptable offering.

"'With respect, I am yours truly,   S. P. E.'"

Two days later the following record is found. Singularly enough it comes in the Journal right between a record of death and of the first intimation of an answer to the prayer for a burial place.

"Among other donations to-day, a little girl about seven years of age brought in fourteen cents, giving it instead of buying candy."

THANKSGIVING DAY.

"*November* 26. To-day is Thanksgiving. I trust I am thankful to the Lord for all his blessings to me and mine during the year past. I daily pray for a heart wholly wedded to Christ, that I may live entirely to his glory. When I review all that the Lord has done for the Home, I cannot but exclaim, 'What hath God wrought.' When the work was commenced in August, I had but little over three hundred dollars, and out of this must come my own business and family expenses, and the Home to be supported. But I knew in whom I trusted, — that I had a rich Father who always honors all drafts upon him. In him I have never been confounded. Daily he has supplied each need. The Home is established in working order; eight patients are abundantly cared for, having all their need supplied, and many luxuries; a matron, two nurses, two domestics, and a man to assist, are supported, all but one (Miss K.) being paid weekly wages ; all the expenses of the house have been paid ; and to-day I have more money on hand than when the work was commenced. Have I not reason to give thanks ? 'Bless the Lord, O my soul: and all that is within me, bless his holy name.'"

FIRST STEP TOWARD A BURYING PLACE.

See how the prayer before recorded begins to be answered! See also how the first prophecy of death in the faith is fulfilled in another death, itself a second prophecy for days to come!

" *November* 27. Yesterday one of the patients left us for a house in the Father's mansion, she having found Christ since her entrance into the Hospital. I thank the Lord that she departed in the faith. May he open the hearts of all the inmates, that Jesus may be precious to their souls.

"Within two or three days a petition has been prepared and signed by nine clergymen and five other gentlemen, asking the City Government for a lot in Mt. Hope Cemetery for the benefit of the Home. This petition will be presented on Monday. May the Lord guide and direct it to his glory. To the Lord I give the praise of all the blessings of the week. May he give me more and more grace that I may know him more.

DONATIONS SMALL.

Another of the prophecies of the first weeks was a time when the donations though continued daily became exceedingly small, none reaching above twenty cents (think of it!) for eight days. This brought special prayer and speedy answer, abundant to satisfy the heart that God had not forgotten, yet not enough to go far in sustaining the work. Another object God had in view which we shall presently see. O how often afterward were these same things substantially repeated! This is the record : —

" *December* 8. The donations this month have been quite small. Perhaps the Lord is trying my faith. Each day something is given, though I think no one has reached twenty cents. Since writing the above, Mrs. F. has given me two dollars. I thank thee, O Lord, that thou dost hear and answer prayer. Not fifteen minutes before this was given, I knelt and asked the Lord not to let the day pass without a donation."

EXPECTATIONS GREAT.

In the midst of this period of diminished gifts, we have the extraordinary record of prayer for double the work. · Another house. This too is one of the first things in the work which has been often repeated since that day. A strait for means, and prayer in that strait, less for deliverance from that in particular, than for some enlargement which would require much greater means. Then some token of loving care from the Lord, and soon prayer answered both for larger means and for an enlargement of the work. A strait — increase of faith while yet in the strait — enlargement asked, more given than has been asked, and God glorified alike for the strait, the increase of faith, and enlargement of the work. This has been the oft repeated course. The record of this first instance bears date four days only after the one concerning the meagreness of donations, and contains in itself the evidence that there had as yet been no relief, no considerable increase of gifts when the second house began to be asked for simply on the ground that the first was full. This record is as follows : —

"*December* 12. I have been praying for more extensive accommodations, as we are now full. Either that one of the adjoining houses may be obtained, or that a larger building somewhere else may be secured. ' Therefore I will look unto the Lord, I will wait for the God of my salvation, my God will hear me.' My prayer at the beginning of the month was, that God would give me greater donations this month than ever before. Thus far they have never been so small. But I am still believing, remembering that ' all things are possible to him that believeth.' Yesterday, when taking a friend over the Home, I mentioned the fact of the falling off in the gifts, and he replied, ' This is the way with all our charities ; when the novelty is worn off, people lose their interest.' Immediately my heart swelled with

gratitude to our Heavenly Father, that this charity was founded
on faith in Christ Jesus, and not on the gifts of the world. I
said only this, ' My trust is in the Lord, he will take care of it.'
My prayer is, as it has ever been, that the Lord will prove that
he is a faithful hearer and answerer of prayer. He will supply.
I do not fear. I have received a note from a lady containing three
dollars, and saying that she feels conscience stricken that she
has prayed so little for the Home recently, and with so little
fervency — that in conversing with another, she found it was
true in her case, and thought that was the reason the funds had
fallen off more than usual. She concludes by saying, ' God
grant that from all your friends, earnest, effectual prayer may go
up to his mercy-seat, and then he will surely answer.' "

SIGNAL ANSWER FOR MEANS.

Two days only passed after that in which the
prayer for another house as well as for enlarged donations has its record, then comes the following : —

" *December* 14. ' I waited patiently for the Lord, and he
heard my cry.' A day or two ago I received a note from a
stranger, asking me to call on her to-day. I have done so, and
found a young lady sick with consumption. She said she was
going to die soon, and as she had a little money, she thought
she would like to give it where it would do most good. At her
request her mother had visited various charitable institutions,
and the Lord had shown her that the Consumptives' Home was
the place to give her money. She made some inquiries regarding the work, and then, taking her purse, she presented me with
five hundred dollars. May the Lord abide with her in all her
sickness, give her perfect peace in Jesus, and make her ' dying
bed feel soft as downy pillows are.' I was not surprised at the
gift, although it was so large an amount, for I expect great things
of the Lord. I had asked for large donations this month, and
though they had been small up till to-day, yet I felt they would
come. To thee, O Lord, belongeth all praise and honor. ' I
will bless the Lord at all times. His praise shall be continually
in my mouth.'

THE BURIAL PLACE GIVEN.

" *December* 20. This evening's paper spoke of a meeting of
the Board of Aldermen, this forenoon, and among their doings
the following order was passed : —

" ' That the Trustees of Mount Hope Cemetery, under the ad-
vice and with the concurrence of the Committee on Cemeteries,
set apart for the use of the " Home for Indigent and Incurable
Consumptives," four lots or twelve hundred square feet in said
Cemetery, upon certain conditions.' Thus the Lord has heard
prayer, and given a burial place for those who die in the Home."

So ends the history, full of promise, full of praise,
of the first three months of the Consumptives' Home.

XVI.

THE PURCHASE OF THE SECOND HOUSE.

CONTINUED STRAIT.

THE first month of the year 1864, the fourth after the opening of the Home, like the preceding one, proved to be one of very small donations. Yet each day brought some reminder of God's care for his work. One day during this day of small things, Doctor Cullis spoke of it to a friend, and instead of getting encouragement he received a response calculated to cast a shadow over his faith, if anything could. It was this : " Yes, that is always the way. As soon as the novelty of any charity is worn off, people stop giving to it." A prophecy of utter failure. Yet it affected the Doctor only so far as to send him to the Lord with a more implicit reliance upon him for all necessary means.

The record of January is comprehended in its main features in the following notes of the Journal, the one at the beginning and the other at the end of the month.

"*January* 2, 1865. A substantial token from the Lord reached me to-day — seventeen dollars, fifty cents, — with the following kind note : —

" ' DR. CULLIS : —

" ' *Dear Sir*, — Our little fair for the Freedmen having realized so much more than we expected (five hundred dollars), we take great pleasure in appropriating the inclosed surplus to the " Home," upon which we fervently pray the new year will shower abundant blessings. Not less could we wish that the

. heart of the founder should daily experience the personal power of our Saviour's holy petition: "I pray for thee that thy faith fail not.'"

"*January* 31. To-night I desire to lift up my heart in gratitude to God for the blessings of another month. 'His loving kindness, O, how great!' The gifts to the work have been smaller this month than any one since it began. But there has been enough. No one has suffered, and the Lord has been with me in all things. O Lord, bless the work more and more. Bless me and keep me faithful. I long for more of Christ, and want to be more and more sanctified through him. I thirst for more work for Christ, and am not satisfied with doing so little for him who hath done so much for me. O Lord, I am in thy hands. Use me as it seemeth good in thy sight, only keep me near thee."

THE FAITH JUSTIFIED.

The Lord always glorifies himself by justifying the faith of his servants. February opened with small gifts and large expenses, but about the middle of the month the Lord began to pour in the means in a measure which not only met current expenses, but enabled Doctor Cullis to make a large payment on the first house, nineteen years before it was due. The novelty had worn off still more, and if it had been man's work, donations might have ceased, but as it was the Lord's, he caused them to increase.

February 9th the Journal says: —

"The Lord still sends his gifts though thus far this month they have been small, while the expenses have been larger than usual. But my trust is in him, and I lift up my heart in thanksgiving that he has given me the means to pay all expenses. My faith is strong in his arm. To him be all the glory."

February 16th, the first token of what was coming was given in the reception of a good return for that precious chain, about which the correspondence brought forth the confession of a faith still more precious. The entry opens with the incense of praise: —

" ' I love the Lord because he hath heard my voice and my supplication.' This morning I received thirty-five dollars for the gold chain given last November. It was placed in the store of Palmer and Bachelders, who kindly put it in order. There it remained, waiting to be sold, till now, in this hour of need, when the gifts have been so small and the expenses larger than ever before, the Lord in his love sends a purchaser, that we may realize the amount when most needed. How good he is! How wonderful are his dealings! Praise his great and holy name."

February 21st brought another token of enlargement in answer to prayer, and another sweet remembrance of the children's interest in the work, and a note showing by little gifts from a number of friends an extending friendship for the Home. The Journal says : —

"My prayer this morning was that the Lord would send a large donation to-day. How faithfully he answered. A firm in this city — strangers to me — sent twenty dollars. Little Freddy and his sister Mary fifty cents each. This evening I received a note without a signature which I will insert : —

" ' An offering for the " Home." From one friend, three dollars ; another, one dollar ; from sixteen others, fifty cents each ; from another, fifty-five cents. Total, twelve dollars, fifty-five cents.'

"May the Lord bless them all. What shall I render unto the Lord for all his blessings towards me."

Four days later the Lord sent a gift, the largest of all received as yet there, save the one of five hundred dollars received from the lady who was expecting soon herself to die of consumption. All the more gratifying as coming from a society, and therefore expressive of the unanimous confidence and good-will of its various members. The record shows the gladness it caused. It is as follows : —

" *February* 25. The Lord be praised ! This evening I received a note from the Treasurer of the Mass. Charitable Fire Society to the effect that the Society had by a vote decided to give the Consumptives' Home the sum of three hundred dollars, which I am requested to call and receive. How faithful he is! A committee from that Society visited the Home a week or two ago, and then called on me for further information, and this gift is the result. How can any one doubt God's hand in this? My desire is that not only my faith, but that of other Christians, may be strengthened by the knowledge of his care of this work. As our expenses increase, he sends us more means.

I have great reason to thank God for his blessings upon the work the past month. Four hundred and twenty-eight dollars have been given in answer to prayer. The Lord's name be praised."

FAITH FOR LIFE AND STRENGTH.

From what was said of the sufferings of Doctor Cullis in his childhood and youth, from constant ill health, some may think of him as a man of physical weakness and subject to frequent attacks of disease. The contrary of this is the truth. The Lord has brought him out into full vigor of health seldom interrupted by sickness of any kind. Yet he keeps him in mind of his dependence. His Journal says under date

" *March* 3. Yesterday I was very much prostrated physically, but to-day I feel better. My trust is in God, who will give me strength to work just as long as it is his will to honor me by permitting me to labor for him. When my work is finished here, he will take me to himself and give me rest. How often he proves to me that this is not my home, and that underneath are the everlasting arms. I am in the Lord's hands, praying for strength of body and soul."

FURTHER ANSWERS BY LARGE DONATIONS.

" *March* 15. This morning, in less than ten minutes after my prayer that a large gift might be sent to-day, twenty-five dollars was forwarded by a lady unknown to me. Thus it is proved that he grants the desire of them that fear him.

" This afternoon a stranger called, and after asking if I were

Dr. Cullis, handed me a roll of bills, which he said was for the Consumptives' Home. I asked his name, but he declined giving it, saying he did not wish it known. After he was gone I found the package to contain one hundred dollars. May the Lord bless the donor.

"*March* 20. Yesterday I received a check for a hundred dollars from a firm in this city. May they be greatly blessed of the Lord. The building now contains fifteen souls to be supported. Ten are patients, — all our present apartments can accommodate, — the others are on pay, and yet the supplies are adequate to the demand. I am kept in perfect peace, free from anxiety lest the means shall fail. To God, on whom I rely, be everlasting praise.

"*March* 28. The Lord has been very precious to-day. While conversing with a friend on our Father's goodness, and of the gracious manner in which he was blessing us, a letter came, containing a check for fifty dollars. My friend had just before given me ten dollars, and in less than fifteen minutes after this, twenty dollars were given. This afternoon, the President of the " Detroit Young Men's Christian Association " called to inquire about our operations. I gave him, in as few words as possible, our history, and the way God blesses us. Before he left, he gave me an order for twenty-five dollars. To the Lord belongs all the praise, the honor, and the glory. What shall I render unto the Lord for all his blessings ? Truly, God is love. How unworthy I am of such favors."

RECORD OF THE MONTH CLOSED WITH TEARS OF JOY.

"*March* 29. It is now half past six, A. M., and my heart melts within me, and finds relief in tears when I think of all God's goodness toward me, so unprofitable a servant. O Lord, I ask thee for more grace, that I may honor thee in all my doings this day. What a comfort to be able to lean upon Jesus always ! I have asked him to guide me in each duty, to lead me beside the still waters, to refresh my soul, and to keep me in perfect peace. I have asked his blessing upon the work, that he will guide me in each step that I shall take, and that he will give me a large donation, that the work may be enlarged. O, the blessedness of prayer ! The Lord has heard, and so faithfully answered, that I cannot doubt his continued presence in all difficulties as well as joys."

April opened, as March ended, in the sweet sunshine of the smiles of the Lord.

The one event of the month which seemed to touch all hearts in the house, was the death of one of the Lord's dear children. She had been six months in the Home, and by her sweet spirit had endeared herself to everybody. All knew and loved her as Fannie. On the morning of April 2d, she "quietly breathed her spirit into the arms of our loving Saviour. She was a general favorite with all. The patients loved her; the nurses cherished a tender regard for her; and visitors often brought or sent little delicacies or flowers specially for 'Fannie.' Blessed are the dead who die in the Lord."

The Psalmist says "Precious in the sight of the Lord, is the death of his saints." Then we need not wonder that the Home is precious to him, for from thence many of his saints have gone and are to go home to him to whom they are precious. In this sense as also in that in which the words were first uttered by Jacob, "This is the house of God and the gate of heaven."

RENEWED PRAYER FOR A SECOND HOUSE.

The reason for asking another house of the Lord with expenses nearly doubled as they would be by the enlargement, was not the superabundance of money, but of applications for accommodations in the Home. The record is as follows: —

"*May* 2. I pray earnestly for another building, as there are applications now from patients who cannot be received. I know my prayer will be answered, for the Lord has promised that 'all things whatsoever ye ask in prayer, believing, ye shall receive.'"

PRAISE WHILE WAITING.

One cannot trace the history of this work without seeing how wonderfully the Lord shut his servant up to himself as the grand centre and source of his joy. Prayer for enlargement or relief in any way seems first to have been answered by causing a deep, sweet, and joyful sense of entire dependence and an entire sinking into the will of the Lord, and finding it " good, acceptable, and perfect," and then came the thing asked for, or something far better. An illustration of this we have in the record of

" *May* 8. A new morning brings peace from the Lord. I would praise him for all things. May this be a day of peculiar nearness to Jesus. I want to honor him in all I do, living wholly to his glory. May he bless the work as he pleases. O Lord, keep me humble, — keep my heart satisfied in Christ. I am praying for one of the adjoining buildings, that we may have more room to accommodate patients who are now waiting to be admitted. May God answer as seemeth good in his sight."

NEGOTIATIONS

for the second house, like every other movement forwarded in the work, had to be commenced, not upon the strength of funds in hand, but of faith in the Lord. The Journal says under date of

" *May* 10. I have made an effort to obtain one of the adjoining buildings. Have found out who is the owner, and intend to-day to see what can be done. As there were four applications for admittance yesterday, I feel it my duty and the Lord's will that the work should be enlarged.

" *Noon.* I have been to see one of the owners of the house below, and find the only way it can be obtained is to buy it. As there are good tenants in it now, the owners do not wish to remove them except to sell, which they intend to do in the fall. There is a mortgage of twenty-five hundred dollars on the house, which can remain. They wish the balance to be cash. The price is four thousand dollars. Thus I need fifteen hundred dollars to pay the amount over and above the mortgage. The house on the other side is leased to a good tenant for five years. I called to inquire if he would relinquish his lease, but he is not willing to move. This is the Lord's work. To him I am looking for guidance, praying him to stop me if I am going too fast, and not permit me to obtain either building unless it is his will, and that if he sees it best that I shall purchase, he will send the means to pay the fifteen hundred dollars, and for what alterations will be needed, also to furnish the apartments. I remember the promise, ' Ask, and ye shall receive.' "

TRIALS OF FAITH

came, as they always do, with this new step for enlargement. Two days after commencing negotiations for the house, Doctor Cullis says, " I am praying yet for the means to enlarge, if it is the Lord's will. Perhaps no donation was allowed, that my faith might be tried. As it seemeth good in the Lord's sight, his will, not mine, be done."

Shortly after this record comes another, showing how the adversary, through good men, and the dearest of friends, as in the case of Job, may assail us to destroy the foundations of our confidence and retard the work of our hands. It is this : —

" Yesterday, a dear friend rather put a doubt into my mind as to the expediency of enlarging. He did not say he would advise me not to obtain the other building, but spoke of the expenses — whether I should have patients enough to fill it, etc. This led me to think and pray more. I am sure I do not desire this unless it is the Lord's will, and if I know my own heart, it is wholly for his glory. I have no fear of the result. If the Lord permit me to enlarge, he will furnish the means. My trust is in him."

FAITH CONFIRMED.

The answer was not far off. It never is when Satan has been defeated in his attempts to destroy one's faith. The Journal says, —

" *May* 13. The Lord has been near to-day, and given me much comfort in leaning upon Jesus. The prayer for enlargement has been answered. This morning twenty dollars were received, and five this afternoon.

"*May* 16. Twenty dollars were given yesterday, and thirteen to-day. I am still praying for the fifteen hundred dollars. Hitherto the Lord hath helped us, and he will still provide.

" *May* 22. Within the last three days I have received one hundred and thirty-three dollars and fifty cents towards the new building."

FURTHER NEGOTIATIONS.

" *May* 25. This morning, with the owner, I examined the house adjoining the Home, and found it in better condition than I expected, and have now the refusal of it for a few days. The cost of altering will be considerable, and many things are needed to render it suitable for our use. I now desire to lean upon the Lord for direction, praying that he will guide me and that I may make no mistakes."

THE DECISION.

" *May* 27. Two more patients have applied for admission, proving to my mind beyond a doubt, that it is the Lord's will that I should go on, trusting in him. I now feel that it is certainly my duty to secure the building, and I pray for the means. I can with my own funds, pay the fifteen hundred dollars, for I have that amount and a little more on hand. I trust in the Lord to supply means wherewith to alter and furnish. Upon his strong arm I am leaning."

THE PURCHASE MADE.

The first house was purchased August 3, 1864. The second May 31, 1865. A little less than ten months intervened between the two. This is the record : —

" *May* 31. This morning I bought the house adjoining the Home, for thirty-nine hundred dollars, one hundred less than the owner asked for it He inquired all about the Home — how it was supported, etc., and then said, he would, in consideration of the cause, sell it for the above price. My trust for the increased cost and expenses is now, where it ever has been, in the living God. Large sums will be needed to make the alterations, but he who paid his taxes from the fish's mouth will supply. I am now praying for large means. I feel that I have done right in making the purchase, for my prayer was that the Lord would not permit me to make a mistake, but if it was not best to enlarge, to stop me."

The payment made at the time the house was purchased, was five hundred dollars. Twenty-five hundred dollars remained on mortgage, and nine hundred dollars was to be paid when the title papers should be ready. Ten days after the purchase the transaction was completed, the title papers given, and the nine hundred dollars paid over. The Lord enabled his servant to make this payment chiefly out of money earned in his profession, *and to thank the Lord for the privilege.* He exclaimed, " O, I am so happy in giving something of my own! and I only wish I had thousands to use for Christ. Yet what a poor offering is gold to him who gave his life for us."

This is one only of the continually recurring instances in which the original design and desire on the part of Doctor Cullis, as it was put in his heart by the Lord and accepted by him in giving a special work to his servant, is seen in its outcroppings. It was sought and accepted as a work to which Doctor Cullis could devote his own earnings, first of all and for which beyond this, he was to ask and receive of the Lord. It is precious to be able to trace this, step by step, as an unbroken covenant of gladness. All is given gladly. More is asked with a faith always gladdening the heart, and all is given that is required.

XVII.

TO THE END OF THE YEAR.

THE month of June was filled up with daily tokens of the Lord's kindly remembrance, but without gifts of money. Amongst the gifts bestowed was a barrel of flour on the 7th, from one who from the beginning had been in the habit of keeping the meal unwasting, by the bestowment of it, barrel after barrel, as often as needed, and it was received with the prayer "May the Lord supply all his need." Also a half barrel of white sugar sent on the 8th, by the Union Sugar Refinery. "A great help when sugar is eighteen cents a pound. Blessing on the kind hearts of those who have thus remembered us." Thus day by day the manna fell, but money did not come in. Was this to bring out the fact more palpably of

THE ABSOLUTE DEPENDENCE

of the work on the Lord himself? There was a double demand for a comparatively large amount. The second house was to be fitted and furnished, and just then came a notice from the Savings Bank in Charlestown, that they wished the mortgage for the twenty-five hundred dollars paid off. The time had fully come to begin on the house, and the time was at hand for paying off the mortgage. What should be done? What was done? The 5th of July the carpenters and masons were set to work on the·house, with the record in the Journal, " My faith is strong. · God can make the wilderness a pool of water, and the dry land springs of water.' In him is my trust, ' For the Lord God will help me, therefore I shall not be confounded. Therefore have I set my face like a flint, and I know that I shall not be ashamed.' O the comfort of abiding in the Rock ! " On the 15th of July the bank was satisfied by the payment of nine hundred dollars on the mortgage, and kindly remitted the extra interest, one and three tenths per cent.

The way this payment was made, gives perhaps the reason for the delay in the bestowment of other money in these days of dearth. Certain United States bonds had been purchased and held as a building fund. These were sold to make the payment on the mortgage.

Meanwhile the men were at work on the building, and the fund was gone. The power of the Lord to keep in peace under such circumstances is shown by the following record made at this time : —

"*July* 17. I praise God for the peace that reigns within tonight. The Lord will provide.

" 'The birds without barn or store house are fed,
From them let us learn to trust for our bread ;
His saints what is fitting shall ne'er be denied,
So long as 'tis written, the Lord will provide.' "

Another matter came up during these days causing no little thought and prayer.

HOW SHALL I REPORT THE WORK

at the end of the year ? Ten weeks remained. It was due to the Lord that his gracious gifts and goodness should be shown forth, and it was due to those in whose hearts he had put the good-will to give of their money and property, that they should be informed as to how it had been used. Yet how should this be done was the question. The first entry about this matter contains the gist of the perplexity.

" I desire for the glory of God that the many wonderful answers to prayer may be published; but to write it myself, and to speak of answers to my prayers might seem to others like boasting. This I would avoid, for my sole desire is that the Lord may be honored. I leave it all in his hands who will make it plain."

THE QUESTION ANSWERED.

Shortly after this perplexity was expressed, light came in the very moment when Doctor Cullis was writing the words, " Thus far I have received no light." The very next words gave the solution of the difficulty.

" It seems to me that the best way would be for a third party to take my journal and edit it. This would avoid all personalities, and I think would have a better effect than if written by myself."

This ' seeming' proved to be the Lord's teaching.

The next question was " Who should that person be ? "

To this the answer came sweetly and quickly. Doctor Cullis's mind was turned toward one who could understand the Lord's dealing in the work, and immediately he put the question to the test by alternative prayer. He prayed that if it was the Lord's will that she should edit the report, he would lead her to give her assent when he should propose it to her ; but if not, that she should decline to do it. When called upon she offered to do it. Thus the Lord decided it and filled the heart of his servant with praise.

HOW THE CARPENTERS AND MASONS WERE PAID.

Out of his own earnings first in part. This was God's order, in accordance with the original covenant of the work. Here is the record : —

"*July* 21. This noon I found myself short of money, and knowing that I should need some for the work this afternoon, I asked the Lord either to send me a donation, or to put it into the hearts of some of my people who are indebted to me to call and pay their bills. Before tea four bills were paid, and a donation of four dollars given to the work. Thus the Lord gave me more than I needed for the anticipated expenses of the day. To his name be the praise."

This, however, though all that was required for the time, was only a small part of the amount to be paid for the work. The end of the month was at hand, and then other bills would be due while the treasury was empty. All anxiety is taken away, however, by a beautiful answer to prayer. Doctor Cullis asked for a proof that the Lord would take care of the bills. He says, "I ask this, not that I doubt for a moment, but for the glory of God." Then he adds, "It is now half past eight in the morning. May the Lord hear and answer."

"*Evening.* A poor widow, who is herself supported by charity, sent this afternoon fifty cents. In the widow's offering I have my proof."

The last day of the month came. The bills would be due the next day. The treasury was still empty. At night the record is made, —

"*July* 31. I am too tired to write to-night, but my heart is full. Jesus has been near me to-day. His mercies have been so marked that I have stood and wondered. Many prayers have been answered, and I can now rejoice in a living Saviour. I prayed this morning for money to meet all the bills becoming due to-morrow. In answer to this some debts were paid."

This enabled him to meet the bills.   Then he adds :

" Another great blessing, for which I would praise the Hearer
of prayer, is, that a young man, for whom I have labored and
prayed, and who had devoted his energies to serving Satan, is
now seeking Jesus.   May he find him precious to his soul."

The carpenters had not yet finished, or the masons
or the plumbers.   The painters had not commenced.
To meet all these expenses the Doctor had not five
hundred dollars, his own included, in the world, and
the house was to be furnished, which would require
several hundred dollars more.   " August 2d a little
girl whose mother gives her a dollar a month spending money, brought in a dollar for the work, as she
had done three or four months before, and the receipts of the day were fifty-five dollars."   August
11th is recorded as " a day of mercies, greater than
ever before experienced."   The first token of the
morning was a note inclosing five dollars.   The second was a letter from a friend who had just found
the Saviour in answer to prayer in his behalf.   A
month before, this friend had spent the day with Doctor Cullis and visited the Home.   He said : —

" ' Doctor, you must either have a large income, or very influ-
ential friends to carry on this Institution.'   I said I had neither,
but that my trust was in a living God, who had promised to
give to all who ask in faith.   He said he could not appreciate
it.   I took the opportunity after dinner to talk to this friend of
the blessed Saviour who had died for us.   He heard me kindly,
and then repeated the old story of the inconsistency of Christians.
I told him that I should pray for him, and to-day he writes me
that he has found Christ precious to his soul."

The third token was one which met the carpenter's
bill before it was presented.

" A gentleman called at the Home and left the cause one hundred dollars.   He would not give his name.   May the blessing
of the Lord rest upon him.   See the goodness of God !   Just at

the time when so much is needed, he sends. Never once have I doubted, so I am not surprised at large gifts. His promises are sure and steadfast. 'Heaven and earth shall pass away, but my words shall not pass away.' "

Two days later the carpenter's bill, two hundred and ninety-four dollars was presented and paid.

The next day the Doctor stopped at the bedside of a patient who was about to die, and said : " You will leave us soon, you will be with us only a little longer." To which he replied " It is better to go and be with the Lord." An only sister of his, the last of his family, followed him to the grave.

Five days later still, August 19th, the Doctor, who had already asked for the bills of the mason and the plumber, because his custom was to pay as soon as work was done, prayed in the morning for a large donation, knowing that the bills might come at any moment. Three young ladies from Lynn came with the proceeds of a fair they had conducted, amounting to four hundred and twenty-eight dollars and fifty cents. Whereupon the Doctor writes in his Journal "how faithful is he that hath said ' ask and receive.' There is no perhaps about this, it is ye *shall* receive. To his name be all the glory." Still larger amounts were needed. Other bills were to come in. The report must be printed. The first house sadly needed repairs, had needed them from the first, and the matter was put off for want of money. A musical instrument was very much wanted to aid in the daily worship, and especially in the Sunday services. Each of these objects as they came up were carried in prayer, and laid over upon the Lord.

The mason's bill of ninety dollars was presented and paid August 24th, ten dollars and twenty-five cents

having been kindly deducted from the full amount by
him.   August 28th the Doctor prayed in the morning for large gifts.   Before nine o'clock twenty-six
dollars were given.   One dollar from a young miss
to whom her mother gave it to use for pleasure, and
the Lord inclined her to give it to him.   In the afternoon two beautiful pictures were sent in.   They
had been promised six months before when not
needed, and now when needed the Lord caused them
to be sent.   They were " The Believer's Vision " and
" The Mother's Dream."   From another person, a
bedstead, mattress, and rocking-chair came in.   It was
a day of mercies, and in recording it the Doctor said :
' My heart is full, I cannot express the deep gratitude that fills my soul.   How numberless are the mercies of the Lord ! and such peace in Jesus ! "

The first day of September the Doctor was asked
to advance a hundred dollars on the work.   Right
thankful for the ability, he did it.   Ten minutes afterward a parcel was handed him containing the proceeds
of a fair held by the children of the Beach House,
Swampscott, two hundred and fifty-six dollars and
forty-six cents.

The painter was requested to bring his bill.   Special prayer was made for fuel for the winter.

September 4th money began to come in for an organ — ten dollars given.   The plasterer's bill was paid.
September 9th the painter's bill of three hundred and
sixty-one dollars came and was paid.   If the plumber's
bill which had been requested, had been sent, it could
not have been met, but the Lord provided by causing
delay in sending it in.   At this the Doctor exclaims,
" How wonderfully God orders all things !   Who
ever trusted in him and was confounded ?   The Lord

is my Shepherd; I shall not want." Five dollars more came in for the organ, and other five promised. September 15th the Doctor records his gratitude to God for a large quantity of crockery, glassware, hardware, and other articles needed for the new house, and exclaims, " How wonderful are his mercies! Truly his name is love. When the house is ready he sends a supply." And then adds, " I am needing a large amount of money, and have been praying for it, and daily looking for answers. As yet but little has come in this month, but I am casting all my care on him who careth for me."

" This was in the morning. At noon, as I needed money to pay a bill, I asked the Lord to send me twenty dollars for that purpose. In less than ten minutes a letter was delivered at the door, which on opening I found to contain fifty dollars, with the following written on a card: ' For the new building, and may the Lord reward thee.' How my heart swelled with gratitude to God for his blessings. I was not surprised, for I expected an answer to my prayer.

" Yesterday a basket of beautiful grapes was left at the door of the Home. To-day, when the basket was called for, the Matron inquired who they were from. ' It is no matter about the name,' was the reply, ' it is a small gift, but it is the first time our vine has borne, and these were all, so we thought we would send them here.' May the Lord bless her for sending the first-fruits to the suffering ones."

This was a gift precious indeed in the spirit and manner of it. Another scarcely less so came shortly after — a gold dollar from a little girl about eight years of age with this note: —

" Will dear Dr. Cullis please accept this small gift from a little friend. I. E. N."

One day six dollars, and the next day eighteen dollars came in for the organ, and it was obtained.

SECOND HOUSE DEDICATED.

The record is as follows : —

" *September* 27. God's great and holy name be praised **for all** his blessings. I thank him that in his infinite wisdom **and** goodness, he has spared my life and health to the beginning of this day. One year ago this evening, the first building of the Home was dedicated to God. I little thought then, that when its first anniversary occurred, a second would be offered to him. But all things are possible with God. Never has he failed to hear and answer prayer. Our wants have all been supplied. And though at this time we are in greater need than ever before, I know he will help us. May the Holy Spirit be with me to give me sufficient grace for the day, and may he abide with us all the evening, that not only the building, but the heart of each one present may be dedicated to the living God.

" *Midnight.* The second building has been dedicated to Almighty God. The services commenced by singing the chant, 'I will lift up mine eyes unto the hills,' by the choir of Emmanuel Church, S. A. Bancroft, organist. After which Rev. Dr. Huntington gave a brief history of the institution. Then followed prayer and another chant ; reading the Scripture, by Rev. J. M. Manning ; dedicatory prayer, by Rev. Dr. Huntington ; and another chant. Remarks were made by Dr. Chickering, Dr. Bolles, Rev. J. I. T. Coolidge, and Rev. Mr. Manning. A hymn was sung, and a poem delivered by B. P. Shillaber, followed by singing of the Doxology. After the benediction the company were invited to the rooms below, where the ladies had prepared a feast for the body. The tables were loaded with good things, and all seemed to enjoy themselves. A friend, on shaking hands with me, left twenty-five dollars in my hand. Others gave small sums, amounting in all to fifty-five dollars. To the Lord I return thanks for all his blessings."

A MONTH'S TRIAL OF FAITH.

Just before the close of this the last month in the first year of the work, the Doctor makes the following record : —

" I have this morning, in prayer, told the Lord of my need for the work — of the large amount required, and the small funds on hand, with the expenses nearly three hundred dollars above the gifts, and my own funds very low. I besought him who both hears and answers prayer, that he would send the means as needed, that I may record the loving-kindness of the living God.

"*Evening.* I found on calling at the house, that the young ladies connected with the fair held at Lynn, had called and left twelve dollars, the further proceeds of that enterprise, and that four little girls of the ages of four, six, seven, and eight, had got up a penny fair, resulting in the sum of four dollars and seventy-six cents. With one exception, this is the largest gift in money since the first day of the month. The Lord is trying my faith more than ever before. Never since the work commenced has the need been greater, and never have I had so little money. In the living God I trust, and I know I shall not be confounded. Six dollars and fifty cents have been given for the organ."

A moment's retrospect will show at once that this trial of faith though not expressed every day, was a daily trial from the beginning to the end.

THE UNLOOKED-FOR RESPONSE.

Not unlooked for in fact but in manner, all the more gladdening because of the manner in which it came. This is its record : —

"*September* 28. A day long to be remembered. How shall I render sufficient thanks to my Heavenly Father for the great blessings he has this day bestowed upon me. This forenoon two ladies called and informed me that a friend had authorized them to furnish the new house with everything needed at his expense. They declined to give his name. But the name of God is always known. His be the praise, and may his blessing rest upon the kind friend. This is a great help, and another proof that God hears and answers prayer. For several weeks I have been asking for means to furnish the house, and the Lord, in his goodness, instead of sending the money to purchase all these things, puts it into the heart of this friend to do it all, with the exception of the articles previously mentioned, thus saving me much trouble and care. What a faithful Promiser !

CLOSE OF THE YEAR.

"*September* 30. Upon this the closing day of the first year of the work, I lift up my heart in gratitude to the Giver of all good gifts, and would praise his great and holy name for his tender care, having supplied all our need so that we have lacked nothing. To all our kind friends into whose hearts he hath given the grace to help us, I would say in the language of Paul, ' We give thanks to God always for you all, making mention of you in our prayers, remembering without ceasing your work of faith, and labor of love, and the patience of hope in our Lord Jesus Christ in the sight of God and our Father.'

"In answer to prayer the Lord has given in cash, five thousand, nine hundred and sixteen dollars, twenty-eight cents. Expenses, five thousand, nine hundred and sixteen dollars, twenty-eight cents. Leaving no balance in the treasury. But there is the never failing bank on which to draw, where the drafts are never dishonored. The work was commenced with only a little over three hundred dollars in money, but with strong faith in God's promises, and never has the promise failed. Not a day since the work was dedicated to the Lord has he failed to send his daily gift of some kind.

" ' O, give thanks unto the Lord, for he is good ; for his mercy endureth forever. O, that men would praise the Lord for his goodness, and for his wonderful works to the children of men !

" ' Unto him that is able to do exceeding abundantly above all that we ask or think, according to the power that worketh in us, unto him be glory in the church by Christ Jesus, throughout all ages, world without end. Amen.' "

THE SECOND YEAR.

XVIII.

TRIAL AND TRIUMPH ABOUT THE REPORT.

ONE of the first things of the second year was the Report of the previous work. This had been fully determined upon, and the Report had been prepared and sent to the printers. Then came

A GREAT TRIAL ABOUT IT.

Doctor Cullis says he felt an irrepressible shrinking from laying bare the workings of his own mind and heart, his hidden daily life with. God, as he had done it in his Journal to the world. Yet there seemed to be no other way of making known the gracious dealings of the Lord with him in the work. Then too he desired from his inmost soul to glorify God as the hearer and answerer of prayer, which could be done in no other way but by telling how he had prayed and how the Lord had answered him. Franke had done the same thing substantially a hundred and seventy years ago and Müller was now doing it from year to year, but all this did not repress — much less remove — the painful shrinking he felt from what some might think to be the parading of himself and his own heart-life before the public. Some would think him a boaster, and others a fanatic.

While Satan was plying him on all sides in this way, he spoke of the matter with several friends, and uniformly got from them the same kind of comfort that

Job did in the days of his trials from his friends
Hardest of all to bear was a silent refusal to write an
introduction to the Report from one highly esteemed,
who had all along counseled, aided, and encouraged
him in his work. He could not blame a man had
in reputation for drawing back from deliberately in-
dorsing him, a young and comparatively little known
man, before the public, and all the more this caused
his own heart to become faint about issuing the Report.

At last the trial became so great that he ordered
the printers to stop their work upon it.

Singularly enough the first light he obtained about
the matter was light out of the darkness itself. His
own record of it is this: " As I have been so unusually
discouraged and distressed about it, *I cannot but feel
that Satan has been busy trying to stop the work.* But
what a comfort to know that God is stronger than
Satan. May the Lord remove the cloud."

Shortly after this he received a letter from a perfect
stranger, who spoke of sending substantial aid as soon
as he should see a report of the work and know the
need. Then again the Lord sweetly opened to him
the second verse of Hebrews xii. : " Looking unto Jesus
the author and finisher of our faith, who for the joy
that was set before him endured the cross, despising
the shame." And great comfort came into his soul
from the words " enduring the cross, despising the
shame." This dispelled the cloud and put him at
rest upon the subject, and he ordered the printers to
go forward. The same hand that gave him peace
changed also the mind of his friend, who without ex-
planation wrote the desired introduction, and the Report was issued.

THE TRIUMPH IN THE TRIAL

was followed by results fully accounting for Satan's desire to prevent if possible the issue of the Report. When the first parcel came from the printers the Doctor says : —

"I knelt down with the bundle in my hands and asked the Lord to bless each one to his own glory, that they may, by his grace, be the means of strengthening the faith of Christians, and of leading many to seek a living Saviour. I prayed the Lord to keep me humble, to give me grace to bear all criticisms, and that the Report, in all its circulation, might redound to the glory of God. I then took the first copy, and mailed it to my mother, feeling that as she first taught me to say, ' Our Father, who art in heaven,' I ought to honor her. Fifty cents have been given to-day, towards paying the expenses of printing."

The ninth day after this the Journal contains this record, —

" *November* 27. Day by day encouraging words come to me regarding the Report. My heart overflows with gratitude to God, for such signal favor upon a work that was cast upon the world with fear and trembling. To-day I heard from a man, to whom a friend had handed a Report; he says, I never read such a book before in my life ; it is wonderful! Tell Dr. Cullis, I will give him five dollars every year as long as I live. Again, a lady told me, this morning, she had never read anything that had done her so much good as the Report ; she thanks the Lord, that he gave me grace to print it. A lady called this afternoon, gave me five dollars for the work, she having read the Report. A friend has paid a note of forty-five dollars, fifty cents, being the increased interest on the mortgage ; he incloses to me the receipted note, with three dollars from a friend who had read the Report."

A fortnight later the mail brought the following letter : —

"*December* 12, 1865.

" Dr. Cullis : —

" *Dear Sir,* — Please accept my thanks for the Report.

" I think nothing except the words of inspiration has ever more interested me than the ' History.'   It is news from near home, and so full of Christ.   Indeed it is a light shining on the narrow path leading fast by the Great Rock, and though it is far ahead, it helps my feeble vision, and makes me stronger for the march. God bless you for giving it to the world.

" The Institution appears to me like a great fountain of good, sending out streams in every direction, and not the least of its blessings is the good it does the donors, those that give for Christ s sake:—such a fine opportunity to invest in the funds of the Home Government, ' the land beyond the sin.'

" I am trespassing on your time and patience.   Forgive me.

" Very respectfully yours."

From this time forth, in continuous stream, evideuces of God's approval came in, some in the form of contributions in aid of printing the Report, others showing that it had opened hearts to give for the work in an extraordinary manner.

" A poor woman, who is one of the many sufferers of this world, but at peace with Jesus, and living a life of faith, having been totally helpless for years, depending wholly upon God's gifts, through his children, for her support, having read the Report, writes : ' Please accept this little for the " Home " ; it has been lying in my work-box, during all my sickness, some ten years; I have had no occasion to use it, as my wants have all been supplied.   It is but a little I know, and instead of sixty cents, I wish it were six thousand dollars.   The " Home " and the founder are the Lord's; there will be no failure.   Praise the Lord for such a " Home l " ' "

" A lady called at the Home, and left one dollar and thirty-six cents in currency, and six dollars in gold; the gold pieces were keepsakes, but after reading the Report, she felt she could not keep them but must give them to the Lord."

Contributions were increased also in number, and in amount by means of the Report.

"One day," says the Doctor, " a gentleman called to see me about the work.   As I was not at home, he left word for me to call at his house, which I did this afternoon, when he told me some one had given him a Report, which he had read with great interest, saying, ' it is the most wonderful book I have ever read.' After some inquiries about the work, he handed me fifty dollars, saying he wished me to consider him an annual contributor, and requested that a Report might be sent him every year. May the Lord bless him! O, how rejoiced I am, that my Father is honored by this little book."

Many had their faith greatly strengthened. The Doctor says, —

" A stranger called, said she had read the Report with a great deal of interest and gained renewed faith thereby.

" A lady in speaking to me of the Report this afternoon said, that owing to a severe affliction, she had lost her faith in special prayer, and had only used the Lord's Prayer until she read the Report, when the Lord blessed it to the *renewing* of her faith and she had again commenced to take God at his word, and pray for all things."

Conversions to God also followed the reading of the Report. The following is an instance. The Doctor in his Journal says, —

" Yesterday I learned that a man was brought to Christ by reading the Report; he has since made an open confession of the saving grace of the blood of Jesus. I praise God for this, and I thank him that he gave me grace to publish the book, when my heart was sinking within me, for fear of man."

It was not long before a second edition was required, the first having been exhausted. How it was paid for will be explained to the glory of God by the following entry in the Doctor's Journal: —

" This morning a dear friend of mine gave me five hundred dollars; as he handed me this amount, I asked him how it should be used, whether towards a new building, to pay for the present buildings, the general expenses, or for the printing of another edition of the Report, the first being nearly exhausted, all of which are subjects of daily prayer. He replied, ' Use it as you please.' I replied, 'I would much rather you should designate,' when he asked which object I preferred. This I refused to answer, silently asking God to guide the decision. He re-

plied, ' I gave it for the printing of the Report.' I have been
praying for many days for the means to print a new edition. See
how carefully the Lord supplies all our need at the right moment. The Reports were nearly gone, the demand for them still
as great as at first, with no money to print more, when the Lord
inclines the heart of this dear friend to give the required sum.
' They that trust in the Lord shall be as Mount Zion, which cannot be moved, but abideth forever.' Psalm cxxv."

And now if it be asked by any one, " Was not the
Report issued as an appeal by Doctor Cullis for contributions to the work ? " the answer is clearly, *No.
It was issued as a part of the work itself, essential to
the glory of God in the work.* And it is so given in
this history of the work.

Let it be borne in mind that no report whatever of
the work was issued until after the second house had
been purchased, fitted up, furnished and paid for entirely, all — with the fitting and furnishing of the
first house — in answer to prayer, without an appeal
to man. And that it was high time that what the
Lord had done in answer to prayer should be told to
his glory. We have seen also the excessive shrinking
of Doctor Cullis from preparing first, and afterwards
from publishing, the Report, as much from fear that
through misconstruction of his motives and unbelief
in the principles and methods of the work the contributions might be decreased, as from any thought of
the contempt it might bring upon him. He and the
work together, as he well knew, must stand or fall
together, and if he should be condemned and rejected
the work would be destroyed.

Against all this and the discouragement from
friends, he, strengthened by the Lord alone, went forward, led by the Lord himself, to complete and perfect triumph.

XIX.

VICISSITUDES AND SUPPLIES.

THE first month of the second year was one of unusual trial for want of money. No day of that or any
other month passed without tokens of remembrance
from the Lord. Some days, however, they were exceedingly small. A dollar, fifty cents, five cents, and
one day one cent only. Some days nothing at all in
money and very little in other things, one day only
two loaves of brown bread, and another a newspaper,
nothing more. Yet to him without whom not a spar-
row falls, and who numbers the hairs of the head,
nothing — not even one cent or two loaves of bread,
or a newspaper, is too small to be noted and to be
used in confirmation of his care for us. The year
opened with less than fifteen dollars in the treasury,
reduced the next day to a little more than three dollars. The contributions were small and the wants
were large. Time after time, after meeting the day's
demands for necessary daily bread, nothing remained
over. But this made no difference whatever in the
fare of the Lord's dear suffering children in the Home.
In mentioning one of these short times Dr. Cullis
makes this remark in his Journal: —

" All things needed have been as carefully provided as if there
were thousands of dollars in the treasury. The matron never
knows whether there is a large amount on hand or not, for the
reason, that if she knew that funds were low, she might be
tempted (and rightly too) to economize, while it is my wish
that all should be bountifully dealt with, and I see that this plan

is always carried out. I have not the least fear for the present or future. I feel and know that this is the Lord's work, and with such promises as these, how can I doubt. ' Commit thy way unto the Lord; trust also in him; and he shall bring it to pass.' Ps. xxxvii 5. ' And this is the confidence that we have in him, that if we ask any thing according to his will, he heareth us; and if we know that he hear us, whatsoever we ask, we know that we have the petitions that we desired of him.' 1 John v. 14, 15. These are not man's promises, but the promises of a *living* God. Here is another: ' What things soever ye desire when ye pray, *believe* that ye receive them, and ye *shall* have them.' Mark xi. 24. ' *Only believe.'* "

STOVES FOR THE UPPER ROOMS.

Early autumn brought with its cool weather, the necessity for means to warm the rooms occupied by the sufferers, and this caused special prayer specially answered. Here is the record : —

" This afternoon, knowing the necessity of stoves for some of the upper rooms, as the weather is quite cool, I went to the Lord in prayer, and told him of our need, praying him in some way to supply us. I then went down town to a friend, to look at stoves, and inquire the price. After deciding upon two that I thought would answer, I asked the price, when he said, ' That's all right, I shall not charge anything,' and said he would see that they were put up. This man knew nothing of our great need; he had never visited the ' Home,' knew but little about it, and not a word did he know of the state of my purse. Did not the Lord answer my prayer and incline the man's heart to give the stoves ? I thanked him, and thanked God for his goodness, praying that his Holy Spirit might be given to this kind friend, that he may know the preciousness of Christ's love."

FURNACE AND COAL.

It will be remembered that just at the close of the preceding year a gentleman, a stranger to Doctor Cullis, authorized two ladies to furnish the second house throughout, and it was done.

As the autumn drew on, Doctor Cullis, foreseeing that a furnace and fuel would soon be indispensable to the comfort and well being of all in the Home, and having no funds to buy with, made it, day after day, his daily prayer that the Lord would provide.

Well, one day, just in good time, the gentleman who had paid for furnishing the house, without having a hint of the want from any one but the Lord, called in person at the house, asked how the house was to be warmed, ascertained the facts in the case, and of his own accord had a furnace put in, with fourteen tons of coal at his own expense, whereupon Doctor Cullis says, " The Lord has answered my prayer. Truly whosoever believeth in him shall not be confounded. His be the glory. May his Spirit be given to the kind donor."

A TWENTY FOLD RETURN THE SAME DAY.

At a time in these days of strait an incident is recorded by Doctor Cullis in the Journal, with evident reluctance, lest, as he said, " it should seem like parading his own private charities." This reluctance was overcome by a sense of duty to acknowledge God's tender care. He says : —

" *November* 11. I think I have never so keenly felt the need of means for the Home, and my own use, as at present. This afternoon a poor woman, whose history I have known for some time, and who has a sick husband, over eighty years of age, called on me, stating that she had only had a ten cent loaf of bread for herself and husband to eat, since Wednesday — and to-day is Saturday. Notwithstanding my own need, I felt that I could not withhold from one in greater straits than myself, so in Christ's name, gave her enough to procure necessary food for a few days. The Lord did not forget it, but this evening has returned the amount with bountiful interest, he having sent me forty dollars for the two that I gave him.   This forty dollars was the amount of a bill unexpectedly paid this evening. ' There is that scattereth and yet increaseth.' "

ANOTHER PRECIOUS RETURN.

From time to time, Doctor Cullis has had occasion to use his own earnings, sometimes to the last dollar in hand, to meet demands for daily supplies, or to pay bills for work done on the Home, and he has rejoiced in the privilege of doing so.   In some instances of this kind he has been deterred from mentioning this in his Journal by what, all things considered, must be set down as false modesty.   False modesty, because it was at his own prayer in the beginning that God gave him the work as one to which first of all his own earnings should be devoted and as much more as the Lord might please to bestow upon it in unsolicited gifts from others.   It is therefore due to truth and to the glory of God to tell of what the Lord has given Doctor Cullis in money to bestow, and grace to give it, as much as if given by any other person.   He has given gladly but recorded it, if at all, with reluctance.

An incident in the first year, which passed in this way without record, was brought out early in the second year by a very precious return.   In one of the first year's straits the Doctor sold his watch.   It was a good gold watch.   A friend of his who was abroad and knew nothing of this purchased for him a watch worth many times more than the one sold, and in the autumn of the second year, returned and presented it to him.   This has always since been one of the glad memories of the early days of the work.   One of a thousand proofs that " he that soweth bountifully shall reap also bountifully."

THE LAST DOLLAR.

" *November* 23. Knowing that the wages of two of the ' help ' were due this morning, I prayed the Lord to send me the amount by nine o'clock, the hour for visiting the Home; at five minutes before nine, the sum came in; after paying the wages, I have left twenty-one cents. While at the Home, a visitor gave me one dollar; soon after, the matron asked for money to buy some flour; I handed her the dollar; thus the Lord cares for each *moment* as well as each day. Nine o'clock, P. M. Within a half hour five dollars have been given."

JUST IN TIME.

" *January* 9. The bill for printing the Reports came in this afternoon. Now see the goodness of the Lord. I sent for this bill some three weeks ago. At that time I had not the money to meet it; twice since, I have inquired, but have seen nothing of i, until to-day. The amount is four hundred and forty-two dollars, ninety cents. I thank the Lord that I have enough on hand to meet this. Truly it is best to ' rest in the Lord,' and to ' wait patiently for him."

A SPEEDY ANSWER.

" *March* 26. Remembering that the gifts for many days have been quite small in money, at noon I asked the Lord to enlarge the supply according to our need; in less than half an hour, a lady called and gave me forty dollars. How unmistakably the Lord proves that he is a living God."

DAYS OF PECULIAR STRAIT.

" *June* 27. The gifts for several days have been very small. Yesterday four cents were given. A friend expressed anxiety because the gifts were so few while the expenses were larger than ever. My reply was, that I scarcely thought of it; I know in whom I trust and therefore carry no burden. It is the Lord's work, not mine. He will provide. I can give no better proof of this than to mention that, at tea-time, a note was brought me with fifty dollars inclosed. ' They that trust in the Lord shall not be confounded.' "

The last of the year, like its beginning, was a time of living by the day.

"*September* 18. Yesterday's gift was thirteen cents. This morning my funds were entirely exhausted. I called upon the Lord, and he heard me. This evening a note with twenty-five dollars inclosed was left at my house. See how good the Lord was at the hour when we had not a dollar in the world. He inclined the heart of a stranger to send to our aid.

"*September* 21. I commence the day without a dollar in the world, yet I have no fear, for I know 'the Lord will provide.' 'Our help is in the name of the Lord, who made heaven and earth.' Ps. cxxiv. 8. We are now buying our provisions and groceries, and paying for them each day, thus obeying the command to owe no man anything. Therefore I am looking to the Lord for our daily need, that we may be able to keep the command. The above was written at eight o'clock, this morning. All day I have been looking for the answer to my prayer. At six o'clock, this evening, a friend called and paid me twenty-five dollars on his account. This man I had not seen for weeks, and he had not been requested to pay his bill. To the Lord belongeth the praise. 'What things soever ye desire when ye pray, believe that ye receive them, and ye shall have them.' This afternoon there was another application, and he a poor colored man, who contracted his disease while in the army."

Among the many contributions there are scarcely any that have not in them, or in the circumstances connected with them, something of special interest, which, if it were possible to do it, would impel an account of them, but that would swell this history to four times the size it should be. All that can be done is to give a few, almost at random, to show

THE SPIRIT OF THE DONORS.

A poor widow called on Doctor Cullis October 5th, in the evening, and related the following story : —

"Her husband died two years ago, in Charleston, S. C.; afterwards, during the bombardment of that city, she lost everything

she had in the world; after great trials, she was enabled to get
through the rebel lines, and come North. Before she left, she
exchanged what little Confederate money she had for gold;
handing me a five dollar gold piece, she said, 'I gave one hundred dollars Confederate money for that, and have carried it in
my pocket for more than two years, but the other evening while
at the dedication of the new building, I resolved to give it to the
Lord.' See how carefully the Lord kept this gold piece those
two years, to be given now in our great need! 'How manifold
are thy mercies.'"

Two days after this the following note was received,
inclosing twenty dollars.

"*October* 6.

"DEAR DR. HUNTINGTON, — When you go again to the
Hospital, will you put my mite into the treasury; and tell Doctor Cullis that a loving heart asks to leave it there, which, like
his, has been bereaved by the disease to which he ministers;
and like his (in lowlier mission,) consecrates itself to give all it
has to give, to the Master, through his sufferers, and so render
back the love which 'dealeth with us as with sons.' Believing

'That God, who takes away,
Yet takes not half
Of what he seems to take,
Or gives it back,
Not to our prayer —
But far beyond our prayer.'

I pray for him."

December 18th, five dollars pinned to a piece of
paper "from an old lady ninety-two years old, after
reading the Report."

Christmas Day, Christmas offering before nine
o'clock in the morning one hundred and sixty-six dollars from fifty-five friends. From New Jersey, one
hundred dollars and a large bundle of towels, stock-
ings, shirts, drawers, skirts, blankets, sheets, etc:
One hundred dollars in money and a bundle of nice
things for the Home with touching words of cheer by
letter from a lady whom the Doctor never had seen.

One " who three times before had been moved by the goodness of God to help " the work.   Twenty dollars from one who called and introduced himself while the bundle was still open.   Five dollars from another visitor.   Five dollars from one of the assistants.   One dollar, two dollars, one dollar, respectively, from others.   Fifty dollars from two ladies and five dollars from another.   Amounting in all to three hundred and twenty-five dollars, besides a constant stream of good things all day long — flowers, fruits, meats, jellies, etc.

The Doctor had been praying specially during several days before Christmas for large gifts, and this was the answer.   For all of which he asked special blessing upon the donors, and gave glory to God.

A poor sufferer sent a small contribution, very precious because it was all she had, and because she had been keeping it ten years.

" The amount was sixty cents in silver. While it lay upon my table, a friend called, who inquired about it, and on being told its history, added to it another sixty cents in silver. During the afternoon, 'a mite ' (five dollars), inclosed by mail, reached me. A young miss called, bringing twenty dollars from her mother, with five from herself, as a ' New Year's offering.' This evening a poor woman called on me, bringing a dollar towards paying for the Reports; at the first I declined receiving it, knowing how great was her own need. Her reply was, ' I must give it, for the book has done me more than a dollar's worth of good ' "

One morning the mail " brought an envelope." the Doctor says, " directed to me, which on opening I found to contain a fifty dollar bill pinned to a piece of blank paper."

One afternoon a gentleman called on the Doctor, and he says, " After a happy talk for Christ he gave me his check for one hundred dollars."

One morning a lady called with four dollars from

four ladies who sat up the night before to hear the Report read, one of them over eighty years old.

One Sunday evening a clergyman, from another State, present at the service, handed the Doctor fifteen dollars inclosed in a note saying it was what he had received for preaching to a neighboring congregation that day.

A gentleman from the West, in Boston collecting money for a p'rpose dear to him in his own city, called, having seen the Report, and presented a little roll of bills to the Doctor, — twenty-five dollars. This, out of his own purse for the Home, from one raising money for a benevolent institution hundreds of miles away!

One who visited the Home, quietly dropped his check for one hundred dollars in the box. Twenty-one dollars the same day was given by other visitors.

A Sunday-school sent in forty-two dollars and six-teen cents.

A note came requesting Doctor Cullis to call on a lady in reference to the Home. He called. She asked him about the work, and handed him three hundred dollars, — money left by her mother in her hands to be given for charities as she might think best.

A second gift was received from the Massachusetts Charitable Fire Society. The amount was four hundred dollars.

From Dutchess County, N. Y., a note came inclosing ten dollars, saying, " Were it in my power to send you one dollar for each year of my unprofitable life you would receive eighty-one instead of the ten."

One hundred dollars was presented by a gentleman, who stated that his daughter had died of consumption, and had requested him to give this amount from her private funds.

One who is not rich, sends from ten to twenty do_
lars a month. He devotes a portion of his income
regularly to the Lord.

At a moment when large donations were needed
and asked of the Lord for the work, a gentleman sent
two hundred dollars, saying, " Since you will not ask
man when you want money I will send you some
without asking if you need it." The Doctor adds,
" God bless him ! I was not surprised, though it is
the largest gift received for months. I called upon
the Lord and he heard my prayer." The largest
gift of money received for the Home up to the end
of the second year was one thousand dollars, the proceeds of a fair held by a gentleman and lady in their
own house.

XX.

SALVATION OF ALL IN THE HOME.

HITHERTO we have been tracing mainly the good providence of God in giving his suffering children a home, and in providing for their comfort. Let us for a few moments see how he cares also for their spiritual well-being. On the 19th of January, 1865, Doctor Cullis, in his Journal, states that " up to this date we have not had one death in the Home without a hope in Christ." This fact is the more remarkable because so many of those received in the Home are from the ranks of those least likely in all human views to be saved.

The same day it was also stated that " among the sick there are three unconverted. I am praying for one near his end, but yet no peace ; he says, he wants to be a Christian but cannot — seems distressed — yet is unable to give himself into the hands of a loving Saviour."

About three weeks after this Doctor Cullis mentioned to a friend the condition of the three patients as nearing death without hope. His friend's response was, " You will soon have to stop saying you have not had a death out of Christ." The Doctor was startled, and with earnestness replied, — " I know the Lord will yet open their eyes that they may see, and he will open their hearts that the Holy Spirit may enter in. I have not a doubt of their conversion.

Each of these unconverted ones have been urged to come to Jesus. To one of them I spoke yesterday, praying that he might give his heart to Christ. His reply was, ' It's of no use for me to repent, for if I should, the next moment I would use profane language.' Yet even for this man I have faith to believe that he will yet be born again."

ONE OF THE THREE CONVERTED.

The second day after this conversation, the conversion of the first one among the three occurred. After mentioning with joy a timely contribution, the Doctor adds : —

"I have a still greater reason to rejoice to-night in that another soul has been born again. A poor colored man, who has been with us about five weeks, and is now near his end, has this day found Jesus a precious Saviour. Yesterday he was in agony of mind, to-day he says, 'I am so happy I could fly.' He is one of those mentioned three days ago. He was then spiritually blind, but now his eyes are open. O, blessed be God in that 'while we were yet sinners, Christ died for us.' "

THE SECOND ONE CONVERTED.

Two days later the second one of the three gave her heart to the blessed Jesus, and her conversion was used of God to awaken deep interest among all in the Home. The account of it as follows : —

" Another poor sufferer is rejoicing to-night ; for many weeks she has been seeking Jesus ; she would read her Bible in bed, and pray for pardon, but the faith to believe was needed, and for many days she has been groping in darkness. On asking her each morning if there was peace, she replied, 'No!' But this afternoon the Holy Spirit entered into her heart, and her countenance was radiant with joy unspeakable. Although very low, yet she wished all who were able to leave their beds, to come to her. She desired even the domestics might be called, and as they came and stood around her bed, she told them of her happiness, and urged those unconverted to come to Christ. She told them that the Lord had stretched down his hand and pulled her out of hell. To-night she grasped my hand, and looking up, said, ' O, doctor, I am so happy, I can die now, I want to go,' and inquired how long she could live. 'Only a little while,' I replied. ' I long to go,' she said. The whole house seems alive at the great manifestation of the Holy Spirit."

THE THIRD ONE SAVED.

The same day, Dr. Cullis says : —

" The third one of the three asked me this morning to pray with him, said he wished to give his heart to Christ, but says, ' I am such a great sinner, God cannot forgive me.' After leaving the bedside of the woman who was so happy, I went to his room, and on asking him how he felt, he replied, ' Most dead, doctor.' ' But have you found Christ?' ' No.' ' Why not ?' ' I am looking for some great change, but it does not come.' I told him to look for nothing, but simply to cast himself upon the mercy of his Saviour. I asked him, ' Do you repent of your sins ?' ' Yes.' ' Have you asked God to forgive you?' ' Yes, many times.' ' And don't you think that he *has* forgiven you ?' ' No, I feel that I am too great a sinner to be forgiven.' ' Then you don't believe the Lord's word, for he has promised to forgive *all* who truly come unto him ; do you realize this, that you are doubting God's word ?' He looked up, and fixing his eyes on me, his whole countenance changed, lit up with an expression, that told in plainer language than his simple utterance, ' I do believe.' O, the joy and peace of a sin-washed soul ! My own heart is full to overflowing ! Truly, the Spirit is with us. I pray he may continue until not only the sick, but all who, in health, labor and dwell with us, may find Jesus precious to their souls !

" What a day of rejoicing ! Now, know I that the Lord saveth his anointed ; he will hear him from his holy heaven, with the saving strength of his right hand. Ps. xx. 6."

DEATH OF TWO IN ONE DAY.

The following day, the Journal goes on to say under date : —

" *March* 14. The poor girl who was so happy yesterday, is happier to-night, she having entered the mansions prepared for those who love God. She died at six o'clock. The man who, last night gave his heart to Christ, died this afternoon. Some one asked him if he had found his Saviour? He could not speak, but smiled and nodded assent. This morning he said he was happy and at peace. This man is the last of the three mentioned under record of March 9. In answer to prayer, all of them were born again.

"I have often wished that those who question the reality of sudden conversions, and death-bed evidences, could witness the radiance that almost instantaneously overspread the countenances of these dying ones, when but a moment before they looked the picture of utter hopelessness. We know how sad it is for a person to live a whole life of sin, and then to give only these last weak moments to Christ; yet is it not joyful that a soul should be saved even at the last? Did not our Lord, in the parable, receive laborers into the vineyard at the 'eleventh hour'?

"This is the first time we have had two deaths in one day. Many persons would think that this visitation would cast a gloom over the household, yet I think the feeling is one of rejoicing to those among us who love Jesus — that the departed have, after many prayers, given such abundant evidence of the presence of the Holy Spirit, with which the house even now seems to be filled. The poor colored man, who was converted a day or two since, was this day baptized, at his own request."

A FOURTH CONVERSION.

Doctor Cullis says : —

" *March* 15. 'Rejoice evermore, pray without ceasing, in every thing give thanks, for this is the will of God, in Christ.' 1 Thes. v. 16, 17, 18. I have great reason to rejoice, to pray, and give thanks. Another inmate told me this morning, that he felt his sins were forgiven through Christ Jesus. This is the fourth conversion since Sunday. Thanks be unto God, who hath given the victory through our Lord Jesus Christ."

Prayer for the immediate .salvation of all yet unconverted in the Home, is recorded under date March 21st.

THE ANSWER.

One week after this record the Doctor says : —

"When I visited the patients, another told me that he had given his heart to Christ, and was at peace. As I had been looking for the conversion of this patient, I was not surprised. I am also waiting for the awakening of others. May the Holy Spirit abide with us until all are brought to Jesus."

This last aspiration shows that then as yet Doctor Cullis had not learned the great lesson of the abiding which was afterwards so sweetly taught him by the Lord.

The first Sunday in April the Doctor records two more conversions. He says : —

"I have had such a feast, and such a sense of the Lord's nearness, that to his glory I desire to record the joy that fills my soul. I found a new patient that had been with us but a short time, and who came without any hope in Christ, feeling that her sins were forgiven, and she washed clean by Jesus' blood.'

The next was a young man who was awakened at the bedside of the woman who called all in the Home around her the day she found the Saviour. The Doctor says : —

"On going to the men's room, I spoke to one for whom I have prayed, and to whom I have talked for many weeks. I said to him, 'How thankful we ought to be for such a beautiful morning, the day on which our Saviour rose from the dead.' I then said, 'If you could know how anxious I am that you should give your heart to Christ, and how long and earnestly I have prayed for you, I know you would think more about it.' To my surprise, he confessed that he was a sinner, and that he had been praying for pardon. Never before would he acknowledge that he was a sinner, or needed forgiveness.

"On the day that the dying girl requested that all in the house might come to her bedside, when she told them of her joy, and urged all to put on Christ, this young man left the room, saying, 'Here is a reality in religion that I never saw before!' and from that time he became more thoughtful, though saying nothing until this morning. I asked him if he felt that the Lord had answered his prayer, and that his sins were forgiven. His eye lit up as he said, ' I *do* feel that I am forgiven.'

"I thank God for the conversion of this young man, who has so long withstood the influences of the Holy Spirit. By the grace of God, I can now make the record, that all the patients have given their hearts to Christ. There have been eight conversions in three weeks. ' What shall I render unto the Lord for all his benefits unto me!' "

Thus was the prayer answered. All in the Home were saved. Two months later two others, young men who had been in the Home about a week, were also won to Jesus. A month after this the Doctor says under date

"*June* 10. This morning, as I went from bed to bed, I talked to each of the patients of the love of Jesus. This is my frequent habit, but to-day I felt a greater need of earnestness, as we have four unconverted with us; one, a poor woman, near her end, and so hardened that she will not listen, or when she does it is only to scoff, and say she don't want to hear anything about it. She has often promised to pray for pardon, but when I asked her this morning if she had, she said, no. I urged her not to put it off too long. It will be too late soon. Another said, she wished to be a Christian, and promised she would pray for a new heart. The others say they want to be cleansed. May the Lord give to each a new heart, and put a new spirit within them."

The next day one of the four said she had given her heart to Jesus. Two days later still another found acceptance with God. Three days still later the Doctor says : —

"I have been much exercised for several days in behalf of one of the patients, who can live but a short time, and without a comforting ray of hope to cheer her dying hour and to give her a safe entrance into the kingdom. I have often plead with her,

.and she has been especially prayed for, but as yet her heart
seems not in the least softened. She will not speak upon the
subject, and refuses to answer any questions put to her, in regard
to her soul. Yesterday I found her so low, I told her she could
not remain with us long, and asked if she was going to die in
that manner. She replied, 'No.' 'But you have no time to
lose.' I spoke of the love of Jesus, and asked her if she would
not pray for pardon, when she promised she would. On asking
her this morning, if she had kept her promise, she would not
reply. I felt too much grieved to talk with her, and saying, 'May
the Lord have mercy upon you,' I left her bedside. Earnestly
I have to-day prayed for her conversion, knowing that the command is, 'Pray for one another,' James v. 16, and not forget-
ting the promise, 'Ask and ye shall receive, that your joy may
be full.' John xvi. 24."

Three days after this the Doctor again talked with
her. He says : —

"'Blessed be the Lord, who daily loadeth us with benefits, even
the God of our salvation.' Ps. lxviii. 19. On going to the
bedside of the poor woman mentioned yesterday, I asked her if
she had prayed? No answer. I then said, I am more anxious
for your soul than your body. Won't you pray? 'Yes.' I
then talked to her of the love of Christ, and of her nearness to
eternity, and said that the whole household were praying for
her. Soon tears filled her eyes and coursed down her cheeks,
and she exclaimed, 'Lord forgive me my sins for Christ's sake.'
Tears continued to flow, while she told me that she did repent,
and again exclaimed, 'Lord forgive me my sins for Christ's
sake.' With a heart filled with gratitude, as she grew calmer, I
left her, praying that she might have 'perfect peace.'"

The next day but one the Doctor says : —

"June 21. On going to the bedside of the patient mentioned
above, she exclaimed, 'O doctor, I am so happy, I feel now that
I am ready to say the Lord's will be done, to get well or to die;
I feel that all, all my sins are forgiven.' I replied, I am very
thankful, but why did you not give your heart to Christ before,
when we have been pleading with you, for so long? 'I don't
know, I was as hard as a stone. I cannot praise the Lord

enough for this woman's conversion.   She is the one mentioned some days since as a scoffer.   How manifold are God's mercies."

Still later we have this record, —

" One more patient told me this morning, that the burden was taken from his heart, and that he was trusting in the Lord."

XXI.

THE HOME APPRECIATED BY THE INMATES.

Two things in the Home cannot fail to impress those who visit it and converse freely with those who in it enjoy the Lord's hospitality. One is the preciousness of Jesus to them and the other is their appreciation of the Home.

A gentleman called one day and was shown the chapels and the rooms. Some questions of his about the inscriptions " Jesus Only " and " Christ the same yesterday, to-day, and forever," indicating that he did not understand them, led his guide to ask him about himself, whether Jesus was precious to him? This called forth from him a frank confession of his entire ignorance of the saving power of Christ, and of his unbelief in the Bible. Shortly after, as they were exchanging kind words with one after another of the sufferers, the gentleman asked one how he was. The answer was, " I am suffering in body, but O, Jesus is so precious to me ! " A similar question to another was answered, " O, I am wasting away ; I shall soon die ; but Jesus is with me and makes all my bed in my sickness." The gentleman was deeply moved, and when taking his leave expressed with much emotion his interest in all he had seen and heard and in the work.

At another time another visitor asked some kindly question of one who had lately been received in the

Home, to which he replied, " Why, it seems to me that
I have got into heaven here."   One day two patients
were received.   " One of them was a colored woman
in the last stages of consumption.   The only place for
her was in the room with three white women.   Before
she was sent up-stairs, I asked the patients if they had
any objection to having a colored woman occupy a
bed in the same room with themselves.   Each replied,
emphatically ' No,' and one said, ' I feel so thankful
for so good a home, that I would not keep out any
one, black or white.'   Another patient entered to-
day, who has worked for five years in a tailor's shop
in this city ; since her sickness, she has spent the little money she had saved, in trying to get well ; she
is an orphan, with no friends in the world.   She will
stay with us but a little while — almost ready to
walk the golden streets.   A poor German woman,
whose husband is in the institution, called to see him
this morning, but before going up-stairs, said she
wished to see the matron, when she took out her
purse, handed her five dollars, saying, ' It is not for
my husband ; I wish to give it to the institution.'
The matron replied, ' I cannot take it; you have
yourself and three children to support by washing,
and cannot afford to give away so much.'   The poor
woman insisted, and said, ' Don't you know, if I give
this to the Lord, he will give me more strength to
work ?   You must take it for the Lord.'   The money
was received, while I pray God to give her strength
equal to her faith."

Of course no great amount could be expected in
contribution from those directly benefited by the
Home.   The poor hopeless, homeless ones come to it
as a last tenting place in their journey already nearly

at its end. A few, however, recover sufficiently by means of its kindly shelter and skillful nursing and medical aid, to go out again into active life, and some get entirely well. From these many cheering words come back accompanied by such substantial tokens of gratitude as they are in circumstances to give. These contributions are small but worth a great deal. The following note inclosing two dollars is one of these, and all that space will allow to be given.

"*June* 30, 1866.

" Dr. CULLIS : —

" *Dear Sir*, — Please accept, with this small offering, the heartfelt gratitude of an inmate for what God, through you, has done for her, both soul and body.

" That you may, in the world to come, reap a rich reward, is the wish of one who will ever kindly remember the founder and the Home."

Orphanages, schools, colleges, and all institutions for the benefit of the young may reasonably look for benefactions from them in return, but the Home for homeless, hopeless consumptives, from which most of its recipients go out into the home above, must look alone to him whose children they are for its support.

XXII.

A THIRD HOUSE ASKED OF GOD.

LONG before the end of the second year it became apparent that the Lord purposed an enlargement of the Home. The first suggestion to Doctor Cullis was one which has since been wonderfully realized, — that of a building specially for a Home in some place where there would be ample room, both within and around. This, however, was rather a prophecy than a plan for the time then being. The Lord's immediate plan was for the purchase of another house in connection with the two which were already occupied. But when, after a time, the Doctor was convinced of this, his own mind went out after one or other of the houses on one side or the other of the Home. But here again the Lord had another and a better thing in store, a house in the rear fronting another street, and so situated that the intermediate space could be occupied by a building, the lower part of which should be very useful for domestic purposes while the upper part should be a beautiful chapel into which all three of the houses would open.

THE NECESSITY FOR A THIRD HOUSE

was pressed upon Doctor Cullis over and over again by the Lord in various ways, causing him to wait on the Lord week after week and month after month in prayer about it. The first entries in his Journal about it are the following :

" *February* 12. Within two or three days have commenced to pray regularly for the means to erect a new building, one that shall every way be suitable for the work.

"'*February* 13. I am more and more convinced of the need of a building for the work. To-day two applicants were refused for the want of room : one of them it seemed to me we must take, his surroundings being more wretched than any I had ever witnessed before. Besides the want of room for patients, there are other reasons why it seems to me right and proper to build. One is, where so many sick people are gathered together in a house, the arrangements for cooking, washing, and ironing, and all such matters, are inadequate to the demand ; another reason for building is that God may be glorified, that his promises may again be verified. ' All things whatsoever ye shall ask in faith, believing, ye shall receive.'

" The beginning of a fund for a building commenced about one year ago, at which time I picked up a five cent piece in the street. The thought came to me, I will dedicate this to the Lord, as the first offering towards the erectioh of the new building. Many friends added, as they said, ' a brick ' until the sum of nine dollars was reached. This may seem like the grain of sand in comparison with the amount needed, yet our gracious Lord ever loves to magnify his power, by choosing the ' least ' things, the ' grain of mustard seed,' ' the foolish things,' to ' confound the mighty.' "

From this time on one daily prayer seems to have been for " the new building," for already the assurance seems to have been given that a new building would be bestowed. For example, under date March 2d, the Doctor says in his Journal, —

"I am feeling more and more the need of a new building ; I pray for it with the assurance that it will be erected, for the promise of God is, if we ask *we shall receive.*"

Application after application was made, twelve at one period, within a few weeks, but there was no room to receive the suffering ones. Some of these applications were wonderfully touching, and it was painful to be compelled to refuse them. Here is one, —

" *May* 22. This morning a poor widow, with five children, applied at the Home. I could only give her medicine, and tell her to call again. I have called on the parties occupying the houses adjoining the Home, in regard to obtaining them. One party cannot possibly give up his house, and if he could, would not let, but sell it. The party in the other house is willing to dispose of his lease, provided he can obtain one to move into. I pray the Lord to direct this matter. It is to his glory, not mine. As I feel that my prayer was answered by the increased applications of patients, I cannot refrain from trying to carry out the plan to enlarge."

All the negotiations for an adjoining house failed. The Lord reserved the consummation for the next year. The final entry in the Doctor's Journal for the year in reference to it was this : —

" *September* 27. Two years ago to-day the first building was dedicated to the Lord ; one year ago the second. I had hoped that another would have been offered to him to-day ; but it was not **his** will, therefore I am content."

XXIII.

THE SECOND HOUSE PAID FOR.

THE first house was purchased without any payment in cash down whatever. The whole amount
was secured by mortgage. The second one was paid
for, in part, at the time of the purchase, the balance
being secured by mortgage. Doctor Cullis had been
taught by the Lord himself that this would not be in
violation of the ·principle essential to faith work,
" Owe no man anything." He was compelled to
purchase in this way, instead of renting, by two
things — want of money to buy or build with, and
continual failure to find any suitable building which
he could rent for the purpose. In each instance the
property was its own security for the purchase-money,
so that in case of failure there could be no loss to the
former owner ; the property would simply revert to
him enhanced in value, or be sold and paid for out of
the proceeds of the sale. Meanwhile, the interest
upon the purchase-money would be less than the rent,
and the houses could be freely altered in any way
requisite for their purpose without having first to get
the consent of another party. These facts decided
the principle upon which all the purchases of houses
and lands have since been made. Toward the close
of the first year, after the second house was bought,
the Lord laid it upon the heart of his servant to ask
and receive the money to pay the remaining mortgage

9

on the second house. No sooner had Doctor Cullis begun to pray for this than the Lord began to give him tokens that his prayer would be answered.

At last, one day, a gentleman came in with one thousand dollars, the proceeds of a fair held by his wife and himself, in their own house, for the benefit of the Home. This was just the amount of the mortgage. So the next day it was paid, and the title made clear.

The second house was thus paid for first. One of the mortgages on the first house had yet more than eighteen years to run before its maturity, and the other could be continued indefinitely ; but the Doctor began asking the Lord for means to pay them off. July 19th he made the following record : —

"For many days I have been praying for the means to pay for house No. 4,[1] this being wholly mortgaged, nothing having been paid on it. This morning I received a note from a person whom I had seen only once, and she knew nothing of my prayer. I take this extract from the note. ' I send two dollars in this, if you please, towards the payment of the mortgage, wishing it were thousands.' "

But, although encouraged by this to continue praying, in full confidence that the Lord would answer, he was kept waiting until the next year.

[1] The first house purchased.

XXIV.

A NEW BRANCH OF THE WORK FORESHAD-
OWED.

A CHILDREN'S HOME.

As early as the beginning of June, in this the second year of the work, Doctor Cullis began to be
impressed with the feeling that the Lord would have
him commence a Home for the children of consumptives. On the 16th of June he made a record in his
Journal of his thoughts upon the subject, as follows : —

"Within a few days, I have thought much of establishing, in
connection with the Home, an Institution for the care of the
children, whose only parent may be an inmate of the Home.
In case of the death of the parents, the child or children, if there
are no relations or friends to provide, to be adopted into the
Institution, religiously educated and cared for, until they are
able to support themselves. My reason for this is, that we have
had many applications for admittance to the Home, from poor
widows, who have felt they could not part with their children,
and who have labored for their support, until they themselves
have become too sick to properly provide for their future welfare.
Some persons may think such an undertaking wholly unneces-
sary. Yet, since this Home has been in operation, there have
been at least thirty children (belonging to mothers or fathers
who have been with us, and many of whom have died) who have
been scattered in different parts of the country, brothers and
sisters oftentimes being unavoidably separated. Knowing as I
do, the anxiety this has caused many a sick one, I feel that such
an institution would be a boon to not a few of those whom the

Lord places under our care. In many instances the sick who have desired to enter the Home, have been deterred by the fear of what seems to them a final separation from their children; whereas if it were known that the little ones could be under the same care and management, and would be restored to the parents on their recovery, even should it take months to accomplish the same, they would gladly avail themselves of the privilege. If not restored to health, they have ample opportunity to decide what they propose to do with their children, as they are always candidly told their condition, in season to do this. If there are no friends to take them, it will be a comfort to the poor mother to know that the Lord, who has so kindly cared for her, has moved upon the hearts of his servants to provide for her children, for God has promised to 'save the children of the needy.' Psalm lxxvi. 4.

" This may seem like a great undertaking, for it will be readily seen, that a succession of developments must follow a work that has for its object the physical and spiritual welfare of the homeless. May the Lord guide and give me wisdom, that I may know his will."

These thoughts speedily, through prayer, ripened into purpose deferred only until the Lord should provide the means to establish the Children's Home. Meanwhile the Lord moved the heart of one who well knew how to feel for both the mothers who must die and leave their children homeless, and the motherless ones left with no one to care for them, to write once and again to the Doctor upon the subject. This is her second letter : —

" VERMONT, *September* 11, 1866.

" DOCTOR CULLIS : —

" *Sir*, — Since I was so ill last spring, I have thought very much about the mothers that died at the Home, and of the children that are there made motherless. What must those mothers suffer in leaving them? and who will watch over, as well as pray for those children, and strive to bring them up for Jesus? I know few as sad sights as children ' going to live out.' I know they sometimes find good homes, seldom loving hearts, much oftener they are made beasts of burden. May God pity them and give them firm hands to guide them, and warm, loving hearts to shelter them. Surely, happy are they who have the means and inclination to provide for them."

This lady had once before spoken of this matter, but did not know of the plan to provide for the little ones.

Thus foreshadowed, this new branch of the work awaited its successful commencement in the following year.

THIRD YEAR'S ENLARGEMENT.

XXV.

ANOTHER TIME OF STRAIT.

THE third year opened without a dollar in the treasury, but with perfect peace in the heart of the Lord's servant.

Daily wants were met by daily supplies in answer to special prayer. The supplies often came in such ways as to melt the heart into grateful tenderness. This happened the very first day of the new year. The record of it is as follows : —

" One of the patients came to me as I was leaving the Home and said she had had eight dollars given her, also clothing enough for her winter use ; she wished to keep one dollar of this, pay two to a person from whom she borrowed that amount, and five she desired to give to the Home. I asked her if she had prayed about it; she replied that she had and that she had found Jesus since she came in and had been so kindly cared for, she felt that she wanted to give this five dollars to the Lord. I accepted it and prayed God to bless her. A lady from New York gave me one dollar."

This period of living by the day lasted several weeks and came sometimes down to living by the hour or even by the moment. Records like the following frequently occurred in those days : —

" After paying for the necessary articles this morning my funds were entirely exhausted. At the Home the matron asked me for money to pay the domestics. I had to tell her I had not a dollar in the world. On reaching my residence I found a lady waiting to pay a bill for professional services. That enabled me to send the amount needed to the Home. Thus the Lord cares for us. I can praise him that he keeps me in perfect peace in all the trials."

Another day : —

" After paying daily expenses this morning my purse contained less than ten cents. One of the demands that emptied it was for eight dollars to pay the domestics. I gave the matron all I had, seven dollars. In less than an hour there was paid in two dollars, enabling me to make up the deficiency."

Another day : —

" All the expenses have been met to-day, but we had to purchase articles in small quantities."

Journal entries like these run through many days. Why did the Lord so try his servant ? He tried him yet more.

We have seen in the past how the Lord in a great many instances touched the hearts of his children with such pity for his poor suffering ones, and with such sympathy for his servant in the work, that they gladly brought forth their hidden treasures and then jewels and their keepsakes and gave them. And we have seen how not only in the devotion of all his earnings, and time, but at one time in the sale of his watch, the Lord brought his servant into the like glad sacrifice with those who in this way evinced their sense of the preciousness of the work.

Now again in this new time of strait the Lord brought Doctor Cullis to bring forth heart treasures for him. The records of the fourth and fifth days of the new year tell the story.

" *October* 4. The day closes with my having but one dollar and forty-eight cents in the world. The Lord is trying my faith as it never has been tried before, yet he keeps us in the hollow of his hand and we are safe. There have been two applications but no room for them. Our winter's fuel is not in, and last year's Reports are to be printed, yet I have no fear.

"*Nine* P. M. A friend has just been in to pay ten dollars on his account. I am as thankful for this as if it had been a donation to the work, for it is all the Lord's.

" *October* 5. This morning five dollars were paid me; on going to the Home fifteen dollars were required for provisions; this with a demand for one of the domestics' weekly pay took all I had in the world except ten cents; afterwards there was another call for some necessary articles. To meet this demand, when I returned to my home, I sent some keepsakes to be sold which had been *treasures* for many years. I had to pray for the needed grace to do this and the Lord gave it; knowing that all I had was his, could I withhold anything from him? With my dear wife I have called upon the Lord to come to our help, for he only knows that we have never been in such straits before. Our need at my own house is even greater than at the Home, for everything is supplied for the poor sick ones, while we deny ourselves. This afternoon two dollars were received from Providence."

One of the things which increased the trial of faith during those days, was that it was mid-autumn and the cold weather gave notice of winter at hand while, like the treasury, the coal-bins were empty. Where was the winter's fuel to come from?

One morning, as the climax of all, the inmates of the Home were thrown into great consternation by learning that the first house was on fire. Its roof was burning over their heads. The fire caught from a spark which fell from a neighbor's chimney into the gutter, and the fire burned on underneath the slates some time before it was discovered. Thus the Lord tried the work. The roof was mostly destroyed and some of the furniture, and the whole house was badly damaged by water. But the patients were all provided for. They retreated to the second house, and were afterwards removed to a house below that had been vacated a few days before. Stoves were soon set up, the rooms warmed, and although less comfortable than the Home, the house answered well until the damaged one was repaired. Of course a considerable amount of money was required to repair it. How did all this affect the faith of Doctor Cullis and his helpers in the Home? He says, —

"We have great reason to thank God that the fire did not occur in the night, and that all the patients were able to walk. After quiet was restored we knelt together, and lifted up our hearts in gratitude for this signal mercy, thankful for the assurance that 'all things work together for good to them that love God.'"

One fact shows that, like the worthies of old, who by faith "waxed valiant in fight," the Doctor grew stronger under every trial. He had been praying before the close of the second year, both for an enlargement of the Consumptives' Home by a new building and for the addition of a Children's Home to the work. Did these varied trials quench the fervor of his zeal? Nay, rather they kindled it to flame. Or rather the Lord did in spite of the trials.

Applicant after applicant had to be refused admission to the Home. Sometimes two, and once or oftener, three in one day. At last the trial for want of the new house and of the Children's Home outgrew that for want of money to meet the expenses of the work as it was. Such records as the following evince this. A bed having been vacated by a peaceful death, —

"A new patient applied this afternoon and was received, although I had not money enough in the world to pay the postage on a letter to England, which I desired to send. I am looking to the Lord, and he will not disappoint. 'Thou shalt know that I am the Lord, for they shall not be ashamed that wait on me.'"

THE NEW HOUSE.

" *October* 17. I am daily praying for the means to build; the Lord only knows how much we need more room. Yesterday there was an application from a poor man, living in a most wretched place, with scarcely a single comfort. We can do nothing for him. Two hundred pounds of salt fish and a keg of mackerel have been given to-day."

THE CHILDREN'S HOME.

" *October* 18. This morning a lady called, requesting me to go and see a poor woman, sick with consumption. She wished her to go to the Home, but the sick woman felt that she could not part with her two children. I pray for the speedy establishment of a home for these needy little ones."

The Consumptives' Home was fitted for twenty patients, but the pressure and the peculiarities of the cases induced the reception of two more than the full number, with the best provisions for them possible under the circumstances.

About this time the Doctor says in his Journal, —

" It is with sorrow I am daily turning from our doors the sick who apply for admission. God knows this. He will, I am sure, in his own good time supply a building."

Again : —

" My heart aches for the poor people that we are daily obliged to refuse admittance to the Home. We have now twenty-two patients, — two more than our complement. Others are waiting."

Again : —

" I am praying for the enlargement of the Home, for our need is so great that it makes my heart ache to turn the poor sufferers from our doors, and with our crowded condition our assistants are seriously troubled for the want of room for household purposes. My only desire in enlarging is that God may be glorified and his sick cared for. I pray that ' patience may have her perfect work.' "

One day one of the patients touched the Doctor's heart, in regard to the Children's Home, and led him to pray more fervently than ever. He asked if the Doctor thought he would recover. The answer was in the negative. Then he expressed great anxiety about his children. "Who will care for them? My wife is dead. What is to become of them?"

We may well understand how this gave a new spur to the daily supplications in behalf of the helpless little ones, robbed by death of their parents. The most remarkable thing about this whole matter is, that by such means, and by his Spirit in the heart of his servant, the Lord so raised him above the pressure of the daily wants, as to make him ask in the very strait, so earnestly for the twofold enlargement of the work.

XXVI.

SIGNAL ANSWERS TO PRAYER.

ONE day, during the trials in the early days of the new year, Doctor Cullis invited in four friends to help in claiming the promises to united prayer. Three of them came. During the time they were together, the fourth one sent in a note with twelve dollars inclosed.

This was Saturday. Monday afternoon a gentleman called and inquired about the work, and gave fifty dollars. Tuesday a bill of one hundred dollars was to be paid. Special prayer was made for means to pay it. "At two P. M.," says the record, —

"A friend called and gave five dollars, and in less than an hour, a check was sent me for two hundred dollars. How faithful is he who hath promised! O that we could *always* ' ask in faith,' nothing ' wavering,' for ' without faith it is *impossible to please* God.' "

THE TURNING POINT

of the peculiar straits mentioned in the preceding chapter seems to have been the prayer of thanksgiving after the fire. That very day, first a neighbor offered to take some of the patients, and handed the Doctor five dollars. Another — an unknown donor — sent twenty tons of coal, ending the question about fuel for the winter. Eleven dollars came from Newburyport, and ten from a gentleman who called. The next day the carpenters were at the roof. A lady called and left forty dollars, another twenty-five dollars. Two friends gave a dollar each, and another five dollars and twenty cents, and from that time on, donations came in more freely from day to day.

SPECIAL PRAYER FOR THE CHILDREN'S HOME

was made by Doctor Cullis, Sunday morning, November 18th, and he gives the answer as follows: —

" After this evening's Sabbath service the following note was placed in my hand : —

" ' BOSTON, *November* 18, 1866.

" ' Dr. CULLIS : —

" ' *Dear Sir*, — I present you with the inclosed fifty dollars, which has been laid by for you for some time.

" ' I wish you to use it for the purpose you have most earnestly prayed for this day ; I always feel strengthened in my *faith* and *trust* (both of which I daily need) by the perusal of your Reports.

" ' That God may continue to bless and prosper you in your *blessed* work, is the wish and the prayer of

" ' Yours truly.'

" ' I cried unto God with my voice, even unto God with my voice, and he gave ear unto me.' Ps. lxxvii. 1.

" Another lady placed ten dollars in my hand.

" *November* 19. My prayer this morning was, that God might be glorified in the work ; that means might be given for the Children's Home, also for the new building ; that all our needs might be supplied. On returning to my house in the forenoon, I found a clergyman waiting, he having brought a gift of one hundred dollars, from an invalid lady, for the Children's Home. Another gentleman was also waiting, and gave five dollars. At noon, I received a check for one hundred dollars, from a firm in this city, ' for the daily requirements of the Home, or for the new building, as you may determine.' As my prayer this morning was more particularly for the new building, I placed it to that object.

" An envelope containing fourteen dollars, seventy-seven cents, and a quantity of pins, the latter the proceeds of a chil·dren's pin fair, were left at my door. God bless the little ones !

" ' A friend ' who writes he has known what poverty and des-
titution is, having lost both parents of consumption before he
was seven years old, incloses fifty dollars."

ANSWERS TO PRAYER FOR MEANS TO PAY FOR THE FIRST HOUSE.

The second house was paid for last year, and at
that time, as it will be remembered, Doctor Cullis
began praying for means to pay for the first one.
The amount was large, as amounts were then looked
upon in the work, but not hopelessly so. At one
time, about the middle of November, there is a record
of this kind : —

"It has been my prayer, for many months, to be able to pay
the amount due on the first house. This day my prayer is answered, in so far as that I have been permitted to pay five hundred dollars upon it, and I hope to be able, before the close of
the year, to thank God that it is entirely paid for."

This was his prayer and expectation, because,
although the money would not be due yet for more
than seventeen years, " The silver and gold are the
Lord's, and he will provide."

Not many days passed before a package was handed
the Doctor containing eight hundred dollars from an
unknown donor, and the same day a " thanksgiving
offering from members of Emmanuel Church," of one
hundred dollars.

Two days after this a gentleman called and gave
Doctor Cullis one thousand dollars from " a Bostonian
in London," whose name he declined giving.

One day some one left one hundred and fifty dollars, and the same day the Brokers' Board sent in
five hundred dollars, with a kind note from its Presi-

dent, saying that it was presented by a unanimous vote of the Board, at that morning's session.

Another day, when the Doctor had been praying for large gifts toward paying for the house, a gentleman called and gave him his check for five hundred dollars, — ninety-three dollars to pay his bill, and the balance for the work.

Shortly afterward the " Massachusetts Charitable Fire Society " sent in six hundred dollars.

About the same time a lady arranged a concert in Music Hall, and secured by it eleven hundred and five dollars, for the benefit of the Home. This, like all other contributions, was the unsolicited offering of pure good-will.

The next day, after the last of the proceeds of the concert was given, while as yet the end of the year had not nearly come, the prayer of hope at the beginning of the year that the first house might be all paid for before its close, was answered. This is the record : —

"*June* 25. By God's love I have been enabled to-day to pay the balance of the mortgage on House No. 4; both houses belonging to the Home are now paid for. To the Lord I return thanks."

CONCERNING PAY FOR PRINTING SECOND EDITION OF SECOND REPORT.

On the seventh day of March, the following prayer is recorded : " May our Heavenly Father grant means for another edition of the Report, the first of which is nearly gone, while the demand continues." Shortly after this the first edition having been exhausted, Doctor Cullis ordered a second, looking to the Lord to supply the means to pay for it. The Reports were sent in. A little money had been contributed toward paying for them, but not much. At last the bill came in. To the Doctor's surprise the man to whom the order was given, said that all who had done or furnished anything for this second edition, except one man, had freely given all, so that there was only five dollars and thirty-eight cents out of several hundred dollars to be paid. The special contributions fully covered this amount.

XXVII.

PECULIAR DONATIONS.

CHILDREN'S gifts like children's praises are the perfection of incense to the Lord. One day a mother
wrote : —

"Will you please accept from dear little Gracie on this, the
first anniversary of her birthday, the inclosed five dollars towards
the fund for building a new Home, also ten dollars from the
grateful mother."

The same day " Little Mary " sent the contents of
her savings bank — one dollar.

Christmas day, " Little Eddie," who had a dollar
given him, sent it to Doctor Cullis. " God bless him,"
says the record.

A little boy sent his Christmas money, ten cents,
asking Doctor Cullis to pray for him, because " father
doesn't pray." " Surely," says the record, " our
Heavenly Father will not turn from such. an appeal."

" My little girls," says a mother, " have been listening to your Report (the eldest is only six), and
with tears in their eyes they send their little offering."
The mother adds five dollars. The children, not content to have the mother alone write, pen for themselves, in rude characters, a note inclosing their treasure, *thirty-nine cents*. The eldest is the scribe, and
says : —

" DEAR DOCTOR CULLIS : — Sister and I send all the money we
have, for a little help towards your Home for the dear little children whose mammas are sick."

" Little Carrie" sent of her spending money, twenty-five cents. A little girl made book-marks and sold them for one dollar and ninety cents, and sent it to the Home.

A little boy sent a dollar saying, " I heard your Report read, and have saved my spending-money for you."

A little boy who listened to the Report, sent a dollar, increased to five by his mother and grandmother.

One day sixty-seven dollars came in, the proceeds of a concert started by a boy in Charlestown. " God bless," says the Doctor, " the dear boy who started it."

The same day five dollars came also from a little girl who had collected it amongst her friends. Also thirty-five cents currency and twenty-five in silver from a little boy. Also six dollars from a children's sewing-circle. Another day one dollar, the produce of dandelions, was given from a little boy of six. It was inclosed in a note written by a lady eighty-two years old.

THE GIFTS OF YOUNG CONVERTS

are very precious, both as thank-offerings to Jesus from those who have been recently born again, — tokens of their gratitude for his love, and as expressions of their own love to him in return. One sent five dollars ; others other sums. One wrote dating

" ——, MICHIGAN, *March* 28, 1867.
" CHARLES CULLIS, M. D. : —

" *Dear Sir,* — Having spent so much of the Lord's treasure foolishly when in a state of sin and rebellion against him, I now desire, in view of his great goodness and mercy toward me, to do all that I can for his honor and glory, and the good of my fellow beings. I have just finished reading your Second Annual

Report, and words fail to express the good it has done me. It brought the tears to my eyes many times. It has strengthened my faith and created new desires within me after holy things; and above all, it has enabled me to rely upon and trust more in the power and efficacy of prayer. And that is what I need, for I have been praying some time for the Lord to open a way for me to preach his gospel, firmly believing he has called me to this holy and sacred profession. O, how much your Report has helped me in this matter.

"A YOUNG BROTHER IN CHRIST."

GOLD AND SILVER.

It is a singular fact, not noticed in its place, that the work was commenced after the suspension of specie payments, when gold and silver had risen to more than double the par value, and provisions of all kinds were enhanced in price in proportion. The time was chosen by the Lord himself. His servant was not at liberty to begin a day earlier than he did, nor to delay any longer. Was this to show, in the beginning, that the Lord was able to sustain the work, as he caused it to be commenced, in the most unfavorable times?

Another fact, not unlike this, oft repeated, is the gift of silver and gold to the work by those who had treasured it, as long as their hearts would let them, because more precious than bank-notes.

One man was long in the habit of dropping in the box at the Home, at intervals, five dollars, or ten dollars at a time, in gold. Some one, unknown, dropped a twenty-dollar gold piece in the box, January 6th. A ten-dollar gold piece was sent from a distance, at one time, and another at another time, and a five-dollar gold piece was sent at another time. A gold dollar and fifty-five cents in silver, with several three-cent pieces, and the following note, came at a certain time : —

" A dear young daughter, who died of consumption, laid up this money for some good object. Having read with much interest your Report of the Consumptives' Home, I send it to you."

A clergyman's little daughter came to the Doctor, at one time, with two gold dollars, one from her sister, the other from herself. The following note tells its own story : —

" Acton, *March* 18, 1867.

" Dr. Charles Cullis : —

" *Dear Sir,* — The inclosed dollar has a history. It was given me by a young girl of this place who died in consumption early in the present year, with the request that I should give it to some good object. She became a Christian before her death, and gave many messages to friends of the same age who came to see her, urging them to prepare to meet her in the ' better land. Her father proposed that this money should be applied to procure, as a motto for our Sunday-school, the words of a favorite hymn with her, —

" ' There'll be no more sorrow there,'

and to this she assented. On inquiry I found that this was not published as a motto, and that to print it in large letters suitable for the school-room, would cost $3.00. Some cardboard was therefore procured, and a younger sister painted this motto upon it in quite an ornamental style, and it is now in our S. S. room.

" The dollar yet remained with me, and a friend having lent me a copy of your last Report, in whose perusal I have been exceedingly interested and profited, I conclude to send the bill to you to be applied, if you will, to the special object referred to under dates of June 6th, and July 5th.

" Wishing you all success in your most benevolent enterprise,

" Very truly yours."

If the history of every precious dollar, and of every peculiar gift, freighted with sacred associations and emotions, should be written, there would be no end to it.

Amongst the most valuable of all, according to our Saviour's estimate, are

THE POOR WIDOWS' MITES.

They are not few. Smallest — perhaps, also, largest — among these was one of thirty-eight cents, with the following note, —

"Dr. Cullis : — Please accept this small offering as a poor, sick widow's mite. It is little pieces I have had for twenty years. I know it is a small gift, but the Lord will not despise it. I have great reason to bless his holy name, that he has not cast me off forever."

Another was sixty cents "from a poor widow who is desirous of doing what good she can in the service of her Lord and Master." Five dollars came from " an aged widow in Dorchester."

Three dollars, by a gentleman, as " a widow's mite," from one whose name and place he declined to give.

From New York, by mail, another of five dollars, with these words, —

"I have been one of the Lord's children but one year, and that year is worth *all* my previous life."

A lady from Minnesota sent five dollars as "faith money," and the same bearer brought two dollars and fifty cents "from a poor widow" who herself lives by faith.

A BAND OF MISSIONARIES

sent in the following note, with the amount of money mentioned in it : —

"City Missionary Rooms,
"16 Tremont Temple, *January* 7, 1867.

" Dear Dr. Cullis : — The band of missionaries with which I have the privilege of being connected, have read with interest the second Report of the 'Consumptives' Home,' which you were kind enough to send us. Deeply impressed, by our constant intercourse with the poor, of the necessity of such an insti-

tution, and admiring the unwavering faith by which it was
founded and has been sustained, we desire to make the inclosed
small contribution ($15.05) towards defraying its current ex-
penses.

"Truly yours in behalf of the Missionaries."

THANKSGIVING DAY

some one left at Doctor Cullis' house, anonymously,
one hundred dollars, with the text, Haggai i. 8 : " Go
up to the mountain, and bring wood and build a house,
and I will take pleasure in it, and I will be glorified,
saith the Lord." Whereupon the Doctor said in his
Journal, —

"This word from God filled my heart with joy. Surely he
will build for his suffering people! And will he not be glorified; will not each stone be an offering from grateful, pious
hearts?"

Nor was this all. "Two turkeys, two pairs of
chickens, bread, jellies, apples, ice-cream, and other
luxuries," says the Doctor, "were lavished upon us."
And there were yet other gifts in money. The
record of the day opens with the words of Joel ii. 25 :
" And ye shall eat in plenty and be satisfied, and
praise the name of the Lord your God, that hath
dealt wondrously with you, and my people shall never
be ashamed."

Consumptives enjoy one compensation for their
wasting, — a good appetite. And O, how differently
would most of those in the Home have fared if they
had not been the Lord's own guests on that day, but
had been homeless !

CHRISTMAS DAY

brought also its hundred dollar gift, with clothing and
bedding, and another gift of sixty-one dollars, and

another of five dollars, and yet another of twenty-five dollars, besides the proceeds of a fair held by a little girl, which amounted to one hundred and fifty-seven dollars and seventy-five cents, and a dollar from a poor woman.

Nor was the dinner forgotten. A quantity of good things were sent in.

NEW YEAR'S DAY

one gentleman presented twenty dollars and another twenty-five, and the same poor woman who gave the dollar Christmas, sent another, saying, " The Lord returned the dollar I gave you with interest, so I can afford to send another."

An Easter gift of one hundred dollars was also presented.

PRECIOUS THINGS OF BEREAVED ONES,

left by those who have passed away, when presented by those who loved them, have in them, every one, a whole volume of heart history, and are tokens of the deep interest in the work, kindled by the Lord in the hearts of those who present them.

One day five dollars and ninety-eight cents came, accompanied by a note from the father of the one to whom it had belonged, saying that his daughter had died of consumption.

"In her purse were currency and pennies which are here inclosed. Her mother, after reading your Report, thought it specially proper that these little *relics*, though small in amount, should take this direction."

Specially appropriate indeed!

A lady sent twenty-five dollars, with these words : —

" In memory of one who would have done so much for the sick, had that life been prolonged."

A mother handed in one dollar which she found in the purse of her deceased daughter.

A lady left some silver in a wrapper upon which was written, —

" Silver left in a savings box, by a lady who died of consumption four and a half years ago, two dollars and sixty-three cents."

In the same box there was found also for the Home, in a separate piece of paper, two five-dollar bills.

One afternoon a lady called and presented " a little basket," says Doctor Cullis, " containing four dollars in silver. This amount her aunt, on her death-bed, requested might be sent to me for the ' Home ; ' besides this was her Prayer-book and Testament."

The following tells its own story : —

" *August* 13, 186.

" DR. CULLIS : —

" *Dear Sir*, — Three years ago to-day my dear husband wrote to me for *the last time*, though he was then expecting to be home in a *very few days*. He sent me ten dollars to use, if I wished, to go and meet him, as he would be delayed in Concord with his regiment. Instead of the long locked for telegram to meet him, came the sad news of his death. I could not use that money for any *other* purpose, therefore it has laid by me till this time, as I placed it in my sadness and disappointment. I could not use it for myself, so it has remained idle. To-day, the third anniversary, I send it to you, to be used for the ' Children's Home ' in any way you need. May God bless it in your hands.

" I think you were very fortunate to secure a house for the children so near the ' Home.'

" May God bless you in all your labors for him.

" Yours, with interest and sympathy."

GIFTS BY PATIENTS

might be expected as tokens of gratitude to God and
the Home for all the benefits received without money
and without price — benefits which cost money and
benefits which no money could buy — if they were
rich, or even if they had wherewith to bestow and
have a competence left : but when they give like the
poor widow all their living, it comes unexpectedly and
is deeply touching.   Patients never hear anything
about the straits of the Home for lack of money.

On a certain day Doctor Cullis made the following
entry in his Journal : —

"I was much pleased to learn that twelve dollars, which I
found in the box at the Home, a few days ago, were put there
by one of the patients ; it was all the money he had. He told his
nurse 'it ought to be given to the institution, for if he got well
he could earn more ; if he should not recover, he would not need
it.' "

The following, concerning one of the patients,
shows the appreciation of the Home borne by them
in their hearts, if in any case, as they sometimes do,
one recovers sufficiently to go forth and enter into the
labors of life : —

"One of the patients who left us about two months ago, so far
recovered as to be able to work, called this afternoon and gave
me five dollars for the Home. I at first declined, knowing
him to be poor, but he said he had got five more and must give
this to the work. Does any one doubt but that this poor man
will be richer both in this life and in the one to come, because
he gave it for Christ's sake ? "

A FATHER FOR HIS BABE

gave twenty-five dollars, saying that she was according to this token, thus early consecrated to the work
of the Lord.

THE FIRST LEGACY

was one hundred dollars, less government taxes, received February 27, 1867, left by a deceased lady. When this was received Doctor Cullis in recording it gave expression to the fullness of his heart in the words of the Psalmist, " O that men would praise the Lord for his goodness, and for his wonderful works to the children of men."

THE FIRST MONEY EARNED.

The amount was small, — ninety cents, — but like the widow's mite it is large as the first money earned, and all of it. The donor unknown.

FOR A HUSBAND'S RECOVERY.

A wife sent ten dollars as a thank offering for her husband's recovery from severe illness.

LAST NOT LEAST.

" A poor sick woman who has been confined to her room for more than thirty years, has, with her feeble strength, worked thimble cases and earned a dollar. As she had formed the resolution to give one tenth to the Lord, she sent me ten cents for the Home."

XXVIII.

THE PUBLICATION DEPARTMENT.

No special attention was given during the year to this part of the work, yet it was cared for by the Lord and also bore precious fruit. The gifts to it were not large, one or two dollars at a time, the largest ten dollars, yet they were enough and came at such intervals as to keep interest in the work from failing. The Lord's chief means, however, of increasing desire for the enlargement of this department was the reports of signal blessing upon the little books circulated.

In connection with the record of gifts received January 11th, Doctor Cullis mentions the fact that one of them requested the little book, " A Saviour for You," and adds, " this little book is constantly called for ; a gentleman this morning wished some to circulate in his neighborhood, where he said, they were accomplishing much good. May the Lord send the means to print more, as my stock is fast diminishing."

This little book was the one only work as yet published by Doctor Cullis though many others were kept for distribution. A small beginning for a department which has since grown so much. One of its precious fruits is shown in the following, from the Journal.

"*June* 26. Some weeks ago I received a letter from a stranger requesting me to send her a copy of ' A Saviour for You,' saying she wished it for a friend sick with consumption and without a hope in Christ. This afternoon a young lady called and told me the result of the reading of the little book ; the young man read it and by God's Spirit it was blest to him so that he found Jesus a living Saviour to his soul. The little book he kept with him constantly, and after death the worn copy was found in his pocket."

Shortly after this " Faith," by the author of " A Saviour for You," was added. August 28th, Doctor Cullis makes the following entry : —.

"It is with gratitude to God I record the conversion, in a neighboring city, of five persons by the blessing of God upon the little book ' A Saviour for You,' and one by the same author, S. M. Haughton, entitled 'Faith.' The writer thus narrates this latter conversion : —

" ' A young woman told me last week that the little book " Faith," opened her eyes and brought her to Jesus. She remarked that one night she took up the book and read along until she came to the thirteenth page, commencing " Many anxious souls," etc.; as she read on her own case was described. Then she read "that everything is already done, and that for them nothing remains but to *receive the gifts and be thankful*." " That is my case," said she, " now *I will receive the gift*," and that moment light and peace broke into her soul, and she has rejoiced in Jesus ever since.'

" Both of these books I am having stereotyped for gratuitous distribution, so that many more souls may be blest."

XXIX.

CONVERSIONS IN THE HOME.

PRECIOUS were the various answers to prayer, precious the daily supply, precious the means of paying for the two houses purchased, precious the gifts towards a third one, precious the constant and generous tokens of a Children's Home at hand, precious the keepsakes and the gold and silver, and the many other special tokens that the Lord had given the Home a remarkably deep hold upon the hearts of his beloved children ; but of all the precious things given of God, that of the conversion of all the inmates of the Home, one at a time, all along through the year, was the most precious, because it indicated the constant presence of the Saviour in the Home, as other things did his constant providence for it.

From month to month Doctor Cullis's Journal records conversions as they came to his knowledge.

" *October* 27. It was refreshing this morning to hear one of the poor sick ones say, that he felt his sins were forgiven. For two months I have earnestly prayed for this young man. Thanks be to God we can now rejoice together.

" *November* 4. ' O, give thanks unto the Lord, for he is good, for his mercy endureth forever ! ' Ps. cvi. 1.

" This morning a patient near unto death told me that Jesus was her ' all in all.' O, the joy that filled my heart to know that another soul was rejoicing. Blessed Jesus ! His blood cleanseth from all sin.

" *November* 26. Yesterday twenty dollars were given.

" The Lord gave us a greater blessing than a gift of money this morning, when his Holy Spirit filled the heart of one poor sufferer, who entered the Home about a week ago without a hope in the blessed Jesus, but who now says, ' I feel that the Lord has taken a great burden from my heart, and in its place given me peace through my dear Saviour.' "

At that date Doctor Cullis was able to record the fact that the Home then had in it, as patients,

NOT ONE SOUL UNRECONCILED TO GOD.

Nor was salvation confined to the patients. All who came within the sacred influence of the work were affected by it and touched by the Spirit.

December 11, the Journal says : —:

" A young man who has been employed in the Home told me this morning he had given his heart to Christ. ' Unto thee, O Lord, do I lift up my soul.' "

Others, meanwhile, having been received as patients, the Journal says : —

" *January* 14. The best news of yesterday was that one poor patient, who, previous to entering the Home, had been for years an intemperate man, and whose disease was probably induced by liquor, told me he had ' given his heart to Jesus.' There are three others seeking the ' pearl of great price.' May they cherish these strivings of the Spirit ! They who ' seek ' *shall* ' find ! '

" *January* 19. One more soul is rejoicing in Jesus.

" *January* 25 Two more souls have confessed Christ, feeling that all their sins are washed away in his most precious blood.

" *February* 25. This morning a young man at the Home, who has lived without Christ in the world, told me, rejoicingly, that he had now the assurance of sins forgiven, *all washed in that most precious blood.*

" *March* 4. Yesterday another of the patients told me that she was rejoicing in Jesus. When she entered the Home, a little more than a week ago, she had no hope ; but to-day, the joy that overspread her countenance, as she spoke of the blessed new birth, told more plainly than words of the perfect trust in a

11

living Saviour.   Another, lately converted, says ' it doesn't hurt
so much to cough, now that Jesus is with me.'

" *March* 7.   The best gift of yesterday was a new heart to
one of our patients.

" *March* 9.   One patient more has confessed Christ as her
living Saviour.

" *April* 4.   It rejoices my heart to record the witness of one
more repentant soul, to the power of forgiveness and love as it is
in Jesus.

" *April* 15.   Another patient rejoices in the new born hope of
salvation through our Lord Jesus Christ !

. " *May* 25.   Yesterday's gift was a new heart to one of our
sick ones.

" *May* 27.   A young man is rejoicing to-day in Jesus.

" *June* 11.   The Lord has answered prayer in the conversion
of another of the inmates.   His be the glory.

" *July* 22.   One more soul rejoicing in Jesus. '

The final record of conversions during the year,
occurs on the twenty-fourth day of September, the
last week of the year, and three days only before the
dedication day, when the Children's Home was publicly recognized as the Lord's.   The Doctor's words are,
'· With thanks to God, I record the conversion of two
more of our sick ones."

In closing this remarkable record, the reflection
comes, what if in every church and every household
in Christendom there should be the same dependence
upon God, the same simple trust in Jesus, and the
same following of the Spirit ?   Would not the Lord
add unto them daily such as should be saved ?   Would
not the earth soon be full of the glory of the Lord ?

XXX.

THE CHILDREN'S HOME ESTABLISHED.

ALL through the year evidences multiplied showing it to be the Lord's will that there should be a further enlargement of the work in both the addition, in some way, of more room for consumptives, and in the establishment of a Home for children.

Contributions for both purposes were frequently made, and circumstances often occurred which called forth more and more prayer, and led finally to endeavors to procure houses so situated as to answer the desired purposes.

Doctor Cullis's idea, at first, in respect to the enlargement of the Consumptives' Home was that of the erection of a building somewhere, large enough to receive all who should apply for admission, and for this purpose carried contributions to a building fund.

Finally, however, he gave up that idea, or rather postponed it, and then sought a third house adjoining the two already occupied as a Home. Failing in this, he added one story to the L of the second house, which afforded a room more retired for patients who in their last hours were in need of it more especially. Further enlargement in any way had to be put over for another year.

Not so the Children's Home. Contributions for this thickened in number and increased in amount The Lord, by his providence and Spirit, pressed the matter more and more upon his servant. At last, on the fifth of June, when all things were ripe for it, the intelligence was brought to Doctor Cullis that there was a house for sale just across the street from the Consumptives' Home. That day he arranged to meet the agent the day following, and did so. He found the house sadly out of repair, requiring several hundred dollars expended upon it, to make it tenantable. The price was six thousand dollars, one thousand to be paid down, and a thousand annually thereafter until all should be paid. He purchased it, and on the eleventh, six days after learning that it was for sale, he made the first payment of one thousand dollars, and soon had the carpenters and other mechanics at work upon it.

One fact in this connection, will serve to show how deeply and truly the Lord had impressed the matter upon Doctor Cullis.

The house in which the Doctor lived was rented, and the owner gave him notice that he wanted it vacated at the expiration of the lease. This would throw the Doctor out of a home for himself and family. A boarding-place would not well answer for one so constantly occupied and so much needing a home to rest in, what time he could have for it. Of course he greatly desired a house for himself, but the Lord put him to the test as to which he desired most, a house for himself or for a Children's Home.

The day he examined the house for the Children's Home a friend said to him (O, how often one's friends come in, as in the case of Job, between us and the Lord!), "How can you take this care and go to all this expense when you have not the means and are in need of a home for yourself?"

Doctor Cullis replied, " The Lord who has taken care of us so'well, will not forsake us now."

An hour afterward, a friend gave the Doctor one hundred dollars. " How shall I use it ? " asked the Doctor. " Just as you please, your judgment will be best," answered his friend. " Then I shall place it to the Children's Home," said the Doctor. Then follows this simple record : " This morning as I called upon God in regard to my own need, a sweet peace of assurance that my wants should be supplied, filled my breast. I wait now in perfect confidence."

Thus the Lord brought his servant not only to prefer that the children should have a home rather than himself, but to be filled with peace in view of being himself thrown out of a home.

The repairs went forward. Contributions came in, one gentleman gave two hundred dollars ; young ladies brought in five hundred dollars, half for the Children's Home; and many other sums of considerable amount and a large number of small gifts, some of them wonderfully precious in their heart value. The mechanics were paid. A gentleman of New York, interested in an organ manufactory, gave an organ ; the gentleman who had given the curtains and fixtures for the Consumptives' Home, did the same for the Children's Home. Another gave part of the furniture. And these are only specimens of the generous kindness with which the Lord inspired the hearts of many of his dear children, to aid in the establishment of a home for the children. So when dedication day came round, all things were ready. The following is the account of the dedication : —

" *September* 27. At 7½ o'clock this evening, the rooms were filled to overflowing with kind friends who met with us, to make one more offering to him who gave his life for us.

"The Rev. F. D. Huntington, D. D., who cheerfully took charge of the services, very appropriately suggested that our first utterance should be the voice of praise and thanksgiving. The choir of Emmanuel Church, led by Silas A. Bancroft, with our new Cabinet Organ, then sang the anthem, 'Glory be to God on high,' after which appropriate selections from God's Holy Word were read, followed by prayer consecrating the house, its laborers, the friends assembled, its future inmates, the dear children, to the Giver of all good gifts, in whose name we now commence our labors, and to whom be all the glory. Kind words of sympathy and encouragement were then uttered by Rev. R. H. Neale, D. D., Rev. J. H. Means, of Dorchester, Hon. Henry Wilson, Rev. E. M. P. Wells, D. D., Rev. O. T. Walker, Rev. E. Edmunds, James W. Kimball, Esq., after which our never-failing friend, B. P. Shillaber, Esq., read a poem prepared for the occasion, entitled 'The Cry of the Children.' After this a word and then the benediction by Rev. W. R. Nicholson, D. D. The company were then invited to partake of a bountiful collation which had been prepared by our lady friends. During the evening many kind friends took me by the hand and wishing me God's blessing gave me substantial proof of their sympathy; their gifts amounting to one hundred and twenty-one dollars. I thank the Lord for the happy evening and the proof of his continued and abiding care. Henceforth, by God's grace, not only the 'Consumptives' Home' but the 'Children's Home' shall be embraced in 'A Work of Faith.'"

Thus was the Children's Home established.

THE FOURTH YEAR.

XXXI.

STRAIT AND PLENTY REVERSED IN THEIR SEA-SONS.

THE fourth year of the work, as compared with the third, presents some notable contrasts. Not in the principles of the work, — they have remained unchangeably the same from the first; nor in the peacefulness of the trust in which it has been pursued, this has been steady, — the peace of Christ given not as the world giveth, ceaseless as his love; nor in the wonderful care of the Lord in supplying both the daily wants of the work, and the larger occasional necessities of enlargement from time to time, — this never was more wonderful or bountiful; but in its seasons of strait and of plenty. The periods were completely reversed. The seasons ·of strait in the third year were the seasons of plenty in the fourth, and the seasons of abundance the seasons of strait. During all of the first weeks of the third year the frequent record was not a dollar in the treasury, while during those very weeks in the fourth year, more than three thousand dollars flowed in over and above the current expenses. While the later months of the fourth year found the treasury often empty, as the year before it had been full in the same months. This same contrast is presented between the seasons in the work and in the commercial world. In the fourth year, the early autumn when business men strain every nerve and employ every dollar, and the money market is close, and also the 1st of January, when the books are balanced, and bills made out, and money is in peculiar demand for the settlement of accounts, the contributions were frequent and large, and money in advance of expenses accumulated in the treasury. Why was this? Was it to show that the Lord is not straitened by the straits of human affairs, nor dependent for means to carry on his work upon times of commercial plenty?

One thing is certain. As he withheld his servant from commencing the work when gold was par, and sugar eight cents a pound, and impelled him to begin when gold was more than double its nominal value and sugar three times the price it had been a few months before, — commercially the hardest of all times in human view, — so often and often in the history of the work, the Lord seems to have reversed all human calculations as to times and seasons.

It is interesting, too, to mark the sources of plenty in the work, in these times of scarcity in the business world. The Lord laid his hand upon the hearts of people in different and distant parts of the world, and caused them to send liberally to his servant.

The first Journal entry of the year notes twenty-five dollars received from Paris, France. Four days later one hundred and fifty dollars came from Berlin, Prussia. A few days thereafter, five hundred dollars came from Rosaris, Argentine Republic, the more delightfully surprising because that, of all regions in Christendom, is the last one from which so large a contribution could have been looked for. Another and smaller sum came from Honolulu, Sandwich Islands; and yet another of one hundred and twenty-five dollars, from London, England.

Not all, however, that went to make up the plenty of the season in which the year before there had been scarcity, came from over the waters and far off lands. Much more, in the aggregate, came from equally unexpected sources at home. For example, October 10th, Doctor Cullis, having in the morning asked the Lord for means sufficient to furnish the new building, went to the Home from his boarding-place. On the way he inquired the price of certain articles of furniture. The dealer was interested, and offered credit until it should be convenient to pay. The Doctor thanked him, but replied, saying, " I buy only for cash. My principle is, ' Owe no man anything.' " At the Home, a friend called, and the Doctor showed him over the new house. Before he left he gave his check for five hundred dollars, to be used in furnishing. So was the prayer of that morning answered, and the large necessity of the moment met. Not long after this, two hundred and forty-eight dollars and eighty-five cents came from Woburn, the proceeds of a concert; three hundred and fifty from private tableaux given by a lady in her own house, and one hundred dollars from New York, and other sums too numerous to mention, making up during the first three months of the year, more than three thousand dollars over and above ordinary daily expenses, and the extraordinary expense of fuel for the winter, and furniture for the new house.

XXXII.

THE GREAT TRIAL AND TRIUMPH OF THE YEAR.

CHRISTMAS EVE the great trial of the year came like a thunderbolt from a clear sky. It was as un- precedented as it was unexpected. Gifts had flowed in and accumulated in deposit, in the safe, to the amount of more than three thousand dollars, including what had been received for professional services. Doctor Cullis had been negotiating for a building in rear of the Home, conveniently situated to connect with it, and looked upon the accumulated gifts as for the purchase of that house. Christmas Eve he went to the safe to deposit the gifts of the day, and found to his amazement that it had been robbed of every dollar it contained ; all belonging to himself, and to the Children's Home, and the Consumptives' Home. He was left with only the gifts of the day — less than one hundred and fifty dollars — on hand.

This loss was a great trial. It was enhanced, too, by the fact that there were daily applications for admission to the Home which had to be refused for want of room, and the Doctor had been greatly in hopes of adding the rear house, by means of the funds that now had been stolen. Then, too, he well knew that there were those ready to blame him, and use the loss to impair confidence in him as a man for such a work. He saw that from the human standpoint, few things would be more likely to destroy public trust in him and dry up the streams of beneficence to the work than this event. His, however, is not the human, but the divine standpoint, and it is instructive to mark how the loss affected him and the work.

Doctor Cullis's first words recorded after the robbery were, " It is with sorrow I record this event; *sorrow for the guilty one, but with peace in Jesus, because his promise fills my heart:* ' All things work together for good to them that love God.' "

And he adds, " O, it is blessed to know and FEEL that the Lord reigns. ' God is our refuge and strength, a very present help in trouble. Therefore will not we fear, though the earth be removed, and though the mountains be carried into the midst of the sea.' Ps. xlvi. 1, 2."

How unlike human nature! Sorrow less for the loss, less for fear of impaired confidence in himself and in the work ; more for the poor unknown guilty one who had robbed God of what had been given for the benefit of his poor suffering children !

The next day's Journal breathes the spirit of Christ in like manner.

" *December* 25. Again, Christmas Day gives us cause to rejoice and give thanks for God's best gift to man, his own dear Son, an ever-present and living Saviour ; so present that we can rejoice in this, our trial-season. He has permitted it for good, and I will not question. The money was his, and if he allows it to be diverted from the purposes intended, I can only say, his will be done. My portion of the lost money was reserved to pay for the building in the rear, which I had aimed to purchase for the enlargement of the Home. Though ' thieves break through and steal,' if the work is owned of him, ' he will provide.' "

This of itself was a great triumph. Was it justifiable? Did the Lord justify it? Gloriously. He gave back the loss and some thousands more; even more than had ever been expected, insomuch that the work was enlarged far more during the remaining months of the year than in any whole year before. And the very first day after the robbery the Lord gave tokens very cheering. The Doctor says in his Journal : —

" A friend, almost the first one to hear of the robbery, gave her check for one hundred dollars, and another friend, meeting me on the street, gave ten dollars; both sums designated for my personal use."

The robber proved to be a young colored boy who had been in Doctor Cullis's employ, and was discharged about three weeks before. He was traced to his place in the South, arrested with a false key of the safe in his pocket, brought to Boston, tried, found guilty, and sentenced to five years in the State Prison, but no part of the money was found, or recovered.

XXXIII.

THE LORD'S BOUNTY.

THE Lord added to his work after the robbery, in a few months, two houses to the Home in rear fronting the next street; a chapel in the Home connecting all four of the houses in one, and a house for a Chapel and Tract Repository at the bottom of the street, a Bible Reader, an Evening School, and a Dispensary. The history of each may be given in a few words.

One of the remarkable things about it is that after such a loss the Lord should have strengthened the faith of Doctor Cullis immediately to begin asking and accepting these enlargements one after another.

THE FIRST HOUSE IN REAR.

Doctor Cullis had been praying for this before the loss, and had made an offer for it which was declined. He prayed on. The offer was to give the price the owner had named as the one he would take for it if he should conclude to move out of it, — paying three thousand dollars down. Soon the robbery occurred, and it was known that he had lost all. Then came the owner, saying, " Well, Doctor, now you have lost all your money, you will not be able to buy my house, if I should conclude to move out of it, will you ? " The reply was, " When you are ready to sell call on me; I know the Lord has not forsaken us, and

he loves his suffering children too well to turn a
deaf ear to their cry." A week passed and the
owner came again asking how much would be paid
down, but saying that he had not decided to move
from the house. Doctor Cullis answered, " As soon
as you decide to move let me know, and I shall
then be able to inform you what I can do." Two
days after that the owner called again and said his
mind was made up to move, and asked " How much
can you pay down?" The Doctor replied, " Three
thousand dollars." As soon as the owner went out,
the Doctor knelt and asked the Lord to enable him
to pay that amount whenever the owner should be
ready to vacate the house and make out the title.

Soon after he gathered faith to ask more. The
price of the house was seven thousand dollars. It
was mortgaged for twenty-five hundred, leaving forty-
five hundred to be paid to the owner, and he prayed
for the forty-five hundred instead of the three thousand dollars. When the day came the Lord had
given him thirty-five hundred and shortly afterward
he gave him the remaining thousand dollars, thus in
his bounty fulfilling his largest petition. .This was
not all. Shortly after the purchase the Lord put it
into his heart to build in the rear between this newly
purchased rear house and the two fronting Willard
Street, connecting all,

A CHAPEL IN THE HOME,

and in answer to prayer gave him the money to do
it, so that the Chapel and the new house were dedicated at the same time on the thirtieth day of March.
The dedication, like those before, seems to have been
a happy time. Bishop Eastburn and Rev. Dr. Hunt-

lngton of Boston, Rev. Alexander McKenzie of Cambridge, Rev. Mr. Heaton, an English clergyman, and Hon. Alexander H. Rice and Mr. J. W. Kimball all took part in the exercises, and at the close all enjoyed the bountiful and beautiful collation kindly provided by the lady friends of the Home.

A SECOND HOUSE IN REAR.

Just while the dedication of the first rear house and the Chapel was pending, the owner of another house in rear, along-side of the one already purchased, offered it for sale to Doctor Cullis. Three days after the dedication the bargain was made at seven thousand dollars and the title secured. One thousand dollars was paid down and the balance remained on mortgage to be paid in equal annual instalments, one thousand dollars each.

Thus within about four months after the robbery, the Lord gave to the work two more houses, upon which five ·thousand five hundred dollars had been paid down, and the Home Chapel all paid for, connecting these two rear houses with the two in front, making all into one convenient Home for his suffering ones.

But enlargement did not end here. Willard Street is a short one, shut in at the foot, all but a narrow walk through, by two houses which front up the street and abut in rear on a street thronged with men, women, and children, for whom there then was no suitable place for Sunday-school and worship. The situation of these houses was admirable for a Chapel. Doctor Cullis had seen this and thought much about it before. The Lord so strengthened his faith that only one week after buying the second house in rear of the Home he went and made an offer

12

of five thousand dollars for one of these houses at the foot of the street, — one thousand down and the balance in equal annual payments.

Three days after this offer his faith was put to the test by its acceptance. Evidently he hardly expected it, certainly not so soon, for he says : —

"For a moment I felt a little shrinking from incurring such an increased expense, but shall I not believe when he says, ' Open thy mouth wide, and I will fill it ' ?

" My prayer was that the Lord would prevent my obtaining this house, if not in accordance with his will, and he knows that my only desire is to work for his glory in the saving of souls ; at the longest there is but little time left me to serve him, and I would be ' about my Father's business.' "

A little more than a fortnight passed and the purchase was consummated as proposed. Thus the Lord added yet more to his precious work a house for

A CHAPEL AND TRACT REPOSITORY.

In connection with this new branch of the work, two enterprises already some time in progress found better accommodations.

AN EVENING SCHOOL

had been in existence all winter long. And

A BIBLE READER

appointed early in the year found here also an excellent centre for her work. Soon also

AN ASSISTANT

was employed, a Sunday-school started, and what evenings the Chapel was not already occupied, the people were invited in for prayer-meetings and preaching services, and many souls were saved.

When the house for the Willard Street Chapel was purchased, scarcely a dollar was left in hand for the next day's expenses. Yet, O how blessedly the Lord sealed his approbation upon the heart of his servant that very day! The first gift of the morning was a gold dollar, " sent in memoriam of a precious one in Paradise." That alone touched the deep springs of feeling. The next was from California, twenty-five dollars, from a man and his wife, " on behalf of our little daughter some seventeen months old," and twenty-five dollars more from the same persons to the Doctor for his own personal expenses. These precious gifts, all from entire strangers, caused his heart to overflow with gratitude to God.

A DISPENSARY.

For a long time Doctor Cullis had been desiring to open a Dispensary in connection with the Home, for gratuitous medical and surgical treatment of the poor. Dr. G. M. Pease kindly offered his services, and was placed in charge of this branch of the work. The Dispensary is open from one to two o'clock each day.

The Lord sustained and blessed every branch of the work new and old, and bountifully supplied all wants so that although expenses were largely increased they lacked nothing.

A HOUSE FOR HIMSELF.

Shortly after the purchase of the Willard Street Chapel, in the course of the same month, the Lord gave the Doctor what he had long looked for before in vain, a house as a home for his own family. He took it upon lease for five years. Not until the Children's Home had been established, and the Home for Consumptives had been doubled in capacity, and the Chapel for neglected ones outside had been purchased, did the Lord give his servant even a hired house for himself. Yet all the while the Lord filled his heart with peace, and when a home was given him, he filled him with gratitude for his goodness.

The history of this bounty of the year would be incomplete if something of the story were not told of how it was that the Lord so much more than made up the loss, by such unprecedented enlargement. At the very time of the robbery, a fair was in progress at Roxbury, from which was shortly afterward presented to the work eight hundred dollars, and before the robbery a number of friends of the work, wholly without the knowledge of Doctor Cullis, were already arranging for a fair in Horticultural Hall, Boston, which was held soon after, and from it about five thousand four hundred dollars was presented, making in all from the two about three thousand dollars more than was lost. A great many other contributions, large and small, came in, accompanied by words of cheer and sympathy, a thousand fold overbalancing all reproach from any and every quarter.

XXXIV.

THE LORD'S FAITHFULNESS.

THE history of the work is that of the spirit of grace and supplications given, and of gifts from God in response. Many volumes would hardly suffice to tell all in detail; a few instances at most are all that can be narrated.

FURNISHING THE CHILDREN'S HOME.

October 7th, earnest prayer was made for means to furnish the house just before dedicated as a home for the children. Next day fifty dollars came all the way from beyond the Atlantic, designated for the children. Also one dollar from five little girls in Dorchester, and eleven from a young ladies' class in Vine Street Church, Roxbury.

October 10th, prayer was renewed for the same object, and that very morning a gentleman came, saw what was needed, and left his check for five hundred dollars.

A SEWING-MACHINE

was very much needed. November 6th, Doctor Cullis asked the Lord to send one. Afterwards reflecting that he had money in hand enough for the purpose, he concluded to buy one. Just then a new and very complete machine came in, sent by the company that made it. Whereupon the Doctor says, " How like a tender loving Father as he is, does the

Lord supply every need; no want is too small **to** reach his ear."

January 10th, in the morning, Doctor Cullis prayed for large means towards the purchase of the new house. That day besides smaller gifts a gentleman sent his check for one hundred dollars. The next morning a lady sent her check for one hundred· dollars, and various other gifts came during the day, amounting to one hundred and sixty more. Four days later the Journal entry, without design, gives substantially the answer to the prayer of· the 10th. It is as follows : —

"*January* 15. ' God is love.' The daily gifts are proving God's care for us, and the required amount of three thousand dollars is rapidly accumulating, for the purchase of the new house."

The very next day the prayer was enlarged by asking for forty-five hundred instead of three thousand dollars, and very soon answered.

PAYING WORKMEN.

The treasury was emptied by the purchase, and the workmen engaged in altering the new building must be paid. Doctor Cullis asked the Lord for means to pay them. The Lord gave all that was needed in good time. There was paid, February 22d, two hundred dollars; February 26th, one hundred, and February 28th a gentleman called and gave his check for four hundred and fifty dollars. The Doctor asks, " Is not the promise true, ' Whatsoever ye shall ask the Father in my name, that will I do, *that the Father may be glorified in the Son* ' ? "

ANOTHER LEGACY.

One fact should be clearly understood, or we may fail to give the glory due to God in many instances of prayer answered. The prayer is from God as well as the answer. In many instances, when the Lord has already prepared the answer before the prayer has been made, he puts the prayer in the heart just on the very eve of the answer. The answer has been long preparing, but comes at the moment the prayer ascends. This is the principle of the promise, " Before they call I will hear, and while they are yet speaking I will answer." All this was verified in the following instance : —

"*June* 29. It is now noon. I have asked the Lord for large gifts.

" Three P. M. To God be the glory. A stranger has just called and handed me a check for five hundred dollars, a legacy left by a lady lately deceased in Brookline. ' They that wait on the Lord shall renew their strength ; they shall mount up with wings as eagles ; they shall run and not be weary ; and they shall walk and not faint.' Isa. xl. 31."

PROPOSITIONS DECLINED.

One interested in such matters proposed to give a dramatic performance for the benefit of the Home. Doctor Cullis thanked him for his kindness, but declined the offer, saying, " I could not ask God's blessing upon it, and therefore I could not receive the money it would bring in."

At another time notices were published that on a given day a race would be run for a certain sum, and the winner would give the amount to the Consumptives' Home. Doctor Cullis saw the notice and addressed a note to the one who was arranging for the race, declining the intended benefaction and requesting that the notice should be withdrawn. His note was couched in kind and gentlemanly terms, giving full credit for the generous feeling that had prompted the proceeding, but it gave great offence. There was no race, and two or three weeks after ward the horses of the one who proposed it were sold by the sheriff for his debts.

All gifts are accepted with gratitude, without respect to the sources from whence they come; but when propositions are made by others to get money to bestow upon the Home, by means questionable or demoralizing, Doctor Cullis has felt bound to decline having it done, however generous might be the impulse causing the offer.

CAR FARE.

He who walks by faith, asks alike of God small things and great as they are needed, and sometimes when little is truly asked, much is given. Here is an instance : —

"*August* 7. After paying for provisions this morning, I had not a cent left. Knowing that I had to go into a neighboring town this afternoon, I immediately asked the Lord for the means to pay my car fare. Before the hour arrived to depart, two dollars came in ; while at this place, a lady knowing nothing of the condition of my purse, handed me a check for one hun- dred dollars. On my return home, two hours after, I found a note from the lady who compiled ' Golden Truths,' containing fifty dollars more, her share of the profits from the sale of the book. From a gentleman, three dollars. ' O praise the Lord, all ye nations ; praise him, all ye people. For his merciful kind- ness is great toward us ; and the truth of the Lord endureth for ever. Praise ye the Lord.' Psalm cxvii."

CONVERSIONS IN THE HOME.

At a certain date, Doctor Cullis records the fact that he is " praying for the outpouring of the Spirit upon the inmates of the Home, as there are several unconverted." This was the prayer whenever there were unsaved ones in the Home. Undoubtedly, also, prayer was made daily by helpers in the work for the same thing, and by the saved ones in the Home for those unsaved. Probably special prayer was made for each one converted. The record shows the answers to these prayers from month to month. For example : —

"*October* 14. Precious news to-day 1 A soul rejoicing in Jesus who entered about a week ago.

"*November* 22. The Lord has revealed his nearness to-day in the conversion of two of our poor sufferers.

"*January* 16. A glorious gift to-day, — a new heart to one of the patients.

"*March* 27. Two.

"*March* 28. I rejoice to-night over another.

"*April* 24. Two.

"*June* 9. One.

"*June* 29. Three.

"*July* 22. One.

"*August* 29. Two.

"*September* 12. One.

"*September* 20. One."

These, probably, were not all. Yet these are the recorded ones with their dates. Again, as in former years, it was true that not one died in the Home, or went out from it partially or wholly cured, without good hope in the Lord Jesus.

IN THE TRACT WORK,

it is worthy of special note that a large number of conversions were, from time to time, reported as resulting from the reading of tracts sent out.

Several hundreds of the two tracts, " A Saviour

for You," and " Heaven," were sent to Williamsport, and the good news came back that " a number of conversions are traceable directly to their agency." Individual cases more than one were reported. A missionary wrote from Providence, R. I., " More than twenty conversions have resulted from the distribution of the books you have sent."

DEDICATION DAY

was honored as usual: The Willard Street Chapel was publicly and heartily given up to the Lord as all and only his own. The services were conducted like those of similar occasions before, and participated in by Rev. Dr. Nicholson, Rector of St. Paul's Church, Boston; Rev. James H. Means, of Dorchester; Rev. W. McDonald, of Grace M. E. Church, Boston; Rev. Dr. Gardner, of the First Baptist Church, Charlestown; Bishop Eastburn, Rev. Dr. Kirk, Rev. Mr. Fox, of England, and Mr. J. W. Kimball, of Boston.

Such are the most remarkable features of the fourth year of the work, its reversal of seasons of strait and of plenty, its great trial and triumph, its bounty and its faithfulness. In some respects it was the most remarkable of the four. A great many things in which it was a repetition of the preceding years, such as the precious gifts of widows and children, the poor, the aged, the bereaved, and the like, in which it was not at all behind the preceding years, remain untold for fear of tiring by sameness and for want of room.

THE FIFTH YEAR.

XXXV.

STRAIT ALL THE YEAR ROUND.

In all preceding years there were seasons of strait and seasons of abundance, but the fifth was one of strait from the beginning to the end. Yet in it the Lord was glorified. He was glorified by the seven years of famine in Egypt, as truly as by the seven years of plenty. His bounty in the seven years of plenty, would have gone for little towards the fulfill-ment of his purpose concerning Israel if it had not been for the seven years of famine which brought his own chosen people down into Egypt to be nurtured upon the fatness of the land.

It may well be doubted whether the faith of Doc-tor Cullis would have stood the year-long test to which it was put in the fifth year if it had been thus tested three or four years earlier. And on the other hand it is quite as certain that it would not have had the strength required for the subsequent enlargement of the work but for that year-long trial.

The trial was severe as well as long continued. As often as every other day of the whole year the record shows an empty treasury with immediate wants to be supplied. Yet it was by no means a case of brick required in full tale without straw. Every day brought its supply for the absolute neces-sities of the day, whether large or small; the large

just as easily and just as certainly as the small —
with nothing over. Some days indeed brought double
supply, but then the next day brought next to nothing ; always something, for every day since the work
begun has brought its token of God's love and care.
No one year before the fifth gave as that did record
of so much special prayer answered, and we all know
how wonderfully God is glorified in such cases. Commencing with the first day of October, and running
through till the last day of September, nearly or
quite half the days of the year gave occasion for some
special prayer specially answered, sometimes for little
things, sometimes for large ones. Now for a day's
supply of food or for a single dinner or supper for
the purchase of which there was no money in hand,
and then for two hundred dollars to pay workmen or
a thousand dollars to pay an annual installment due
upon a mortgage. And in either case the answer
was often delayed until faith was put to the greatest
strain, yet the answer came at last, and God was
glorified.

The first day of the year opened without a dollar
in the treasury. There were more than forty souls
in the Consumptives' Home, eight in the Children's
Home, and two connected with Willard Street Chapel,
to be fed, besides Doctor Cullis's own family expenses
to be. paid. The first day's provision was asked of
God and supplied by a gift from two Sunday-school
Classes in Providence, R. I. The second day there
was neither money in the treasury nor provisions in
the larder, prayer was made for the day's supply, answered by twenty-five dollars received from over the
waters, sent by a lady travelling in Europe. The
third day every dollar was gone at noon, — the day's

supply having been purchased out of what was received the day before. The fourth day's history is
unrecorded, probably it was like those before it. The
fifth day there was nothing with which to purchase
dinner, until the following note was received : —

"AMSTERDAM, N. Y., *September* 24, 1868.

"DEAR DR. CULLIS : — I am sure you will be interested to
know the history of the inclosed six dollars. I circulated a
report sent to me by my friend Miss Bacon, keeping it lent for
months and then mailing it to a friend, who would continue to
circulate. One of the ladies who read it was deeply interested
and sent a dollar last year.

" About three weeks since she said to me 'I am thinking much
of Doctor Cullis and his work of late, and I think I shall have
something to send soon. I don't know when, or where it is
coming from, but I hope soon, from some quarter.'

" To-day I called to see her, and she greeted me with ' O, I've
been *praying* you might come to-day. See what I have ;' and
she laid two dollars in my hand, and went on saying, ' My son
gave me a vest to wash that had been out of use for some time.
I washed it, and put it through the wringer three times, then
starched it, and finally hung it out on the line to dry. As I
placed it on the line and the light fell upon it, I noticed a dark
spot in the pocket. I instantly thought *Ah, there is Doctor
Cullis's money ;* and I determined the amount (*whatever* it was)
should go to him.' She had not even hoped for more than one
dollar, but *this* was a *two dollar* bill. Her daughter-in-law over-
heard the story, and came into the room and handed me fifty
cents, saying, ' Yesterday I thought this was lost, but I have
found it, and will put it with mother's.' ' It shall come right
back to you, daughter,' said the mother, handing her another
fifty cents, ' for I owe this to you.' ' Take that also,' said the
daughter, placing it in my hand. I left, with the *three dollars,*
receiving the mother's parting injunction to send it *immediately,*
for *she* believed you were in *need just now.* This mother is a
widow. Her husband was a minister, and she is a woman of
prayer, and powerful faith. On my return I related the incident
to my sister, who said, ' Let *me* add a dollar, and tell sister
Fannie and *she* may give something too.' So I told the story

again, when my second sister instantly rose and handed me another, which with my own made this mite, six dollars.

" God bless you more and more, and add to the number of those who walk by faith.   Your sister in Jesus."

The sixth day came, and again Doctor Cullis was penniless. These words mean just what they say. He had no money of his own, none from donations, nor any earthly resource whatever without doing what would have contravened the principles upon which he had received the work from the Lord. Over and over again he felt compelled to assert this fact in his Journal, lest the glory of the Lord in giving the faith and in furnishing the supply should be obscured. He was literally and entirely shut up to the Lord as his only source, and to prayer as the only means of supply. So, being absolutely penniless, he called on the Lord, and the Lord answered him. Visitors came and left two dollars and a half, one dollar came from Belmont, five from Dorchester, and five from Haverhill. So the day's necessities were met. But now came, prospectively, a larger want. The last house in rear of the first in the Home had not yet been fitted up or furnished, and on this day of the new year alterations were commenced. It was greatly needed ; many had to be turned away, but several hundred dollars would necessarily be required to put it in condition to receive the Lord's suffering children. So again, for means to make these alterations, Doctor Cullis called on the Lord, and that very day the Lord sent him two hundred dollars for professional services.

So ran the days, and so came the supplies through the entire year. Once only, during the year, an article, specially valued, had to be sold to meet pressing demands. Sometimes the payment of dues to laborers was necessarily delayed, to which they cheerfully submitted, — nay, more, they, of their own accord, freely gave money out of their own pockets, just when it was specially needed, without any knowledge of the special necessities they were thus relieving.

The one trial, however, of all others most severe, was that of inability to pay the annual installment of one thousand dollars, on the house converted into Willard Street Chapel. Like payments on other houses were not delayed. The Lord supplied the money, as we shall see, in a manner signalizing his hand in it, but he withheld the money for the Chapel as signally, yet strengthening faith, and so glorifying himself in the withholding in the one case, as he did in giving in the other.

The installment came due, but the money, though asked of the Lord, did not come. The party to whom it was due asked for it, but granted time. The time expired and he asked again. Daily prayer failed of bringing the money. Finally Doctor Cullis felt constrained to offer the Chapel for sale. Cheerfully he advertised it, saying in his heart, " It is not mine, but the Lord's, and if it is his will that it shall be sold, it is all right." Nevertheless, he did not believe it to be the Lord's will that it should be sold, and it was not. The wonderful work which the Lord was doing in the Chapel, in saving many souls, and strengthening the faith of his own dear children, convinced Doctor Cullis that he did not intend to have it sold. Well he knew that a mint of money would not compensate the loss of such a precious work to the cause of Christ. So, while for a whole month the Chapel was offered and advertised, his faith grew stronger all the time, and ultimately, when the trial had wrought its fruits, the Lord gave the money.

13

XXXVI.

SUPPLY METED OUT.

BOUNTEOUSNESS characterized the preceding year ; measured supply the fifth year of the work. Was it not wise ? was it not necessary ?

The first months of the fourth year the Lord poured in money in contributions, and in the payment of bills for professional services, until, when Christmas came, more than three thousand dollars had accumulated in advance of the daily necessities of the work. And then, when Doctor Cullis was robbed of this, the Lord again and yet more abundantly bestowed upon him, day after day, gifts over and above meeting all the daily expenses, insomuch that the additions to the work were larger than in any preceding year. Suppose this had continued in unbroken streams, would not the tendency have been unduly exalting ?

However that may be, it was not continued. We all know that bounteousness in advance, though gratefully received at the time, *may* lead to forgetfulness of the giver, or to undue profuseness in the use of that which is given. A succession of checks in supply, by measuring it out as to time and amount, giving only when needed, and only what is required, however humbling to him who receives it, is wonderfully beneficial. A wise father understands this. God is our Father, and love is the law of his gifts. He gives bounteously in advance when love dictates. He gives by measure as to time, or as to both time and amount, when it will most benefit and bless his beloved children.

This fifth year, in his wisdom, he supplied his servant for the work by measure, always as to time, giving only when the moment of necessity had come, and usually, also, as to amount, giving no more than was absolutely required at the moment. One of the ways in which the Lord cheered his servant on through all this year of stress and strain upon his faith, was just this of letting him see his hand in the supply as to timeliness and amount. The great trial of the preceding year swept over the work and the worker like a tornado, but instead of uprooting the faith of the one, and overthrowing the other, they were borne up and prepared for the unprecedented abundance and growth of the succeeding months. The year long trial of the fifth year, to a weaker faith, would have been too much, but as it was, the faith stood and grew strong, rooted and grounded more and more firmly in the loving faithfulness of God by the stress and strain of each day of the year.

PAY OF WORKMEN.

Alterations in the last house purchased, of the four which finally comprised the Consumptives' Home, while it remained on Willard Street, were commenced on the sixth day of the year. A week passed on. The workmen were to be paid, but the money had not come. Daily gifts had barely met daily expenses. Five dollars over was all Doctor Cullis had in the world. He asked the Lord for the money, and soon after he had prayed, a check for two hundred dollars was received from a man who could not have known

anything about the strait he was in. So the workmen were paid.

THE PURCHASE OF COAL.

At a certain time when the autumn was far advanced, on a day when every dollar had been paid
out, the matron of the Home informed Doctor Cullis
that she had not coal enough to last through the day.
He said nothing to her about being out of money, but
asked the Lord to supply what was necessary. On
returning to his house he found a note from a friend
inclosing fifty dollars, and four dollars from other
sources, so the coal was bought and God was glorified.

ANOTHER WANT.

At another time, being in need of this comparatively large sum, and not finding it in the letters
awaiting him at his own house, Doctor Cullis, with
his wife, knelt and asked the Lord to come to his
help, telling him that they were doing his work, and
that their only hope was in his word, which they had
so often proved to be a living word. This was at
eleven o'clock in the morning. The Doctor went out
again upon professional visits. He came in again at
one o'clock, and found awaiting him a check from a
friend of the work, in the city, for two hundred and
fifty dollars.

A SPECIAL SACRIFICE.

Through all the autumn of this fifth year, just the
time in which, in the year preceding, the large sum
was accumulating of which the safe was robbed, the
stress of daily want, met only in answer to daily special prayer, continued. Finally, on the first winter
day, a climax came. No supplies were sent, and in

the course of that day a valuable article was sent out by the Doctor and sold for forty-six dollars and twenty-five cents, and so that day was provided for. Evening came, and behold a gift of one hundred and fifty dollars came in from two sisters and their brother, personally unknown to the Doctor, and who could not possibly have known anything of the peculiar strait of the work at the time. This again was in direct answer to prayer.

At another time, as the Doctor sat in his office, tired and worn in body from overwork, his thoughts turned to the great necessity, at that moment pressing, having no money, while much was needed on every hand, and as he tells us in his Journal, a little heart weariness came over him, yet *only for a moment*, for he looked up saying, " Lord, this is thy work, not mine, and *I know thou wilt take care of it*, and of me." Soon after, fifty dollars came from a gentleman of Boston Highlands.

Let me here say that in all my researches through the annals of this year of continual stress in regard to supplies, this is the only word indicating heart weariness even for a moment, and this was only for a moment. The habit of Doctor Cullis's mind was that of looking up, — or rather shall I not say it and give the glory to God, the quickening Spirit of Christ in him kept him constantly looking up to the Lord, and not down at the billows, and so kept him from heart sinking. The frequent record of being kept in perfect peace *all the time*, leaves no room for doubt about the fullness and faithfulness of the Lord's keeping power through all the trials of the year.

EXACT EXPENSES OF THE DAY.

One morning Doctor Cullis had not money enough
to buy provisions for the day, and was looking to the
Lord for it, when a lady called, and gave him five
dollars, and one of the laborers gave him two, neither
of them knowing the pressing need, yet the two
together meeting the day's expenses exactly.

FIFTY DOLLARS FOR THE CARPENTER.

Soon after on that same morning a carpenter at
work on the house, asked if he could have fifty dollars the next day, and the Doctor answered " Yes,"
although he had not so much as one dollar of the
fifty at the time, and did not know where a dollar of
it was to come from. He simply asked the Lord to
supply the amount, and believed he would do it.

The next day's record gives the result. After
recounting his morning at the Home, and some precious tokens from the Lord, the Doctor says : —

" On reaching my house I found a lady waiting, who, handing
me a package, said, 'My son has lately returned home, bringing
this valuable fur collar. Having become interested in the work,
he wishes to give it, to be sold for its benefit.' After the lady
had gone, I said to myself, this is not the fifty dollars, I promised
yesterday, but I thanked God for the gift, and asked him to send
speedily, a purchaser. During the afternoon a friend called ;
and showing him the fur, I told him it was for sale for the benefit of the work. He immediately said he would buy it, but went
out without farther comment. Later in the afternoon, he returned, took the fur, and without asking the price, sat down and
filled out his check for one hundred dollars."

SEVENTY-FIVE DOLLARS TO PAY THE MASON.

While at the Home one morning, Doctor Cullis was
asked by a mason at work on the house to pay him

seventy-five dollars in the afternoon. Twenty-five dollars had been sent in by a lady, a dollar came from Eugene City, Oregon, and two dollars and fifty-eight cents from a Sabbath-school, and twenty-five dollars came from a friend. The daily provisions were supplied, and just forty-five dollars remained over toward paying the mason. Doctor Cullis then asked the Lord to supply the remaining thirty dollars. At noon a bill for just thirty dollars for professional services was paid. This enabled him to pay the mason the seventy-five dollars, nothing over. This filled the Doctor's heart with joy in the Lord, and he wrote in his Journal, " O, it is blessed to live by the day on God's promises."

SATURDAY AND SUNDAY'S SUPPLY.

Saturday always brings Sunday's supply with its own. The two days' manna on the sixth day of the week in the wilderness, was not more certain. The double supply came one Saturday in answer to prayer, first by the sale of some pieces of silver, and gathering every penny from all the boxes, increased by a small amount which came in for professional services, and completed by two dollars and a half, received from New York. This was for the Consumptives' Home. Afterward at the Children's Home, Doctor Cullis found that flour was needed. He told the matron he had not a cent, but expected some money from the Lord before the day was past. Just as he finished these words, the door bell rang, and a lady from Framingham entered, and handed him fifty cents, saying, " I came much out of my way to bring this to you. I *was* impressed that I *must* do it."

THREE DOLLARS TO PAY A BOY AT THE HOME.

On that same day when the Saturday and Sunday's supply had been purchased and not a cent remained over, a boy at the Home was to be paid three dollars. Doctor Cullis sent a bill out for collection. It was not paid. He called on the Lord. Half-past seven o'clock P. M. came, and only fifty cents had been received. He started for the Home, praying for the remaining two dollars and a half. On his arrival he found a note from Clifton Springs, with just the two dollars and fifty cents inclosed.

IN TIME FOR THE EXPRESS.

One day a bill for butter came in, the pay for which was to be sent by express. Doctor Cullis was very busy, and had no money. So he asked the Lord to send the money, and wrote a note, directed the envelope, and left it open to receive the money when the Lord should send it. In about an hour a lady called and paid a bill for services which amounted to a little more than was required. So the money was inclosed in time for the express.

A BILL OF THIRTY—TWO DOLLARS.

The third day after this, little by little an amount came in, sufficient barely to buy the dinner for the day. In the afternoon the Doctor asked the Lord for money to pay a bill of thirty-two dollars; a number of small amounts came in for services, and others also as donations. At five o'clock the whole amount in hand was thirty dollars and fifty-nine cents, which lacked one dollar and forty-one cents, of being enough to pay the bill. The Doctor then asked the Lord for this, and in fifteen minutes a gift of one dollar and fifty cents was received; nine cents over the amount required.

Most of the instances thus far given, taken almost at random from the multitude as they have been, are those of no great amount, ranging from two hundred and fifty dollars, down to fifty cents; and lest some question whether in this continued year of strait and trial, a larger amount would not have staggered faith, the following is also given.

SIXTEEN HUNDRED DOLLARS ON MORTGAGE.

Doctor Cullis noted in his Journal, April 12th, that on the last day of the month, sixteen hundred dollars would fall due in payment for the fourth house of the Consumptives' Home, and added, " I am looking to the Lord for the amount." Five days after this, upwards of two hundred dollars was received. Three days later still, one thousand dollars more came in. Eight days more passed, and a check for two hundred dollars was received. When the day came, the whole amount was paid.

Large amounts are as easy for the Lord as small ones, if it is his pleasure to send them.

These are only a few of the many instances of supply, suited to the wants of the work in time and amount, in answer to special prayer during the year; and what does it prove? If it does not prove that God's hand, and God's counsel are in the work, and that he does hear and answer prayer, what could do it? When supply is measured out every day of the year, and every Saturday doubled for Sunday, when half the days of the year it is asked and received, by special prayer; when occasional demands ranging from fifty cents to sixteen hundred dollars are also paid, by money given in answer to prayer; if that does not show the Lord's hand in the matter, pray can it be shown by anything under heaven?

XXXVII.

ADDITIONS TO THE WORK.

NOTWITHSTANDING the perpetual strait for money, some important additions were made to the work during the fifth year. The house in the rear of the Home, which was purchased near the close of the preceding year, the fourth house of the Home, was fitted up, furnished, and filled. How the money came to pay the workmen who made the alterations, we have seen. It was completed and dedicated January 24th, in the evening. Bishop Eastburn, and Rev. Drs. Huntington and Nicholson, Episcopalians, of Boston, Rev. D. R. Cady of Arlington, Rev. J. P. Hubbard of Rhode Island, Rev. George Washburn from Constantinople, and Rev. E. M. P. Wells of Boston, assisted in the services.

Furnishing was a heavy item for a hard year, yet the Lord made it light and easy. The young ladies of Wheaton Seminary, at Norton, voluntarily furnished one room; a lady from Medford furnished another room; friends in Wellesley another, calling it "The Wellesley Room;" a lady furnished the large ward; another lady furnished a bed; and friends in Middleboro' furnished a bed. In this way it was all done, in answer to prayer, and the capacity of the home was increased about one fourth.

The Tract work steadily grew and was wonderfully owned and blessed of God.

The Willard Street Chapel work, through all the trial about paying the installment of the year on the house, was strengthened and increased.

The most important addition of the year, however, was the establishment of

A DEACONESSES' HOUSE.

Perplexity attended the supply of nurses for the Home ; Christian laborers for the different branches of the work were required, but not easily found ; the want of educated trained women was imperative ; and after much prayer in regard to the matter, Doctor Cullis was led to the conclusion that a home must be offered to Christian women willing to give their services and wishing to be trained for their vocation.

The noble work at Kaiserswerth, Germany, afforded an example. An essay by Rev. George Washburn of Constantinople, showed the existence of an order of deaconesses in the Apostolic Church, as mentioned by St. Paul, and also later in the days of Chrysostom, as shown by his letters to the deaconesses of Constantinople, and thus gave the authority of Scripture confirmed by history for such a house.

For more than a year Doctor Cullis had been praying about it, when at last on the 16th of January, 1869, he received one dollar, the first gift for the Deaconesses' House. Three days after this he received a five-dollar gold piece for the House from one who had valued it as a keepsake for years, and also a gold breast-pin from a lady. And from that time on gifts were received, until during the last week in February a house adjoining the Consumptives' Home was vacated, and the one who had occupied it called and offered to transfer his lease, which had a year yet then to run.

This was accepted as a direct answer to prayer, and the house was taken.

It was not strange that after the matter was settled, faith should have been for a moment staggered by the thought of the magnitude of the work as a whole, and the question of expediency in adding to it another house, especially at a time when every day was one of strait for means to pay daily expenses. Encouragement, however, came quickly in the thought that, led as he had been, step by step, walking by faith, not by sight, he' could trust in the Lord. Then came to him the precious words of the Psalmist, "What time I am afraid I will trust in thee," and he was established, strengthened, settled.

On the 11th of May, the house was dedicated. Bishop Huntington presided. The presence and voice of Prof. Washburn of Robert College, Constantinople, whose essay had influenced the decision to establish the house, added greatly to the interest of the occasion. Rev. Mr. Coolidge of South Boston, Rev. Mr. Means of Dorchester, and Rev. Mr. Tucker of Newton, also took part in the service, and all seemed to coincide with Prof. Washburn in the conviction "that the opening of this house marked an era in the history of the Christian Church of New England, which will be looked back upon as one of the most important in the history of the Church."

Thus was the House opened, and soon it was occupied, and before the close of the year it had already shown its usefulness, not only by the work of the deaconesses at home, but also abroad; and thus another branch of the work was born in a time of trial, and so the work grew even in the year of its greatest strait for means.

Another addition to the work was the monthly paper,

"TIMES OF REFRESHING."

Its first number was issued April 24, 1869. Since that, "Loving Words," a monthly for children, has also been added, and now at this writing, the first number of "The Word of Life," a monthly to present Jesus to sinners, has been issued.

Meanwhile, the "Times of Refreshing" has risen in character, greatly grown in circulation, and become a power in unfolding to Christians their present privilege of complete and abiding union with Christ, as made of God, by faith, unto them, wisdom, righteousness, sanctification, and redemption.

God is also glorified in the time and manner in which its publication was undertaken.

Doctor Cullis had felt the need of such a paper, as he tells us, "almost from the beginning of the work," but had not undertaken it in any time of plenty, and now in one of the longest, hardest times of trial for money, he commenced its publication. Why? First he felt more the need of it, and prayed more and more about it, yet mentioned it to no one. Then when the Lord had filled his heart, a letter came from Mr. G. C. Needham, offering to edit such a paper as a work of faith. This the Doctor took as God's answer to his prayer, and the paper was issued immediately. Mr. Needham after a while, at his own request, ceased to edit it. When the first number came, Doctor Cullis "knelt and asked God's blessing on every number," and that prayer has been wonderfully answered more and more from year to year.

THE SIXTH YEAR.

XXXVIII.

THE PURCHASE OF GROVE HALL.

THIS was the great event of the sixth year of the work.

Comparatively early in the year the want of more room in the Home became pressingly apparent to Doctor Cullis. The following record shows it : —

"To-day, December 9th, I was obliged to turn away a man, every male ward being full. The Home now contains forty-four patients. What shall be done now? I remember what the disciples of John did when they lost their leader. They went and *told* Jesus. I will wait and see what is his will."

The first recorded intimation of the way in which the Lord was answering the question, and leading the mind of Doctor Cullis, is given in his Journal January 17th, "Two more patients turned away to-day for want of room." Then he goes on to say, " After much prayer, I am convinced that our best plan would be to build at a little distance from the city, where land enough can be obtained for the erection of suitable buildings for each branch of the work.' The reasons given for this are, first, to secure room . second, greater quiet; third, freedom of the children from bad influences of the city ; fourth, pure air with shade and space and seclusion from heartless scrutiny for the patients.

The one thing thought of as weighing against this plan, was the large amount of money required to

14

carry it out, but this was far overbalanced by the thought of the exceeding great and precious promises, and of the boundless love of God, and by the assurance that the desire to care for God's poor, was " the outflow of his indwelling love," and that he had but to ASK, AND RECEIVE, and to WORK, FOR IT IS GOD WHO WORKETH IN YOU TO WILL AND TO DO OF HIS GOOD PLEASURE.

It is remarkable that the plan here mentioned as the best is the very one filled up to the letter, in the result in everything but one, that of building. The Lord's plan was to furnish the requisite amount of land with buildings already on it needing only to be altered, enlarged, and improved, differing in this one respect only from that conceived and expressed by his servant.

The month following, the necessity for refusing two patients more for want of room, gave occasion for a few words in his Journal, which show that faith was already merging into joyful assurance of the needed enlargement. He says " O, with what joy and assurance I call on the Lord for aid, for the care and comfort of the homeless, for my Saviour has said, ' *Whatsoever* ye shall ask in my name that will I do.' "

The next month comes a record of the first money laid aside for the enlargement. It is five dollars given by a *lady over eighty years* of age to Doctor Cullis for his *own personal use*, as she heard he had been sick, with liberty, however, to appropriate it as he should choose. He chose to have it go for the prospective place.

The month thereafter comes this record, " Within a week five patients have been refused for want of room," followed by these words, —

"My prayer is, ' Speed the time, O Lord, when we shall no longer be obliged to close our doors against one in need ! ' ' We have boldness and access, with confidence, by the faith of him, — his faith, — the faith of the Son of God who loved me, and gave himself for me.' In that faith I ask, and am ' confident of this very thing,' that ' he who hath begun ' this work ' will perform it,' and provide all things, for ' he is able to do exceeding abundantly above all we ask or think, *according to the power that worketh* in us.' "

Hitherto Doctor Cullis had been asking money to build with; now he began asking guidance to the spot, although, as yet, not much money had been received. The next entry upon the subject is this, two months after the last : —

"The need of a new and enlarged Home is pressing upon us, and I pray our Father to enlighten me, *that I may look in the right direction for land.*"

Another month intervened, but instead of discouragement on account of delay, the Lord cheered him with confidence ever increasing. He brought home to his heart the words, " lacked ye anything? " and the answer, " Nothing," with a sweet force that filled him with delight.

During the next two months his prayer for direction to the right place was answered, first by turning his mind toward Boston Highlands, and then by fixing it upon the Grove Hall property. The way in which he was led to think of Grove Hall shows how the Lord overruled his preconceived ideas. Already he had asked two friends in the vicinity to look out for a piece of land or an old estate available. Each independent of the other mentioned Grove Hall. He replied, " No, that will not do." Then a third person said to him, " Grove Hall is just the place." This led him to think whether it was not the Lord's choice. He went to see it; found it contained more land than he supposed, — eleven acres, well situated, and the buildings, though dilapidated, yet such as could be altered and enlarged advantageously for all present purposes of the work, leaving room for others when needed.

He called on the owner. The price asked for it was one hundred thousand dollars, terms easy. For a moment the responsibility of so large an amount seemed a weight, — *only* for a moment, for the Lord assured him by bringing home to him the question, " Is anything too hard for the Lord ? " Great peace, — the Lord's peace followed. He asked and obtained a fortnight's refusal of the property.

The two weeks passed, and his mind was clear without the shadow of a doubt. The owner had told him that he had been offered one hundred and twenty-five thousand dollars for it, but would sell it to him for the work at one hundred thousand. He prayed the Lord that he would cause the owner to reduce the price yet more, and when he met him, on the day appointed, he did reduce it to ninety thousand, and gave him three years to pay ten thousand, and ten years in which to pay the other eighty thousand. The purchase was made, and the Lord gave him perfect peace in it and after it, although, as he tells us, he had not a cent in his pocket, and only a small sum laid by towards building.

Amongst the last words, in the record of the year, Doctor Cullis says, in view of the purchase : —

" Our hearts rejoice looking for the glory of the Lord to be revealed through this abundant gift. As God covenanted with his people Israel, so he doth with us. 'I will rejoice over them to do them good, and I will plant them in *this land*, assuredly with my whole heart, and with my whole soul.' Jer. xxii. 41."

The most remarkable thing about this purchase was that the faith to make it was not the result of an overflowing treasury, for the daily supply was exhausted by the daily necessities almost the whole year round, and very often the morning came with no money in hand for the daily bread, until it was asked and received; nor of any extraordinary teaching or manifestation of God's will in any way, but was induced simply by the evident need of more room, and the assurance that the desire to provide for the suffering ones was the outflow of God's own love from his indwelling presence in the heart of his servant, confirmed by a continual increase in answer to prayer.

XXXIX.

KEPT IN CONTINUAL DEPENDENCE.

WHILE the Lord was preparing the way and moving his servant to ask for and receive the great enlargement of his work, which was to come in its new quarters on Boston Highlands, he kept him daily waiting on him for daily supplies. One of the early days of the year, October 6th, has the following record : —

"This noon I had but twenty cents in the world, belonging to myself or any branch of the work, and money was needed for supper. I asked the Lord to send it, and it came at three o'clock in a check of ten dollars, by mail from Dover, N. H. Truly 'they that trust in the Lord shall not be confounded.'"

Two days afterward the following : —

"*October* 8. This morning, on going to the Home, I had not a cent. As I reached the door, I lifted my heart and asked the Lord to send money before I should leave. An hour later, as I took my hat to leave, a lady called whom I had not seen for a year, and who could not possibly have known my pressing need, and gave forty dollars to be used as I pleased for the work, and ten dollars for my personal use."

These early days represent the first month of the year; the second opened and flowed on in the same channel of daily dependence, as will be seen in the two or three instances for which only there is room.

"*November* 1. To-day the first gift to an empty treasury is two dollars from Brooklyn.

"*November* 2. I retire to-night with but twenty-five cents in the world.

"*November* 4. Yesterday provisions for the day were purchased by the proceeds of a bill for professional services received

"*November* 6. 'Be thou exalted, O God, above the heavens. Let thy glory be above all the earth.' Ps. lvii. 11. This morning I went to the Home without a dollar, yet in peace. Yea, joy filled my heart, for I knew in whom I trusted On reaching the Home, the mail, which just arrived, brought a letter from 'Miss Mary,' inclosing two hundred dollars."

These few days illustrate the constant dependence through the year for daily supplies. A few instances of special necessity, met by special provision, in answer to prayer, will serve to show how the same trust in the Lord was required for the occasional and larger demands of the work.

SIX MONTHS' INTEREST

on the mortgage on the Children's Home came due, and notice of it was received. "On that day," says the Journal, —

"I was entirely without funds. I asked the Lord for the amount (one hundred and five dollars), when a bill for professioual services was paid, sufficient for the purpose."

THE MONTHLY PAY

of the laborers (upwards of one hundred and fifty dollars) was due, when says the Journal, —

"*August* 2. I asked the Lord for the amount. The mail brought one hundred dollars from Rye Beach, N. H., which, with the balance of yesterday, and the payment of a bill, supplied the need."

ONE THOUSAND DOLLARS

on the mortgage upon the Children's Home was overdue.

"The burden of my prayer," says the Journal, "this morning was, that the Lord would send the amount; and while in prayer, the sweet assurance, ' according to your faith be it unto you, filled me with perfect peace ; and every time I have thought of it since, a flood of joy has filled my soul."

A month and more passed by before the money came, but the faith did not fail ; then came just the amount, one thousand dollars, from a single source, and the mortgage was paid off.

CRITICAL ILLNESS OF DOCTOR CULLIS.

Between the 14th and 23d of December, Doctor Cullis was prostrated, and for two days critically ill. On the 23d he was able to leave his bed and resume his Journal, but very weak. In noting these facts, he adds : —

"I would bear record to the glory of God, that he kept me in perfect peace, — free from all anxiety about the work. His own word was so sweet to me: ' O fear the Lord ye his saints, for there is no want to them that fear him.' Ps. xxxiv. 9."

While prostrated, knowing that while recovering he would require rest and need to be away from the scenes of his labor, he asked the Lord that if it pleased him, he would send him the means, as he was entirely without money.

The very next day after he left the bed, some one sent him a twenty-dollar gold piece, for his own personal use, whereupon he says : —

" December 24. I thank the Lord particularly for this, as a direct answer to prayer."

He went to Philadelphia, and returned strengthened and refreshed.

So passed the year in ever-recurring instances, continually refreshing and deepening dependence on the Lord in the heart of his servant.

XL.

LITTLE THINGS.

GOD often touched the heart of his servant by little things, and filled him with gratitude and joy.

THE LITTLE FOLKS

have had much to do in these little things. The first gift of the year was from a fair held by the children in Appleton Street, and although the amount was two dollars only, it told of busy hands and beating hearts, moved by the Lord to supply the wants of the work. In another place, "a little boy of ten" got up a subscription among his friends and relations, and received and sent four dollars. A little girl sent five dollars, saying, "I take great pleasure in sending you this, which I have earned in making a straw castle." One little boy sent the "first fruits" of his earnings. Another sent two dollars, of which a part was earned by him, and a part received in a box for the Home, which he kept on his table. A little girl on Boston Highlands sent forty-five cents and two silver half dollar pieces. Two little girls in East Cambridge saved their pennies for Doctor Cullis, instead of spending them, and sent to him two dollars and fifty cents, the result of their self-denial. The children of *an orphan asylum* in New Jersey, at the suggestion of the matron, gladly saved up, and sent three dollars.

These are only a few of the little things by little

folks, by means of which praise was perfected in the heart of Doctor Cullis, and in the Homes under his charge.

Two or three incidents, in this connection, must not be withheld.

A CHILD, while listening to a Report read by his father to his family around him, said, " I would like to send my silver dollar to the Children's Home." This touched the mother's heart. That silver dollar had been the plaything of her three little ones, two of whom had entered the pearly gates; this one only left, and she said, " Yes, my son, you may." This reacted upon the father's · heart, and moved him to bring forth and send *the keepsakes of an infant sister* of his, taken to heaven more than twenty-five years before, and to add *his own pocket pieces*, making in all five dollars.

A MOTHER in SING SING, N. Y., while talking one evening with her two little children about our risen Saviour, said, " To-morrow will be little Grace's birthday, and I shall send a birthday offering to Doctor Cullis for the Children's Home." They ran for their banks and emptied them. Finding in each only twelve cents, they thought it too little to send. She explained the Saviour's view. The elder one of the two was eight years old. She had given her heart to Jesus seven months before, but during the last few weeks had not shown the meekness and gentleness of Christ. She burst into tears, and when asked the cause, answered with reluctance, " Ma, you know *when* I became a Christian; but lately I haven't been acting like one. I have felt bad for some time. and wanted to tell you, but was ashamed. *I do want to love Jesus more.*" The mother proposed a prayer meeting, which she says was " blessed to us all," and then adds, " Your Report was the means of bringing an answer to my prayers, and an increase of my faith. I had feared that by telling of the early conversion of this lamb of the fold, I had brought reproach upon Christ. My son, hearing part of the conversation, adds his *monthly allowance*, two dollars."

A MOTHER IN NORRISTOWN, PA., sat one evening reading the Report to her two children. The eldest, a girl, gave the contents of her bank " for the babies." The youngest, a boy, brought a tenth of his possessions, twenty-five cents, saying " please ask that I may have a Report to lend to my little friends." The mother herself added " a ring in *behalf of Eliza, our baby, who not many months since went home to Jesus.*" This, however, was only part of the story; the best of it was told in these words in a postscript: " I have such good news that I want you to rejoice with me, and praise the Lord. The interest awakened last night by your Report in my boy's heart, was blessed to his conversion, in answer to the promise, ' Whatsoever ye desire when ye pray, believe that ye receive it, and ye shall have it.' "

THE AGED,

like the children, contributed much cheer by little things.

A LADY OF SEVENTY-THREE earned by knitting, and sent a dollar, — worth, O how much, weighed in the Saviour's scales !

ANOTHER OF OVER EIGHTY, earned also by knitting, and sent five dollars.

THE BEREAVED,

like the children and the aged, contributed out of their sorrows not a little, by *heart-offerings* to the joy of the work.

FROM SPRINGFIELD, one wrote as follows: —

" DOCTOR CULLIS : —

"Inclosed I send you a ring left by my deceased mother; also fifty cents obtained for a coin worn by my baby brother, who went to heaven thirty-one years ago. Not having other means to send, I give these keepsakes as a mite for the good work."

In connection with these things, which have a value far greater than that of mere dollars and cents, may also be mentioned a larger gift. A bereaved husband sent one hundred dollars *in memoriam* for his deceased wife.

THOSE BLESSED,

too, as well as the little ones, the aged, and the bereaved, imparted out of their joys, no little cheer for the work.

A LADY OF PLATTSBURG, N. Y., sent twenty dollars as a *small* token of gratitude to the Great Physician for healing mercy to a dear member of her family.

A LADY OF ATHOL, MASS., sent fifty dollars as a thank-offering for the conversion of her daughter.

These are a few, only, out of many instances in which the gift of things precious, and things out of precious memories and associations were sent, showing how deeply and sweetly the Lord had imbedded this, his own dear work, in the hearts of his own beloved ones.

XLI.

THE SPONTANEOUS DEVICES OF FRIENDS.

THE ways in which friends of the work have gathered money to give for its support, have been various and ingenious.

It is scarcely necessary to say here what has been said before, that all aid is unsolicited, come in whatever form it may ; and all the devices used by those who have, by means of them, happily contributed so largely, are spontaneous.

Amongst the false impressions that have from time to time obtained greater or less currency, has been this, that the fairs and festivals, and other means used in many places to get money for the work under Doctor Cullis, were originated by him. Nothing could be farther from the truth. He asks of the Lord alone the means to carry forward his own work. All money presented to him is received as from the Lord, — alike that which comes directly from individuals, and that which is gathered by the spontaneous devices used by friends.

One cannot fail to see that viewed in this way the gladness and gratitude caused by all these gifts and devices are greatly enhanced. God is seen in each and all ; and the joy in his people, and thanksgiving for their liberality and love, are vastly deeper than if all was viewed as simply between man and man.

Amongst these spontaneous devices this year, was one on the part of friends interested both in the work, and in Rev. Dr. A. L. Stone, who was in Boston on a visit from his home in San Francisco, to secure a lecture from him. The result was two hundred dollars for the Home, and the same amount to Dr. Stone.

Another was that of a strawberry festival, from which two hundred and fifty-three dollars and fifty cents was sent to Doctor Cullis, — just in time, for when it came he was entirely out of money.

A teacher and pupils gave an entertainment, and brought the proceeds, seventy-seven dollars and fifty cents for the work.

A fair was arranged and held at Chickering's Hall, by friends unsolicited, which resulted in the reception of three thousand five hundred dollars, to which must be added the proceeds of a Doré Bible, given by the fair to Doctor Cullis, and sold at his request for the work, — ninety dollars.

Ten young ladies of Lonsdale, R. I., held a fair, and sent for the work, one hundred and eighty-one dollars and thirty-five cents.

Quite a number placed boxes labeled " For the Consumptives' Home," in their halls, or on their tables, and sent whatever was put in them to Doctor Cullis.

These are some of the many ways in which peculiar interest was shown during the year, and money secured by those who willingly offered and willingly worked that God might be glorified in the care of his own suffering ones. By these various devices, many have shown an interest greater than that of giving directly out of their own means, and have greatly aided the work.

XLII.

THE PRESENCE OF THE LORD.

The power of the Spirit in his wonderful works of grace and salvation, marked as it had been in former years, was even more so during the sixth year from beginning to end.

On the fifth day, the significant record was made, "three of the poor sick ones are to-day rejoicing in sins forgiven, and their *beaming faces* attest the fact."

Time after time, the Journal notes the conversion of one and another, and sometimes two in a day, until at last six in one week are mentioned. Then again the record of the next day says, "Another soul rejoicing in Jesus' love." And a few days later, "We are rejoicing over the conversion of two more patients." Still later one who had but just entered said she had "found a new home and new heart."

In February, a meeting for conference and prayer, morning by morning, was substituted for the regular morning prayers. The patients took part in it. Some of the scenes in this meeting were of thrilling interest. One morning a patient rose and in a hoarse whisper, his voice all gone, spoke of his having found the Saviour, and of the love which filled his heart. And then said, "I must testify for Jesus. As long as I can I will speak for him. When I can no longer speak I will stand up for him. And when I am un-

able to stand up for him, I will hold up my hand."
When he sat down all faces were suffused with tears.

In the first one of these meetings a patient who had entered the Home only a short time before, gave this testimony : " I feel that of all men I have more to thank God for than any one else. I have been a great sinner for years. Eleven years ago I thought I became a Christian, I joined the church, but Satan dragged me back into the world. I grew worse than before, committed greater sins, renounced God, and became an open infidel. Then my friends all left me, and, sick, I entered this Home. *The very day I came here* the power of the Holy Spirit took hold of me, and now, I thank God, that he has restored me to myself."

LITTLE TOMMY.

A boy about twelve years old spent the last three months of his short life, as a patient in the Home. He was much prostrated when he entered. He had suffered a great deal. His father was lost at sea, and the fact that a mother can forget her child, was verified in his case, but the Lord took him up.

As he drew near the end of his earthly journey, the Good Shepherd bore him as a lamb in his bosom, gently down to the dark river, dispelling the shadows so that they gave him no fear or gloom.

The last night of his life, he suffered a great deal of bodily pain. The night watcher sat upon the side of his bed, let him lean up against her, and tried to soothe his pain by rubbing him. Then he looked up in her face and said, " It seems as if you were my mother." " Well," she replied, " I'll do every thing for you just as if you were my little boy." " Will you ? " said he, " then won't you put your arm round my waist, and hug me ? " She did so, and he added, " Now I'd like to kiss you." Soon after this he said, " I suffer a great deal, but Jesus helps me bear it." Then he spoke of the fact that there are children in heaven, and said, " I long to go. O, I'm happy, happy, happy ! " About noon the next day his happy spirit took its flight homeward.

MARIA.

The lives of many in the Home have been full of vicissitudes. Maria lived with her mother till she was four years old, then with her aunt until seven, then was sent to a Roman Catholic school five years. At twelve years of age, she was taken from school by her mother, who had married again, to help take care of the children, and after a few years she was thrown out upon the world. She found a situation where she could earn her living, but was taken sick and sent to the Almshouse. After a fortnight there, she was sent to the General Hospital, but *rejected because incurable.* A friend applied for her at the Home, and she was *accepted though incurable.* Her friends did not wish her to be under such influences, and took her away. The dear Saviour touched her heart and gave her a taste of his worship while in the Home, and she was anxious to return, and did so Soon she gave her heart to Jesus and confessed the change to her friends. She became calm, trustful, and happy. Her sweet patience in suffering won the love of all. Her delight in the Word of God was very great. She could not bear to lose a syllable. When it was read in the Chapel service, she was so eager to hear, that in paroxysms of severest pain, she would hold her breath to listen. Her heart yearned for

15

others, that they too might know the blessed Saviour, especially for her mother, and went forth in such expressions as this, " O, that my mother was a Christian." Thoughts of God's goodness in his dealings with her, found expression in such sayings as, " I think Jesus sent this sickness upon me to bring me to himself." " I think God brought me to death's door so many times, that I might be truly brought to Jesus." " How smooth the Lord can make a dying pillow ! " As her thoughts turned more and more to the world above, she spoke of her approaching change joyfully, saying, " No more pain there." " No coughing there." " I shall see Jesus." " I am thinking what a wonderful thing eternity is, never ending." She never tired of hearing about Jesus, and died in perfect peace.

IN THE WILLARD STREET CHAPEL

the presence of the Lord was as truly and powerfully manifested as in the Home. Nightly meetings were held many weeks, and in every one the power of the Lord was upon the people, old and young. Many were converted, and not a few who were already Christians were brought out into the fullness of the gospel by a deeper experience.

THE PUBLICATIONS OF WILLARD TRACT REPOSITORY,

consisting chiefly in small books or tracts, teaching and testifying the Christian's privilege of full present salvation by faith in the precious, ever present, risen Saviour, were greatly multiplied during the year to meet the growing demand for them.

THE " TIMES OF REFRESHING "

also increased largely in its circulation, and like the little books, was owned and blessed of God to a great many of his dear children, as their grateful testimony bears witness.

The work of the Spirit in all these various ways, in the Home, in the Chapel, by the deaconesses and by the publications, has gone forward as steadily and completely as the providential supply of every want. The one is the complement of the other, and it is blessed to see how evenly they have kept pace with each other. No soul unsaved in the Home, many converted in the Chapel and by means of the publications sent abroad, and many more led out into the larger place and richer experience of the abiding in Jesus, kept in perfect peace, and every want supplied in the work throughout all the days of the year to the end.

THE SEVENTH YEAR.

XLIII.

THE GROVE HALL PURCHASE.

CRITICISMS, PUBLIC AND PRIVATE.

QUITE an avalanche came down upon Doctor Cullis soon after the purchase was made. All seemed to centre in three things ; that it was too expensive a property ; that it was low and damp ; and that the price was too high.

The answer of Doctor Cullis to all who came to him, was, that he knew he was following the Lord. He took no step to meet the newspaper comments, but left the defence or justification of what he had done, wholly to the Lord, upon whom he waited in prayer from day to day. One friend offered him five thousand dollars, if he would dispose of the property ; and another proposed to take the bargain off of his hands.

His answer was " No, I cannot sell the place, until God makes known to me, that it is his will to have it sold. When he does I will follow his direction as cheerfully as I did in the purchase. Until he *does*, I should no more dare do it, than to cut off my right hand."

Often it was urged upon him that he ought to respect the judgment of friendly Christian business men, and take their opinion as an indication of the will of the Lord. But when he went with this in prayer before the Lord himself, his mind was filled with warnings from the Word of God, against trust-

ing in man, such as " Cursed be the man that trusteth
in man, and maketh flesh his arm, and whose heart
departeth from the Lord. For he shall be like the
heath in the desert, and shall not see when good
cometh ; but shall inhabit the parched places in the
wilderness, in a salt land and not inhabited. Blessed
is the man that trusteth in the Lord, and whose hope
the Lord is. For he shall be as a tree planted by the
waters, and that spreadeth out her roots by the river,
and shall not see when heat cometh, but her leaf shall
be green ; and shall not be careful in the year of
drought, neither shall cease from yielding fruit. Jer-
emiah xvii. 5–8.

The Lord did take care of the whole matter. Public criticisms as to the situation were silenced by the
facts made known through one of the daily papers by
some one unknown to Doctor Cullis, " that high as is
the ground at the Norfolk House, sixty-six feet above
the water-level, Grove Hall is about twice as high ;
one hundred and twenty-eight feet, and one foot
higher than the State House ; that so far from being
damp, the cellar after being shut up for years was
dry and dusty." And all criticisms as to the price
quickly died, as property there soon doubled in value.

INCORPORATION OF THE WORK.

Until some time after the purchase of Grove Hall,
Doctor Cullis supposed there was no way in which the
work could be incorporated, and he be left free to
carry it on, without the supervision of trustees. He
had done the best he could to secure the property connected with it, in perpetuity to the work. He had
made his will, giving it in trust to two men, with
power to use it for carrying on the Home, after his

death, as a " Work of Faith," or to obtain an act of incorporation, or in any other way they should deem best to use it, in perpetuating the institution as a charitable one.

One of those named in the will as trustees, died. This brought up the question anew. Doctor Cullis immediately took it to the Lord, and the next day a lawyer came to him, as one of three executors of an estate which was to be divided at their option between charitable institutions in Boston, and requested him to make application for a part of the money. Doctor Cullis thanked him, but told him he could not do so, as the first principle of the work was, that nothing for its support should be asked of any one but the Lord. The lawyer asked for a Report, and saw from it that the work was not incorporated, and at once said that although the executors might have great confidence in Doctor Cullis, they could not give any part of the estate to an unincorporated charity. Doctor Cullis said he had desired to have the Home incorporated, but his legal adviser had told him it could not be done, and leave him free. The lawyer after a moment's thought said, " I think it can be done without trouble." After considering it, he told him that " if the work was incorporated, *the Trustees could give a life lease of the property to him, and that would leave him free as long as he should live.*"

This was the Lord's solution of the whole matter. An act of incorporation was obtained. Hon. William Claflin, Rev. A. H. Vinton, D. D., Hon. Jacob Sleeper, and Messrs. Henry F. Durant, Edward S. Rand, Abner Kingman, and Charles Cullis, were made Trustees; and on the twenty-ninth day of April, the property was legally conveyed to them in trust for the work. ▲

PREPARATION OF THE BUILDINGS.

The money required to make the necessary alterations and additions was equal to more than half the
whole amount received for all departments of the
work during the six years it had been in progress. The
stretch of faith required to ask and receive so much in
a few months was not small. How the Lord gave it,
is one of the interesting things of the early days of
the seventh year.

The sixth day bears this record: " I am praying
much about the *new building*." It is evident from
this, that the one main building, the Home only, was
as yet embraced in early expectancy. The Children's
Home, the Chapel, the dwelling for the Assistant,
the Cancer Home, and the Deaconesses' House, were
certainly not forgotten, but only the one building
seems to have been asked for immediately.

Trial somewhat the gravest seems to have been
God's means of strengthening his servant's faith, until
under the severest test it embraced all, and rested for
all as truly as if the money for all had been already
given.

There were not wanting indeed spurs to faith in
cheering forms from time to time. A little one,
greatly blessed, may be mentioned. The very day of
the record above, a note came inclosing only six
dollars, which seems to have spurred his faith as
much as six thousand might have done.

" *Dear Sir :* — My wife heard me speak of your purchase and
thought she would send you whatever might be in her ' *Charity
Box.*' A small matter, but anything helps.
　　　　　　" Yours truly, 　　　　　　T. F. N "

Doctor Cullis said to himself, " how readily we *act*

faith in one another. Hearing of the purchase she responded at once. So would our Father have us respond to his word, for 'faith cometh by hearing, and hearing by the word of God.'" Then our Saviour's words which cover everything, " Seek ye first the kingdom of God, and his righteousness, and *all these things shall be added unto you*," came to him, and he said, "'I seek the kingdom of God, and his righteousness, and so *everything necessary will be added unto me.*'"

Trial in two forms, however, was the main thing in those days of strengthening. Not that trial gives faith — the Holy Spirit alone does that, and does it by the word in the heart — but trial tests it when given, and it is perfected only when it gives rest in the time of the severest test.

Almost daily recurring want of funds for daily bread, was one form of the trial of those days. The other was that of the criticisms public and private in regard to the purchase of Grove Hall.

The first day of the year was commenced without a dollar. Nearly seventy persons were to be fed. Nothing was to be bought on credit.

The third day, and many other days commenced in the same way, and often the morning came with part only in hand for the day's necessities. At last just as the first month was closing, Doctor Cullis men-- tioned the trial to the laborers in the Home at their accustomed morning meeting, that they might with him bear the matter before the Lord. The immedi- ate want in this case, as in every other, was immedi- ately met, but a week later a record is made of the fact that " the gifts had been just sufficient to sup- ply each day's need." Three days still later, as there was at night no money in hand, Doctor Cullis left word at the Home that the usual morning purchases should not be made before his arrival. He could not consent to owe any man anything. That morning the purchases were made for the dinner, by the sale of some articles, and at ten o'clock the matron, the assistant, and he, bowed together to ask the Lord for deliverance from the great need. It is scarcely necessary to say that the deliverance came. Yet a week later and again the daily pressure is seen in the daily Journal. And so on and on through nearly all the days of the first three months of the year.

Meanwhile the days were filled up also with the criticisms of the purchase, which to all human appearance would effectually close the doors of all liberality toward the extensive alterations and additions required to make the buildings what they ought to be for the work.

In the face of this double trial Doctor Cullis prayed on, and the Lord so strengthened his faith that on the last day of December he says: " Two patients were refused to-day." One of the ways used by the Lord to spur his faith was that of frequent applications, while the Home was full. " We have now forty-four sick ones (all the Home would accommodate). *I am looking to the Lord daily for large gifts, that we may commence work on Grove Hall.* THE DEAR JESUS IS MORE AND MORE A CERTAINTY IN MY SOUL: HIS LOVE FILLS ME SO THAT THERE IS PERFECT REST : AND FAITH LOOKS UP WITHOUT A FEAR."

The dawn was at hand. The tide of criticism turned. An architect offered to furnish drawings for the buildings free, and soon completed them. The plan for incorporating was suggested and the act obtained. Ten thousand dollars was given from the Joy Estate. Five thousand dollars was given by one individual, with a request that the name and place of the donor should not be published. A fair was held by friends in Music Hall, Boston, by which they gave to the work twenty-one thousand four hundred and sixty-seven dollars. And a great many sums of lesser amount were given in various ways. So that not only were the alterations undertaken, but the ten thousand dollars, payment on the property, which was not due until the end of three years, was paid on the sixteenth day of May, about the middle of the eighth month after the purchase was made.

Then too, one and another came forward voluntarily with liberal aid in furnishing rooms. A lady in Newburyport sent two hundred dollars for this purpose, in memory of her son, and the daughter of a physician, who formerly owned Grove Hall, requested the privilege of furnishing four wards in memory of her deceased father.

The result was certainly glorious. The Lord gave this year nearly four times the average amount given in each of the six preceding years.

Nevertheless there remained another and a very different trial of faith in connection with the alterations of the buildings. The work of the main building was done by contract. The contractor had altered buildings before in Willard Street for the work and had faithfully fulfilled his agreement : moreover, he was required to give two good sureties. He was to have the building completed by the first day of July, but the time came and it was not done. Every dollar due him by contract was paid him, but he failed to pay those employed by him on the building.

Three things resulted : first, delay of the work, **and** necessity for looking to the sureties to have it com‐ pleted ; second, claims by the workmen upon Doctor Cullis, pressed in some cases by suits at law, for their wages, when he had already paid the contractor for all that had been done ; third, the circulation of a story utterly untrue, that he had failed to pay the contractor.

These trials, however, Doctor Cullis gave to the Lord, and the Lord gave him in exchange for them perfect peace. What the Lord finally did with them remains to be told to his glory, and although it be‐ longs of right to the history of the eighth year, it must be given here to make the thing complete.

As time passed on, and the amount was ascertained to be upwards of ten thousand dollars that the con‐ tractor owed the workmen, Doctor Cullis began to feel more and more the hardship of the case for them. Many of them were mechanics with families dependent upon them, who could ill afford to lose what they had earned. Day after day he prayed for light until he felt that although there was no legal obligation upon him to pay them, it could hardly be pleasing to the Lord to have them go unpaid through the default of the contractor for work done on build‐ ings confessedly belonging to the Lord himself, and he was finally led to the conclusion that the Lord would be glorified by having every dollar paid as soon as he would put the money into the hands of his servant. This conclusion was confirmed by these words brought home to his heart, " I command thee, thou shalt open thine hand wide unto thy brother. Thou shalt surely give him, and thine heart shall not be grieved when thou givest him ; because that for this thing the Lord thy God shall bless thee in all thy works, and in all that thou puttest thine hand unto." Deut. xv. 10.

This conclusion was reached while as yet Doctor Cullis had nothing in hand with which to pay one of the men.

THE CHILDREN'S COTTAGE

was the first of the buildings on the Grove Hall property in readiness. This was taken possession of by the matrons and children on the twentieth day of April. That was a glad day to them. They left behind them the impure air, the din, the pent up quarters, the outside evil influences of the city, and came into their comfortable Cottage Home, with ample lawns, shady trees, large play-grounds, pure air, room out-o'-doors without danger of contact with vice, and all just as the spring was fairly opening out its leaves and flowers under April rains and sunshine. As this was the first fruits of the purchase, in its benefits to the Lord's own precious poor ones, so it was a fair sample, a true wave-sheaf of the future full harvest when the Homes should all be transplanted to the Highlands.

There was no public dedication of the Cottage, but the family with Doctor Cullis and his fellow workers bowed there together, and gave it up to the Lord as his own, and commended it with praise and thanksgiving to his care.

It is in place here to state that before the end of the year Doctor Cullis was led to accept, as the will of God, in the care of children in connection with the work, an important modification. The idea of Cottage Homes, each of which should have its matron or mother at the head of a family of some twelve children only, instead of one general asylum for all, had already been fully adopted as the true one. All along, however, he had refused to take any children except those of the patients, who themselves were received into the Consumptives' Home. Applications were made from time to time, in behalf of other children, and at last these became so numerous and urgent that he was led to go with the question to the Lord, whether it was his will or not that the Cottage Homes should be open to children having neither father or mother living to care for them? On the fifth day of September, in the afternoon, a poor widow, so low that there was no hope of her recovery, called, and in the course of conversation said she had five children who would be left at her death with no one to care for them. "This," he said, "led me again to the Lord in regard to the Cottage Homes, and I prayed him to let me know his will unmistakably. Half an hour after this I received the following : —

"'COLUMBIA, CAL., *August* 22, 1871.
"'DOCTOR CULLIS : —
"'*Dear Christian Brother*, — Inclosed you will find a postal order for six dollars *for whatever object you last prayed for.*
"' Yours in the Lord,
"' A. M. D.' "

This was instantly brought home to his heart as the Lord's answer to the question, and he was filled with peace and joy in conclusion that it was the Lord's will to have him multiply cottages as he should have means, and receive all orphans sent, for whom there should be room.

The Cottage was soon filled up, and since that time applications in behalf of more than twenty children have been refused for want of room, and Doctor Cullis is praying for means to build another cottage.

THE NEW CONSUMPTIVES' HOME

was not finished for the reception of the patients until after the year closed, but enough had been done by the 27th of September, the day so often used in previous years for setting apart buildings for the work, that it could be, and was on that day, publicly dedicated to the Lord.

By means of special cards of invitation, the assembly was limited to such a number as could find room in the beautiful chapel of the Home, which was full.

Rev. Dr. Vinton presided. The services were impressive. Rev. Dr. Chickering and Rev. Messrs. Foster, J. H. Means, S. F. Upham, and W. H. Boole assisted. A poem by Mr. B. P. Shillaber, and singing by Mrs. J. Houston West, and also by Emmanuel Church choir, led by Mr. Bancroft, organist, added interest.

A generous collation prepared by the friends of the work in another apartment, " closed," says the Journal, " one of our pleasantest anniversaries ; jubilant indeed, with the feeling, pervading all engaged in it, of joy that here God's poor suffering ones were to breathe the pure and fragrant air of the country, and enjoy ampler and more perfect accommodations than a city could give."

16

XLIV.

THE GATE OF HEAVEN.

IN a double sense the Home was the gate of heaven
to many. As in years before, so now again all who
came in unconverted, found the Home to them a
Bethel, the house of God, their birthplace into his
family.

ONE EXCEPTION,

however, must be made to this otherwise uniform
fact. Captain G. was received. Soon it was ascertained that he utterly rejected faith in God and the
Bible. He would not allow any one to talk with him
about salvation, and when told, a few hours before his
death, that he could live only a short time, it was
fearful to hear his awful expressions. Much prayer
was made for him, but he died as he lived, rejecting
mercy.

THE CONTRAST

presented by this sad exception to the many happy
instances of salvation is very striking.

A POOR MISERABLE DRUNKARD, for example, was
set free from his chains and made happy in Christ.

In *one morning prayer-meeting*, in the Home, three
were converted.

Two of the patients were baptized, one day, at
their own request, by the Rev. Phillips Brooks. One
of them was

BETA, A CHINESE GIRL.

She gave precious evidence, at the time, that she was trusting in Jesus. Within less than two months, the Home, which had been the gate of heaven in her conversion, was made also the gate of glory to her soul. Those present *saw it*. She called them to her bedside and bade them " good-by," and said, " I am going home to Jesus." Then she sang, " I am going home to die no more." When finally she breathed her last, she raised her eyes toward heaven, and the glory beamed in her face in a beautiful smile.

ABANDONMENT TO JESUS.

One of the patients gave in a letter the following statement : —

" Nine months ago I came to this most blessed Home. I do love it and its matrons, they are so kind, so interested for the soul as well as to make the body comfortable. I was told by three physicians that my case was hopeless, and I came here to die ; but my Father has blessed the means here so that I am better.

" The best however is this. Last Sabbath morning's teachings were blessed to me. Every morning's prayer brings new light. From my heart I thank God I was ever placed here. Again and again I asked Jesus, as you said we must, what he would have me do, and in my helplessness I plead with him. But I *had not* been *wholly* resigned to all circumstances. You and Mr. B. made it so plain I *felt* what I had never thought before. I thank God he has made me to see. I had not before thought of Jesus as *ever present* to save and deliver. I did before think of him as a Saviour, but afar off. Now, in the anguish of my heart, I cast myself *wholly* upon Jesus, and, if I may so say, *abandoned* myself to him, to do with me, and in me, and by me, just as he pleases, that henceforth I may love only him.".

GRACE AND ITS FRUIT.

A CHILD had been in the Children's Home while his father was in the Consumptives' Home. The father was so far restored as to leave and go into some light employment, and he took his little boy with him. The evidence of the good received by the child at the Home came out in this way : —

"One night," so wrote the father, "last winter, my wife read in a newspaper an account of a terrible accident on the Hudson River Railroad, in which many were drowned and burned to death. My boy was in bed, but heard the account. He called to me, and said, 'Papa, that was a bad accident,' and after waiting a moment he resumed, 'It doesn't make any difference if a man is smashed up on a railroad if he is converted to God, and prepared to go to heaven. I am going there, and I hope you and mother will come too.' I asked him what it was to be converted ; he replied, 'To have Christ in your heart.' "

MONEY RESTORED.

A man died one day in the Home. A lady who frequently visited him, had given him ten dollars a few days before his death, and after he died, this lady inquired of the nurse, "If the patient had used any money since she gave it to him, or had left any at his death ? " The nurse answered " No," and gave the matter very little thought, because she supposed the man had given it to his relatives who had been with him ; so nothing more was said or done about it.

The room-mate of the man who had died, was a poor Irishman who had entered the Home about three months before, and a few nights after the inquiry was made by the lady about the money, he called the nurse to his bedside, and asked " if she ever suspected him of taking that money ; " to which she replied,

" No." " Well," said he, " here it is ; a man cannot keep that, after reading the Bible." The word is indeed quick and powerful!

KATIE.

The following is one of many touching stories of those who find the Home to them the gate of heaven. The matron took it down from her lips.

" The first thing I remember is the death of my father. We were living in a poor part of New York city. My brother six years old, my sister eight, and I, were left in the care of a maiden aunt. She managed to keep us together four years, by what she could earn washing, and we by doing errands for the neighbors. Then she obtained a place (to take care of a child) for my sister. My sister strained herself by over-lifting, was taken sick and died. After two or three years more, aunt found a place for brother, in a copper foundry, as an apprentice till he should be twenty-one. He attended night school, and when he saw me, he used to say, ' O Katie, I wish you could go to school.' Aunt needed my help. I knew nothing about school — where it was, or what sort of a place — and I used to tell him I couldn't go. When I was twelve, aunt found a place for me where I took care of a baby. I knew nothing of God or of Jesus then, and was wholly ungoverned. I was so rude and saucy, that the lady sometimes thought she could not keep me ; but she talked to me and I did better, and she taught me to read. When I had been there two years, I thought myself old enough to earn something, and got another place where I had a dollar a week. The lady had daughters who studied evenings, and I listened to them, and learned a good deal of history and arithmetic. I was very anxious to have an education. I saw that I had neither friends, nor money, nor position in society to help me, and I must make myself a place in the world, for I did not wish to be always a servant. So I used to study nights when I ought to have been asleep. I lived in the same place for two years, when I made the acquaintance of some people who wished me to go to New England with them. I went to talk with my brother about it and he said, ' Katie, I would go ; I have heard a great deal about the people in New England, and they are very kind. If you were sick in their houses, they would not turn you out. If you were sick here you would have to go to a hospital. I have a home with my employer until I am twenty-one, and until then I can do nothing for you.' He put his arms around me and said, ' I shall miss you Katie, but go.' I went to Connecticut when sixteen years old, and had never been to church. I began to go now, but the preaching was dull to me. I could not get interested in the Bible, and Christians used to come into the family where I lived and talk so much slander that I was disgusted, and did not wish to be a Christian. I was restless, too, and wanted to see more of the world. I left the family I was living with, and went to work in a factory. My associates there were rough; I didn't like it, and next found work in a shop, where I remained until I was taken sick. I never cared for religion until a lady from New York came where I was and told us what she was doing for Christ in that city. With an assistant, she went into the dark attics and cellars of New York, ministering to the wants of those wretched ones, and talking and reading of Jesus. Sometimes she found them sick in a bed that was in the water upon the floor, and she sent out and got bricks to put under the bed to keep it out of the water. When I heard her story, I rose in meeting and said that was the kind of religion I wanted — a religion that would prompt one to give all for Christ. I gave myself to Christ then, but I have become a great deal stronger Christian since I came here." Last evening she was very weary and longed for sleep. She asked Jesus for it, and told him he had promised " Call upon me in the day of trouble," etc. After a little while she opened her eyes and said, " O, I have slept so sweetly ! Dear, dear Jesus." At eleven o'clock she asked to be turned, then exclaimed, " O, I am going home." In a moment she was gone. To-day she has the sweetest smile I ever saw left upon lifeless clay.

XLV.

REMOVAL AND ENLARGEMENT OF THE PUBLISH-
ING DEPARTMENT.

THE Lord fills the hands of any one with work who
fully trusts and obeys him. The husbandman is not
slow to give an abundance to do to one of his laborers
who does just what he wants him to do in the way
he directs, and does it promptly when commanded.
There are so few in the Church who walk and work
by faith, and there is so much in the world to be done,
that the Lord is sure to lay to the hand of the few all
they can do, working with all their might. To go
no farther, this is exemplified in such instances as those
of Franke in Germany, Müller in England, Mrs. Ran-
yard, also in England, and Dorothea Trudel, in Swit
zerland. Franke was no sooner settled in the principles of trust life and trust work, than work grew
upon his hands apace. His great Orphanage of
twenty-two hundred children commenced in an offer
on his part — which was quite a launch of faith at
the time — to take one child for maintenance and training. In response to his offer four children were presented, and he instantly and gladly said, " I will take
them all." This was a fourfold increase of his faith,
which was yet only as a mustard seed. From this
beginning the Orphanage grew until it contained
twenty-two hundred children. Very soon after it
began fairly to be developed, a home for indigent

students of the University of Halle was added, and soon after that also a publication department. Thus it ever is in trust work. To speak philosophically, there is a tendency in the hearts of those in whom Christ dwells as a fountain, ever springing toward every good word and work, an impulsion to round out the whole circle of service, by works of faith filling up the entire sphere of need, to meet all the needs of the Church and the world by faith in Jesus, even as they have found all their own personal needs met in him. Or to speak in terms of the higher philosophy, the Lord the Spirit moves the hearts of those who are gladly obedient to see and to do whatsoever their hands find to do, and so to fill up in trust work the entire orb of Christian work around them. This is remarkably apparent in the case of Doctor Cullis.

The real faith work of Doctor Cullis had its mustard seed germ in the consecration of his earnings to the Lord at the bedside where his wife was sleeping in death. And the first germination of this mustard seed faith, was in the profuse distribution of tracts all along his pathway. His " tract work " really began before the Lord directed him to the care of homeless, hopeless consumptives, as his " special work." Nor had he been long engaged in this special work before the necessity was laid on him to care for the homeless children of the consumptives, both for the children's sake, and that of their parents, and this gave birth to the Children's Home. Then came the necessity for helpers in the work and volunteers to meet this necessity, and so sprang up the Deaconesses' House. Then came the Deaconesses' work outside of the Home in the highways and hedges, and out of this rose up the Willard Street Chapel, with its meetings, schools, and the salvation of so many perishing ones. In intimate connection with all this came the deeper, sweeter personal experience of Doctor Cullis in the acceptance of the keeping power of the Lord Jesus, as an ever present Saviour from sin, resulting in abiding peace, and entire freedom from fret, and worry, and irritation, and harsh words ; and the introduction of teaching in accordance with this experience into Home and Chapel and publications ; and with this the commencement of a meeting every Tuesday afternoon in Doctor Cullis's own residence, for the express purpose of leading others into the like precious experience given him by the Lord ; and out of this, through the great interest in it, and the overcrowded condition of the meeting, came the suggestion of the proposed Faith Chapel and Training-school for Christian Workers in the higher life ; and by the frequent applications of those suffering with cancer to be admitted into the Home for Consumptives, came the suggestion of the anticipated Cancer House. These last are not yet, but soon will be in existence, considerable amounts having already been contributed toward them. And what next? The Lord of the vineyard knows ; the circle is enlarging and filling up ; yes, and it requires no gift of prophecy to enable one to predict with the assurance of its fulfillment, that the circle will enlarge and fill up to the full measure of the enlarging capacity of Doctor Cullis for work as long as he lives and trusts wholly in the Lord.

The " Tract Work," was in truth Doctor Cullis's first work as a servant of God. He began it very soon after laying away the body of his wife to await

the resurrection; and although it had been partially ·
eclipsed for a time by the Homes for Consumptives
and Children, it had steadily grown into a publication
department or house.   Several tracts or small books,
were embraced in its catalogue, and had been so
blessed in circulation that the demand for them and
for others like them was pressing and constant.
Then, too, the " Times of Refreshing " was issued
monthly and sent out to the number of five thousand
for ten times that number of readers, and for that
the list was enlarging from month to month, while
testimonies were all the while coming in of the blessing to souls which attended it wherever it was sent.

The Lord was at the same time impressing Doctor
Cullis with deepening desire to publish also a monthly
paper for children which should hold forth the word
of life in purity and simplicity.

Meanwhile the place was too strait and too obscure
for this work.   The time had fully come for a change.
It must have room and a business centre for its expansion, or be dwarfed and enfeebled by being muffled
up and kept in its cradle.   If Grove Hall had not
been purchased for the Homes, Willard Street could
not have retained the publication department of the
work.   And after much prayer and satisfactory teaching upon the subject the Lord led Doctor Cullis to
seek and accept a room at No. 12 West Street as the
next tenting place of this department.   With the
removal came immediate enlargement, by the addition
of such other kindred books little and large, as could
be found anywhere and everywhere, calculated to aid
and promote Bible study and Christian experience in
its higher forms.   Manuscripts for other books were
also provided, with the means to publish them, more

and more frequently, fresh from the heart experiences of those who had received the Lord Jesus Christ as a full and complete Saviour and found in his love the fullness of God. Very soon " LOVING WORDS," the monthly for children, was issued, commencing with January, 1871.

Thus came the removal and enlargement of the publication department.

In closing this statement it may be well to mention three or four changes ; first, a change of name consequent upon the change of location. The word " Street " was dropped out and the other words retained to save confusion and preserve identity ; so the name now stands " WILLARD TRACT REPOSITORY," instead of " Willard Street Tract Repository," as it was before.

Two other changes to be noted are these : Mr. G. C. Needham kindly edited the " Times of Refreshing," without salary, during the first of its publication ; and the Rev. E. P. Hammond generously and freely gave the necessary time and labor to the editorial conduct of " Loving Words " one entire year. Now, however, these papers, in common with all other parts of the work, are directly under the oversight of Doctor Cullis himself. A change has also been made in the plan of supplying the publications of Willard Tract Repository to those desiring them either for themselves or others. The *gratuitous plan* was first adopted as the exclusive one, and this answered well in the infancy of the work. And it is still preserved, but not exclusively. The gratuitous feature indeed is expanded. All the publications of the Repository are bestowed freely wherever needed and solicited, to the full extent of all the means the Lord sends for the purpose, and this feature of the work is growing from month to month. In addition to this, however, in answer to prayer, the Lord has taught Doctor Cullis the wisdom and necessity of a fixed price upon each publication, and this has been adopted. This was done first in regard to books and tracts, and since in reference to the papers.

It is wonderful to me, in tracing these and all other transitions, to see how easily and peacefully, and how readily and delightfully the Lord teaches, leads, and sustains his servant. The frictions and collisions of such changes of course must occur with him all the same as if he was leaning upon his own understanding instead of the hand of the Lord ; yet it is clear that neither frictions or collisions break the continuity of peace and good-will in his heart. And it is also beautifully true that the same oil makes peaceful and kind to a surprising extent the spirit of those with whom he is concerned in these frictions and collisions. There is no manager of hearts, either our own, or those of others with whom we have to do, like our Lord Jesus Christ. " Blessed are they who put their trust in the Lord."

THE EIGHTH YEAR.

XLVI.

ENLARGED FAITH GIVEN OF GOD.

STRENGTHENED WITH MIGHT BY HIS SPIRIT, IN THE INNER MAN.

THE first Journal entry of the eighth year bears the imprint of God's Spirit in the enlarged faith it breathes for still greater enlargement of the work. It is as follows : —

"I am daily looking to the Lord for the means to build a wing to the new Home ; as this is needed, not only to accommodate more patients, but to contain boiler room, for steam-heating apparatus, laundries, etc., etc. We desire also, to complete the Chapel on the grounds, to build another Orphan House, and a house for cancer cases, which was mentioned in last Report. A Deaconesses' House is also immediately needed. Upon my knees I have just asked the Lord to grant these, — the desires of my heart. My claim upon the Lord was this : I am thy child, bought by the precious blood of Jesus Thou hast said, ' All things are yours, and ye are Christ's, and Christ is God's '; and I ask, dear Lord, for the Orphan House, that we may care for the poor orphans, thy children ; for the Chapel, that souls may be sought and saved ; for the Cancer House, that these, thy suffering ones, may be cared for ; and most of all, that thy *name* may be glorified. And now, dear Father, this I ask, to prove to the world the truth of thy promises : ' Verily, verily, I say unto you, he that believeth on me, the works that I do, shall he do also ; and greater works than these shall he do ; because I go unto my Father.' ' And whatsover ye shall ask in my name, that *will* I do, that the Father may be glorified in the Son.' ' If ye shall ask anything in my name, I *will* do it.' John xiv. 12, xiii. 14."

How natural it would have been, instead of this

prayer for still greater additions to the work, to have
limited the Holy One of Israel by such thoughts as
these : " Now I have finished the Cottage Home for
the children, and the dwelling-house for my faithful
helper in the work, with his family, and there is a
great deal still to be done upon Grove Hall, with its
wing to be added, and the amount to be paid for the
property is great ; almost a hundred thousand dollars.
All I can ask of God is that he will give me the
means to complete what is begun. Another Cottage
Home for the children is indeed needed now ;. and the
want of a home for poor sufferers with cancer is very
pressing. We do need the Deaconesses' House very,
very much ; and there ought at once to be a chapel,
with its Sunday-school room, free to all, where the
gospel will be preached without money hinderance, or
barrier of any kind, to young and old, high and low ;
and where the secret of the Lord for inletting into
the fullness of faith shall be unfolded to hungering
Christians ; but for all this we must not look now."
How natural, I say, such a position as this.   O, how
supernatural the faith to ask for all these other additions to the work, with all the additional daily expenses they would cause ! What ! ask for money to
add another Cottage Home and a Cancer House to the
work with the greatly enlarged amount required from
day to day to sustain them ? And also to build a
house for the Deaconesses, and to convert barn and
stable into chapel and Sunday-school room, too, while
almost a hundred thousand dollars remained to be
paid upon the Grove Hall estate, and the treasury was
literally empty ? Yes. Human prudence would have
said " No." The Spirit of God in the heart said " Yes."
Did the providence of God justify the answer of his
Spirit in the heart ?   We shall see.

XLVII.

HOW GOD ANSWERED THE ENLARGED FAITH GIVEN.

Two days only passed after Doctor Cullis, while the treasury was yet empty, recorded his daily prayer for the great and various additions to the work, accompanied with the statement that his rest in the Lord Jesus Christ was never sweeter, when from the vicinity of the new property on Boston Highlands came in one hundred and sixty dollars; and when two days more had passed, the Lord gave from another source, two thousand five hundred and sixty dollars; the early streams of an inflowing providence which brought, within the next succeeding ten weeks, into the treasury more than twenty-five thousand dollars.

Thus bountifully did the Lord answer the prayers of his servant, and justify the faith he had given. The work went bravely on. Grove Hall with its wing was completed; the Home with all its inmates and furniture was transferred to its new quarters. A cellar was dug, and foundation laid for the Deacon esses' House, and the conversion of the barn and stable into a chapel and Sunday-school room was begun and carried forward to the completion of the outside work and the plastering within.

Meanwhile continual encouragements to the faith that God fully purposed the building of the Cancer House, were given in small gifts from a great many

17

different persons, and one present of five hundred dollars from a single individual, together with cheering words from all, yet not enough taken all in all to justify as yet a commencement to build. And the same was true also of the second Cottage Home for children. And the Deaconesses' House is still in abeyance, waiting, like the Cancer House and Cottage Home, the gifts of the Lord for their erection, while the faith that asked them is still bright with expectation, and it is strengthened into patience perfected by waiting. The Chapel and how the Lord gave the money to complete it, must have a chapter in due time by itself.

XLVIII.

HOW THE LORD TEMPERED THE WINDS FOR THE REMOVAL TO GROVE HALL.

THE early days of December were very cold; the 6th was severely so, and the 7th was the day set for the removal of the patients from Willard Street in the city to Grove Hall on the Highlands. Some of the poor sufferers were very low indeed, and were to be conveyed in carriages. Doctor Cullis knew well that they could not be moved without a great and favorable change of weather. This he asked and received, but let him tell it in his own words. He says : —

"I asked the Lord that the weather might be moderated, for, 'by the breath of God frost is given,' Job xxxvii. 10; and 'He casteth forth his ice like morsels; who can stand before his cold? He sendeth out his word and melteth them.' Psalm cxlvii. 17, 18. How glorious that 'Word,' that the winds and waves obey, that are 'turned round about by his counsels; that they may do whatsoever he commandeth them, upon the face of the world in the earth.' Job xxxvii. 12. Now see how wonderfully the Lord fulfilled his word. For many days the weather had not only been intensely cold, but, on account of fierce winds, the dust had blown in clouds, stinging and piercing every pore. During last night there was a slight fall of snow, which served to lay the dust ('for he saith to the snow, Be thou on the earth,' Job xxxvii. 6), and the morning opened mild and pleasant, such as we had not known for weeks, so that scarcely an overcoat was needed. On going to the Home, I found two of the patients so feeble, that it hardly seemed safe to move them; I feared they might die in the carriages. I again called upon the Lord, that his strength might be given them ; 'Seek the Lord and his strength, seek his face continually.' Chron. xvi. 11. 'And the Lord hearkened and heard it.' The patients were moved in comfort and safety, and none the worse for the ride of four miles. They were ushered into a perfect summer atmosphere at the new Home, the heat from the steam apparatus permeating every room with a softness that was grateful to us all."

XLIX.

THE LORD'S PRESENCE IN THE NEW HOME.

MORE than once, or twice, or thrice, I have been deeply impressed by expressions from Doctor Cullis, as we have entered the grounds or passed in or come out of the new Home itself, like this. " I never come here without a peculiar sense of the presence of the Holy Spirit." This feeling is not limited to Doctor Cullis. One could easily account for it in his case, if desirous of doing so upon philosophic grounds, exclusive of faith in any special impressiveness of the Spirit's actual presence. The Home itself in all its parts, and everything about it, has been given him in answer to special prayer. As it stands, it is to him a monument of God's faithfulness to his promises. He has seen the Lord's hand in it every day, and every hour of the day through all the years of preparation for it, in all the ways by which it has been established and sustained. Every foot of the ground, every stone and brick and beam and board and nail in it, is to him instinct with God. Well might he be impressed with a deep and peculiar sense of God's presence, therefore, as he enters and passes through the gates and doors of the grounds and buildings there.

Others besides Doctor Cullis, however, have had and do have the same deep, sweet sense of God's presence there. I have it, and others have spontaneously told me that they, too, have been similarly im-

pressed. It is not, however, in impressions upon any
or all of us that the evidence of the special presence
there of the Lord the Spirit mainly rests. The works
he does testify of him. The first Sunday after the
removal was remarkable for the quiet, melting, con-
verting, transforming power of God in the Home. In
the usual morning prayer-meeting there was an
unusual degree of divine power manifested; " *several
hearts* were so melted, that the peace of our Lord
Jesus Christ found abundant entrance to the saving
of their souls." And others were so wrought upon
by the Spirit that they never shook off their convic-
tions until the struggle was ended by yielding to
God and accepting the Saviour. Many weeks after
that first Sunday, one who had long resisted the
gentle wooings of the Spirit, surrendered at last, and
gained the wonderful victory which comes only by
surrender, and in confessing Christ said that in that
morning meeting impressions had been made which
had never ceased or diminished, but increased until
the precious victory came.

L.

HOW THE LORD TRIED THE ENLARGED FAITH GIVEN.

THE incoming streams of supply which flowed from so many quarters in such abundance during the first ten or twelve weeks after the prayer recorded on the 13th day of October, suddenly dried up to the minimum of *absolute* need for the daily sustenance of the work. The Chapel had to be left for the time in its unfinished condition, and the foundation of the Deaconesses' House left unbuilt upon, while all thought of commencing upon the Cancer House and second Cottage Home for the children, had to be put in abeyance. The workmen had to be dismissed, and when they or any one else asked why, the answer had to be given, " No money." Yet, to the glory of God it must be said that the trial did not disturb the sweet peace which he ever kept fresh in the heart of his servant.

ONE VERY SPECIAL TRIAL mentioned in the history of the preceding year, in connection with the contractor's failure, came upon Doctor Cullis at this time ; *the hardship to the workmen employed*, in that the contractor had not paid them for their labor.

It was hard to have it reported and believed that the contractor's failure to pay his men had been caused by Doctor Cullis's failure to pay the contractor, and all the harder because wholly untrue ; and it was yet more trying to have threats made and suits at law commenced against him, to recover from him the wages due from the contractor. And on the other hand it was hard to think of paying over again to the men so large an amount as ten thousand dollars, which had already been paid to the contractor.

But there was another thing the thought of which was harder to bear than all the rest; that the laborers and mechanics who had put their honest toil into the building of the Home, should have it to say when they looked upon it, " There in that Home I put so many days' hard work, for which I have never been paid. My family has been robbed to make a Home for Consumptives."

This trial, great as it was, did not however bring fret or worry or a disposition to battle it out, and seek justification from the lips of judge or jury. It was accepted as permitted by the Lord, for his own glory, and so it was attended from the first with perfect peace. More than this it brought Doctor Cullis face to face with the Lord day after day, with the question, "Lord, what wilt thou have me to do?" and at last its solution came in the sweet teachings of the Spirit, to leave it with the Lord, and pay over again every dollar due to the men, which had before been paid for them to the contractor, as fully and as fast as the Lord should send the means to do it. Thus ended the trial in triumph.

ANOTHER SPECIAL TRIAL came later in the year, indeed passing over into the ninth year of the work, in the flooding of the boiler room, under the wing of the Home, making it necessary to cut a deep and expensive drain to carry off the water.

The expense of this drain would have been felt

much less at another time, but when it came, the treasury was empty, and the daily supply met barely the absolute necessities of the work, and had done so through many weeks, and it came as a deep drain upon faith for funds not yet received, when it was on the watch-tower for means to build the Deaconesses' House for which the foundation was laid, and the Cancer House and Cottage Home, both of which were greatly needed.

At first when the boiler-room was found to be filling up with water from the earth, saturated with the unusual heavy rains of autumn, it was thought that it could be pumped dry, and kept so by a steam-pump, and all interested in the matter were greatly cheered when a steam-pump manufacturer, who had been asked the price of his pumps, but had not been appealed to in any way, freely said of his own accord, " I will give Doctor Cullis a pump worth a hundred and fifty dollars," and did so.

But it was soon ascertained that although the pump lowered the water in the boiler-room, so that the fires could be kept up, and was invaluable for its purpose while the drain was in process of being cut, it would not save the necessity for cutting it. Then this trial was still further increased, by finding that where it was not anticipated at all, there was a great deal of rock-blasting necessary, by which several weeks' time and no little money were consumed.

Through all this, however, both Doctor Cullis and his helpers in the work were borne in patience and peace. I was on the ground from day to day, and met them in private, and in their meetings, and must bear testimony that, from first to last, I never heard a murmuring word, but every day and many times a

day I heard one and another say, " praise the Lord ; "
and some of the most joyful little gatherings for prayer
and praise I ever participated in, were theirs in those
days at their stated times, in the new Sunday-school
room of the Chapel, and that in the evenings of those
days filled up with heavy toil, and with daily disappointed expectation of the speedy completion of the
drain. And of these happy meetings, perhaps the
most joyful of all was one in which the delight of
Christ in taking all our infirmities, if we would but
let him have them, was the subject of conference.

Finally, however, the drain was cut, the drain pipes
put in, the ditch filled up, and all was complete, *and
all paid for* notwithstanding the emptiness of the
treasury. Each day brought its supply, and at the
end of each week when the workmen were to be paid,
the Lord so provided that there was nothing lacking.

LI.

HOW THE LORD SUPPLIED MEANS TO FINISH THE SUNDAY-SCHOOL AND AUDIENCE ROOMS OF GROVE HALL CHAPEL.

"And he made the laver of brass, of the looking-glasses of the women."
— EXODUS xxxviii. 8.

JUST thirty-three cents had been given specifically toward the completion of Grove Hall Chapel,[1] before the tenth day of August, — no more. This was given one day early in June. It was given by *one of the laborers* and was *all she had.*

This little gift was a type in two respects of the greater ones which were to complete first the Sunday-school room, and then the audience room of the

---

[1] Grove Hall Chapel should not be confounded with the Chapel in the Home, which is for the convenience of the inmates; that was finished with the Home, and the dedication service of the Home was held in the Chapel several weeks before the inmates were taken there from the old Home in Willard Street. A daily service had been held in it at 10 A. M. from the time of the removal in December, ten months before the completion of Grove Hall Chapel, and a half hour's preaching service also every Sunday at 4 P. M., with the communion the first Sunday of each month. These services are continued and open to all.

GROVE HALL CHAPEL is outside on the grounds and is for the people in the vicinity and visitors from abroad.

Doctor Cullis preaches in it every Sunday morning, and there is communion in connection with the morning service the first Sunday of every month.

There is also a Sunday-school in the afternoon at 2½, and a meeting for prayer and testimony Sunday evenings at 7½; and a Bible reading Monday evening, and prayer-meeting Thursday evening at the same hour every week; and a ladies' meeting at 3 P. M. Fridays, — with a warm welcome to visitors in all.

Chapel in August and September. They were given by laborers in the work, and were all they had.

The story is this. There was no concert between the two. Both were deaconesses, one employed in one department of the work, and the other in another, and both without salary. They had first given themselves to the Lord, and then to this special work in his service, yet without any pledge in any way on their part to remain in it longer than they should see it to be the Lord's will for them to do so, or on Doctor Cullis's part to keep them or provide for them a day longer than it should suit him to do so. They and he were equally free.

On the tenth day of August, one of them came to Doctor Cullis, and asked him how much it would cost to complete the Sunday-school room of the Chapel for meetings. The answer was, about two hundred dollars. She said, " Well, finish it and I will pay for it."

This was not all she had ; indeed it was less than half as the event proved, but it was a large sum for one in her circumstances to bestow. It came, too, to Doctor Cullis like a cup of cold water to a thirsty soul, because at the time and long before and long afterward the outside gifts barely supplied daily bread, and because he had been long praying daily to God to send means to finish the Chapel. For months it had been standing in its unfinished condition with no one working upon it, appealing daily to him as he appealed daily to God for its completion. Work was at once commenced upon it, and another fortnight passed by. Day by day the records were, " Only means for current expenses ; " " food for the day ; " " the day's need cared for ; " " to-night not a dollar

on hand;" " three days each day enough to purchase
food, we lacked nothing ;" " this morning not a cent,
and the Homes with nearly a hundred people; but
my heart is glad, for I know in whom I trust,
.and he has promised that whosoever trusteth in him
.shall not be confounded." The twenty-sixth day of
August came, and the other of the two deaconesses
came to Doctor Cullis saying she wished to give five
hundred dollars toward the completion of the audience
room of the Chapel. How she came to do this she
herself tells in the following statement furnished by
special request : —

"Three months ago, we were talking about the Chapel-work
one day, and the Doctor said a piece of work upon it would cost
five hundred dollars. The thought came, *I* should like to pay
for that, and if the Lord would show me that it was best, I would
do it. Days, and even weeks passed, and I had no feeling of
decision about it. Six weeks ago, it came before me vividly, and
I opened the Bible, intending to follow the direction of the first
sentence my eye fell upon. It gave me no idea what to do. I
laid the Bible down, thinking I will do nothing more about it,
until the Lord shows me how I may know his will in the matter.

"I waited there, until a few mornings ago; several persons
were talking about giving away what they had, and trusting the
Lord for the future. I remarked that 'I would not do that, without feeling sure that the Lord called me; for, if I should be in a
tight place in the future, I should want to be able to look back,
and feel *sure* I didn't make a mistake when I disposed of what I
had.' And continued, 'You say, Doctor, that the Lord will
teach us his will from his word; I don't think so, for I have had
a matter on my mind for *weeks* to be settled; and I have asked
the Lord to show me from the Bible what to do; and when I
opened it, the first verse I read has been perfectly foreign to the
subject; and I have no idea what to do.' He replied, 'It may
not be the first verse you read; but go on, and the Spirit *will*
teach you what to do.' That night, when I went to my room, I
thought, — now, if the Lord will tell me by his word, that matter
shall be settled. I took up ' Bible Verses,' a very small collection

of Scripture passages. The first thought was, This is too small; he couldn't show me from such a little book as this; and the second, O, yes, he could show me just as well from this. I then asked sincerely, that he would tell me by his word what I should do. I opened the book, and the first words I read were, 'It is more blessed to give than to receive.' I closed the book, and thought, — *more blessed to give than to receive!* Is it possible? It requires all the economy I understand, to get through the year without taking any salary; and is it more blessed to *give* five hundred dollars, than it would be to receive it? If I had the interest of five hundred more, I could get along nicely. I did not wish to be hasty; I would leave it until the next day, then try it again. The next day I went up to my room, and thought, — I'll take the Bible this time; there will be the whole word that he can use. I asked to be guided to the word for *me* — opened, and read, 'Testifying both to the Jews, and also to the Greeks, repentance toward God, and faith toward our Lord Jesus Christ.' Then these words passed through my mind, — here is an opportunity to show your faith toward our Lord Jesus Christ. Reading on, 'And now I go bound in the spirit unto Jerusalem, not knowing the things that shall befall me there.' I thought, I guess I shall go on, not knowing the things that shall befall me. 'But none of these things move me.' I had the feeling that I had not reached the verse I was sent for; and glancing along toward the close of the chapter, my eye rested upon, 'I have coveted no man's silver, or gold, or apparel. Yea, ye yourselves know that these hands have ministered unto my necessities; and to them that were with me. I have showed you all things: how that so laboring, ye ought to support the weak; and to remember the words of the Lord Jesus; how he said, It is more blessed to give than to receive.' I closed the Bible, nearly sure what I was to do. I laid me down and slept; and awaked, and asked the Lord to have patience with me, and show me just once more what I should do. I told him that I knew I was slow to believe; but that this was an important matter to *me*. To many, five hundred dollars would be only a trifle; but to me it was a great deal; but that I *did* want to do as he would have me; and if he would show me *this time*, it *should* decide it. I opened to 'Whatsoever thou wilt ask of God, God will give it thee.' I said, what is this, an assurance that God will take care of me in the future? Then I told him I was not anxious on that point, I only wanted to know *what to do ;* and now that he promised to give whatever I asked, I wanted wisdom, not to make a mistake in this matter. I then opened to these words, — ' So that ye come behind in no gift; waiting for the coming of our Lord Jesus Christ.' Not waiting for his coming at the last day, but waiting his coming more fully into my soul. I was satisfied; but still went on turning the leaves of my Bible, until at length I stopped to read: it was this, — ' Lend, hoping for nothing again ; and your reward shall be great; and ye shall be the children of the Highest. Give, and it shall be given unto you ; good measure, pressed down, and shaken together, and running over, shall men give into your bosom. For with the same measure that ye mete withal, it shall be measured to you again.' I am very happy in the decision I have reached; have not a doubt but God has led to it ; and by his grace will joyfully follow him into the future, trusting him to care for whatever shall befall me."

With this gift of five hundred dollars, work was resumed in completion of the audience room.

The Sunday-school room was finished so that on the evening of August 29th the workers, together with a few friends, met in it to praise God, and give thanks to him for his goodness, and to ask him to glorify himself by the salvation of souls. Meanwhile one of these friends had beautified the walls with texts of Scripture in chromo, and a clock.

The next day a friend without the knowledge of Doctor Cullis, consulted a painter, who said he was too much hurried to undertake the job, but would gladly present his check for fifty dollars toward it.

Three days more passed by, and the deaconess who gave the two hundred dollars to complete the Sunday-school room, came with a request that she might contribute five hundred dollars toward finishing the audience room. This was the last of her earthly possessions, and she gave it all for Jesus.

Thus the two deaconesses gave all to Jesus with

themselves. The work went on, and was completed in time for the dedication on the usual day, September 27th. Meanwhile the same good friend who had given the chromos and the clock for the Sunday-school room, gave matting, carpet, clock, and other things for the audience-room, and a friend in Philadelphia sent a Bible for the desk.

The day came. Friends sent in plants and flowers to beautify the Chapel for the dedication, and an abundant supply of good things for a collation after the service. Tables were spread for the collation, in the Sunday-school room, and the people assembled in the audience-room.

Doctor Cullis, for the first time in all the many services of the kind during the progress of the work, presided in the dedication, and was assisted by Messrs. Chickering, Means, and Plumb (Congregationalists), Steele (Methodist), Hubbard (Episcopalian), and Boardman (Presbyterian), clergymen, and Mr. Sturgis (Episcopalian), President of the Boston Young Men's Christian Association.

After the service, a delightful social half-hour was spent at the tables in the Sunday-school room.

Thus was the Chapel finished by the good hand of God, to whom be all the glory.

GROVE HALL CHAPEL.

GROVE HALL CHAPEL.

LII.

HOW THE LORD MOVED THE PEOPLE TO OFFER WILLINGLY.

AMONG the most beautiful things in the word of God, are the fruits of the Spirit in the abundant offerings of the people to the Lord for his service. The gold and jewels and precious things given by the people to Moses for the tabernacle of God in the wilderness are resplendent in the record with the brightness of a glory far above that which was their own, a glory which was the Lord's, the glory of a willingness of heart which the grace of God alone could have given them. And one of the loveliest features of the pentecostal morning of the present dispensation as given us in the Acts of the Apostles, is the perfect unselfishness, the unstinted measure of true Christian generosity of those who received the gift of the Holy Ghost in counting nothing they possessed as their own, but all the Lord's, and in time of need selling that which man is slowest to part with, houses and lands, to divide the last penny with those who must otherwise suffer.

Something of this same beauty of holiness in giving pertains, as we have seen from year to year, to the record of the gifts to the work of the Lord under Doctor Cullis. The *willingness* of the people to give *unasked* is indeed one of the glories of the work, for in it is seen the hand of God as plainly as it is in the

18

guidance of Doctor Cullis himself. To this there is a superadded lustre purely divine in the gift of personal ornaments to be sold, and of precious memorials of loved ones gone before, and in the gifts of earnings or gleanings by ways and means which love only could devise.

In these things the history of the work has abounded more and more year after year, the. year just past more than any before. The most that can be done is thus to allude to them in general, and give besides a few instances in detail.

THANK—OFFERINGS.

Very many thank-offerings have been made, and for many different favors from God : for manifest answers to prayer ; for husbands raised up from dangerous illness ; for the recovery of brothers and sisters , from critical disease (five hundred dollars in one instance, from two sisters for the recovery of one of the two) ; for the return of the birthday of beloved children ; for continued health to loved ones (ten dollars in one case for the health and growth in loveliness of a dear child).

MEMORIALS

of many kinds, each with a history and sacredness of its own, were bestowed. Among these were a box of gold and silver, in value about eleven dollars, which belonged to a dear one gone to heaven ; a five-dollar gold piece, kept through all the years of depreciated paper currency while no gold has been in circulation, and left by a very dear one for whom the Saviour came, and given " as a pin in the new Home." savings bank with its contents which belonged to a dear child, a daughter taken home; and the memorial windows in the new Home Chapel.

JEWELS

of various kinds were bestowed. One silver set complete; a pair of gold bracelets; buttons, crosses, pins, and other like things, to be sold for the Home, as a better use of them than to wear them as personal adornments.

OF DEVICES,

to earn or gather money for the work there was no end. One *sold* flower seeds from her garden, which in years before she had given away, and thus gathered a sum of money to bestow upon the work. One who had given up a debt of five dollars as lost, gave it to the Lord for Doctor Cullis, *if it should be paid*, and it was very soon paid, and sent; one gave the proceeds of plants, *kept for* the Consumptives' Home, ten dollars; Grace and Charley earned money to send; Grace, seven years old, earned twenty-five cents by sewing, and Charley, aged nine, fifty cents by taking care of his father's horse; the compiler of " Golden Truths," compiled to put its truths better than gold into many hearts, and to put its profits into the Home, sent twenty-five dollars; these are a few instances only of the many different kinds of devices by which so much more has been added to the precious gifts of the people to the Lord for this work.

THE TIMES AND SEASONS AND MOTIVES

of many of the gifts, as mentioned in connection with them, have added to their preciousness. *A larger gift than usual* was sent by one who was known to have lost several thousand dollars just before. A small but welcome donation came during the *week of prayer* from one who referred to the statement concerning Cornelius the centurion, that his prayers and *his alms* had come up for a memorial before God. A lady as she was dying, said, " I want to give something to God; give Doctor Cullis fifty dollars." And the gentleman who brought this dying gift added fifty dollars of his own ; Carrie and her three sisters did housework at school to pay their way ; their mother is an invalid and has been confined ten years to her bed. Carrie said to her mother, " if I had a hundred dollars I would send half of it to Doctor Cullis." She did what she could, she and her friends made up a dollar and sent it; " Little Grace's " *birthday* brought the accustomed five dollars ; but of all the many things, few were more touching than the following

CONFESSION,

accompanying the amount of which it speaks.

"K——, *November* 22.

" DOCTOR CULLIS : —

" *Dear Sir*, — Some time in the summer of 1867 I read your ' History of the Consumptives' Home,' prompted to it by our pastor alluding to it in the weekly prayer-meeting. I was so much interested in it that I collected a little sum, — a dollar apiece from three ladies, and fifty cents for myself; but you have never received it, because I put it with other money in my purse, and, without thinking much about it, spent it.

" Then I thought I should make it up soon, and time went on; and soon the added expense and care of a baby, and housekeeping, put it partially out of mind; though it would often come up and give me sharp twinges of conscience.

" I had an unconverted husband; and about a year ago I began to be more than usually troubled about his soul, and to have some searchings of heart concerning my prayers for him. I began to see the iniquity I was regarding in my heart, which must hinder the Lord from hearing; and then there came a great struggle with my pride, particularly in reference to this case, whether I would give it up, and confess to you and these ladies what a sin I had been guilty of.

" The struggle lasted for months, not only about this instance, but some others, not quite so bad, perhaps, but bad enough; and then my husband became interested about his soul; and still it seemed as though I never could so put my pride in the dust; but the Lord made me feel perfectly willing, and then my husband found his Saviour. But I did not send you the money, for my husband had been intemperate, and we were in very straitened circumstances; however, I was fully determined, and did not feel any of that unwillingness that I did before. I suppose Satan kept a little hold of me, by putting such a plausible reason before me; and so it has gone on, from month to month, through the past summer and fall.

" To-night our pastor brought us a heavy burden, — the father of two members of our church, lying at the point of death, and in the utmost agony about his soul, having been a skeptic for many years, — and, since the meeting, I have thought perhaps my neglect of this thing might hinder the water of life for that soul. Whether it is so or not, it shall not lie on my soul another day, though I take the money intended for warm winter garments.

" Please find inclosed four dollars; and with it goes such a prayer as I can offer; and may I not have yours for a more consecrated heart in the Master's service?

" Very truly,

" * * * "

LIII.

HOW THE LORD SUPPLIED THE RIGHT THING AT THE RIGHT MOMENT.

THE hand of the Lord seen in all the gifts bestowed from the beginning, has been and is one of the chief glories of the work. Gifts peculiar in kind bestowed without solicitation at the very moment when needed, and those given in money, prepared in advance, but coming in the hour of emergency, or in amount exactly suited to the demand, of course show more conclusively the hand of God *to others*, than the mass of the daily benefactions bestowed. *To Doctor Cullis*, who asks and receives everything from the Lord, all gifts alike show the Lord's hand, yet even his heart is made to glow with greater delight when gifts peculiarly timely, or specially suitable in kind or exact in amount, are given, because he knows that others will be more likely to believe and glorify God on account of them.

THE STEAM PUMP,

worth one hundred and fifty dollars, given by the manufacturers without solicitation, was a gift peculiar in kind and suited exactly to the emergency, when the boiler room was flooded. Yet, as the facts had been made known in connection with inquiries about pumps, that, though not one whit less really from

God in answer to prayer, might be less apparently so to some than some other gifts. For instance,

THE TWO COWS

for the Home. As spring began to open, Doctor Cullis began to ask the Lord for cows, that the children and the patients might have an abundance, of milk.

He asked with all the more confidence, too, because the grounds were ample to afford pasture in its season, and hay and roots for food in winter to keep them upon.

The Lord put it into the hearts of kind friends in Dorchester to send, just as winter was going out, a cow with her calf to the Home. And not very long afterwards another new milch cow was sent by a friend from Manchester.

What gladness these gifts caused at the time may be better imagined than told. Several weeks afterward, as I was passing through the grounds, the cows were pointed out to me by one of the laborers, and the story of their reception told me, with a glow in the words showing how deeply the heart was in it, and he added, "Such cows. Such rich milk, and such quantities; I never knew anything like it. If we had selected the cows ourselves we could never have done half so well as the Lord has done for us."

And this last remark I verily believe is true of many things in and about the Home, — true of the laborers, assistant deaconesses, nurses, and all, — true of the place, — true of the plans, — true of the architecture, — true of the ornaments, natural and artificial, — true of the publications, and of many other things.

THE CARRIAGE

for the Homes, so suited in size and form, and so comely in appearance, was another of the gifts special in kind, bestowed in answer to prayer, just at the time when the need of it began to be felt.

At the cost of five hundred and seventy-five dollars a kind friend gave it as the spring was about to open.

One fact more must be given, showing exactness in the amount bestowed at the necessary moment, as prayed for. Early one morning Doctor Cullis asked the Lord for *twenty dollars* to meet the known de-mands of the day. The eight o'clock morning mail brought him from New York a check for exactly that amount.

LIV.

THE LORD'S GIFT OF WORKERS.

THE excellence of the faith principle is exemplified in the excellence of the workers it has served to bring into the work with Doctor Cullis. I am sure the Doctor himself would say, and I should believe him with all my heart, that if he had been left to himself in the selection of those who should become laborers with him, he could not have done it half so well as it has been done for him by the Lord. The same course in the main has been pursued by him in this matter as in getting money to sustain the work and places for its accommodation; he has simply asked and received. Does this imply that he has asked and then taken every one who offered, fit or unfit? No. Not at all. Does it imply that the first to offer has always been the right one for the particular post to be filled? No; not so. Asking has been the first thing, and. then when one has offered, the next thing has been to ask again, Lord is this the one of thy choice? Thus, rolling the matter afresh upon the Lord, he has *shown* his servant in one way or other whether or not the one offering was his choice. Samuel was sent to Bethlehem, by God's own command, to anoint one of the sons of Jesse to be king in Saul's stead. Then when the eldest was presented, came the question, Is this the one? A question not for Samuel, nor for Jesse, nor yet for any of his sons, but for the Lord to answer. So when helpers offered, Doctor Cullis understood that it was not for him but for the Lord to say whether or not they were his choice.

If the question be asked, How could he know the choice of the Lord? the answer is in the promise, " The meek will he guide in judgment." When a question is meekly *submitted* to the Lord, he will *show* his choice. He will *teach* his will; it will be seen. The submission of a question to the Lord implies, however, the faith that accepts the *showing*, when made to the judgment, *as from* the Lord. The ways in which this showing is done are as various as are the peculiarities of the persons about whom the questions are asked, and the circumstances of the case. Neither should the Lord be limited to our ways, but left free to use his own ways, with entire confidence that he will, in his own way, guide in the judgment.

This has certainly worked like a charm in this precious work of the Lord. Perfection is not to be predicated or expected of any one, but if I may judge from a large observation through many years, extending to Christian works and workers in the Old World as well as the New, it is a rare thing to find so much .good service in a spirit so loving and kind, at a cost so small, combined with so much wisdom as in this instance.

One of the maxims of the world is entirely set aside, reversed indeed in this work, namely, that " If you will have good service, you must pay for it." The best service cannot be bought. The opposite principle, " All for Jesus," was the one upon which the Home was founded, and upon which it has been conducted; and millions of money could not have breathed the sweet spirit of self-sacrifice and kindness into the work which has pervaded it in every department. It has been this sweet spirit on the part of the workers that has convinced the inmates of the Consumptives' Home of the reality and preciousness of the Christian religion, and led them to Christ. The hardest people of the hardest classes of the world have come in, and soon seen for themselves, past all possible question, that there is love in the world, that all is not cold, selfish, sensual, devilish ; that there is a religion which impels people to give themselves and their money, and their best services, cheerfully, gladly, for the good of others ; and a religion which makes people happy without the pleasures, or riches, or honors of the world ; and seeing this they have been softened, subdued, and saved.

It is a remarkable thing that rules and regulations are entirely dispensed with in the work. It is literally not under law, but under grace. Penalty and reward are nowhere held out to induce fear or hope, but instead of restrictions, the walls abound in mottoes such as " God is Love," " All for Jesus," " Trust in the Lord," " Only Believe," and I venture to say there never has been a work of equal extent running through eight years, in which so many people have been brought together in the same family with less friction and greater harmony. During the years of my acquaintance with it, I have not heard the word *discipline* used in reference to any inmate of the Home. There was, indeed, one man received as a patient who remained a few days only, but was such an incorrigible grumbler, that Doctor Cullis sent him back to his friends, and that was the nearest thing to a case of discipline I have seen, and the only thing of its kind.

The instances mentioned in connection with the completion of Grove Hall Chapel, are not the only ones in which the workers have given all their possessions to the work while working in it themselves without salary. Two I know did it years before; one gave all she had, amounting to three hundred dollars, which she herself had earned, and the other gave also all he had, and others may have done the same of whom I do not know, for this thing has been done without much talk about it. And thus there has not only been the service of love freely bestowed, but with themselves they have also given all their earthly possessions.

This is true also in its measure of those who have given the productions of their pens to the publishing department; they have not only given without pay the most precious things God has graciously helped them to write, but some of them having the ability to do it, have given money also to aid in their publication and circulation ; and, setting aside what I have written, I am sure the wide world may be searched in vain to find so many and such precious things, with so few inferior ones in proportion to the whole number issued from any one press. Am I not therefore justified in speaking of the excellence of the faith principle in securing workers as well as money for Christian work ? And am I not right in saying that it has worked like a charm in this instance ? Nay, more, would not the prevalence of this principle work like a charm and demonstrate its own excellence if adopted by everybody, in every line of life? I am sure it would. May God hasten its adoption.

A FAMILY LETTER

will show how the " All for Jesus " principle works in the hearts of those touched by it, both in and out of the Home : —

" CHELSEA, July 27, 1871.

" DOCTOR CULLIS : —

" *Dear Sir*, — Since knowing of your Home by my father being under your care, it has been my earnest desire to contribute something, were it ever so small, in aid of your holy, noble work. Thus far it has been out of my power. At father's decease, his children shared expenses, and the bills being paid, ten dollars are surplus. Is it not God saying to us, ' Here, my children, is your " mite "; it is for my Home ' ? It is useless to attempt to express our gratitude for all your kindness to father ; it is beyond the reach of words. I can only plead, *God ever bless you.* We desire to be gratefully remembered to Miss C. and Mrs. P. for their unwavering attention and care. I shall never forget Miss C.'s remark, ' It is all for Jesus '; it brought to me the *meaning* of your blessed work in a deeper significance than ever before. Both my husband and self are greatly interested in your labors. We are young, just commencing in life, but I *know* God will enable us, from time to time, to send a little aid for *somebody's* father, for what has so nobly been done for mine. Mother unites with us in gratitude.

" Yours respectfully,
" O. and J. A."

LV.

THE CROWNING GLORY OF THE WORK.

THE first and last records of the eighth year of the work are full of significance. " The first record of the year brings glory to God, for the conversion of two souls." The last record of the year gives glory to God for the foreshadowings of another branch of the work, to be added in his own good time and way, — a training-school for Christian workers in the fullness of the gospel.

The seal of the Spirit is the crowning glory of the work. This has been signally given in the forms indicated by these two, the first and the last records of the year; in the conversion of all who have come into the Home, to remain until death, or until recovered in health sufficiently to return to some useful employment in life. It certainly does give glory to God to be able to state truthfully that through eight years he has graciously provided a home for his own suffering ones, numbering in all eight hundred and seventy-two, without money and without price ; and a Home also to the children of these poor sufferers, numbering in all forty-five, upon the same easy terms ; and has given assistants and deaconesses to care for both the consumptives and the children, all for Jesus ; and has given money and houses and lands, as they have been required, from first to last, in answer to prayer, without solicitation from those through whom he has bestowed his gifts, amounting in cash and cash values to well·toward half a million of dollars ; and has given the heart and the money to found a Tract Repository and three monthly papers ; and to publish and scatter broadcast many millions of pages of the purest gospel truth ; and to enter upon the work of establishing a Deaconesses' House, and a house or home for sufferers from the terrible disease, cancer. Yet is there not an additional brightness of glory to God over all this in the fact that, besides the many who have been blessed and saved and strengthened in their faith, outside of the Consumptives' Home, abroad through the land by means of the Reports and other publications, the seal of the Spirit has been set upon the work by the conversion of all save one,[1] who entered the Home unconverted out of the whole eight hundred and seventy-two! and in the fact that the standard of the gospel, as the power of God to *save from sin* has been borne aloft so blessedly, from year to year, in the TUESDAY MEETING, until this now seems to be breaking forth out of its chrysalis form into a Faith Chapel and Training-school.

[1] There is room for question whether this one was not saved after all. He may have been brought to Jesus at last. Drowning men have been saved while still conscious, after going under water, and when resuscitated have described the change, and shown its reality by lives of devotion to God. A remarkable experience of the higher life was given to one whom I know, and in whom I have full confidence, in a moment yet more brief. He was in act to be crushed by a railway car, and supposed he would be instantly killed, but was saved. In that instant the Lord flashed upon him the truth as to his false position in relation to Christ as a Saviour from sin, and as to the true position of entire dependence upon him for fitness for heaven, and led him to accept the truth as thus shown to him. And from that instant dates a new life in the fullness of God. He was a Christian before, but has been kept in perfect peace, satisfied in Jesus from day to day from that moment to the present time. May not the Lord have conquered the rebellious spirit of Captain ——, in the last moments of life upon earth, and saved him? The prayer of Doctor Cullis from the beginning, has been "Lord, save every inmate of the Home," and it has not been an unbelieving prayer.

THE POWER OF THE SPIRIT

was blessedly manifested in the Home, during the
eighth year, as it had been in all the years before, and
in some respects more fully and sweetly than in any
of them all.   In the old Home in Willard Street, as
has already been stated, the first record of the year
was that of the conversion of two souls to God.   Is it
not almost equally significant that one of the last
Journal entries there was that of the conversion of a
patient, and the *salvation of a laborer from sin;
from an irritable temper* in particular?

In the new Home on the Highlands, the first Journal entry is that of a sense of the glory of God in its
superiority over the old one, and a prayer that his
glory might " fill the house, and his peace rest upon
it *even now* and *forevermore*."

THE FIRST SUNDAY in the new Home evinced
God's answer to this prayer.   There were no extraordinary measures adopted.   The usual morning prayer-
meeting was held at ten o'clock, and conducted in the
usual way.   The power of God was present, however,
to save.   All were moved; several were melted; a
number found peace, and Christ was received into
their hearts.

This was the beginning in the new Home.   From
that day onward the glory of the Lord has been continually manifested in the pardon and peace found
by those before without Christ, and in the deeper,
sweeter experience of salvation from besetting sins by
Christians.

THE SECOND SUNDAY in the prayer-meeting *three*
patients and one *stranger* found peace in believing.
Already, then, it could be said with truth, as it was,

our chapel is a hallowed place; many have already been saved in it.

The Journal abounds, from month to month, in such entries as these : —

"Many souls have been made free in Christ Jesus.

"This month closes with a proof that the Lord is with us, — another soul is converted.

"Another washed in the blood of the Lamb.

"Another enters into covenant with a new-found Saviour to-day."

Sketches, also, like the following, were made from time to time by the deaconesses : —

ANOTHER PATIENT HOME TO-NIGHT.

"We shall never forget how quickly and sweetly she learned to trust Jesus. Passing through the large ward one afternoon, I saw her with tears streaming down her face, and asked if she could tell me what troubled her. She said, 'O, I cannot sleep. When I shut my eyes it seems as if there was something piercing my heart; I am such a sinner.' We told her that Jesus was *waiting* to forgive her; the blood of Jesus Christ cleanseth from *all* sin ; and asked, 'Now, will you *give* yourself to him, just as you would give away anything you did not want, and trust him to save you?'

"She said, 'Yes, I will.' The next morning she said she was happy; that she slept last night; and her face wore an expression of peace that was new to her. One morning she said, 'O! I was so happy last night I awoke myself, saying the Lord's Prayer, and I finished it after I awoke; and it was so light about me. I used to think it was a dreadful thing to die; but now I am perfectly willing to go, whenever Jesus is ready to take me.' To-night he came, and she was all ready to follow him. Her history had been dark and sad. Praise to the Lamb of God, who hath made her clean in his own blood!"

GLAD TO BE BROUGHT BACK TO THE FOLD.

"About dark this evening, a new patient came. She looked pale and weary, and as she sank into a rocking-chair, exclaimed,

'Thanks to Jesus for a home again.' 'Have you given yourself
to Jesus?' was asked. 'Yes,' she replied. 'How long ago?'
'When the Doctor talked with me about it.' 'When did you
see the Doctor?' 'This afternoon, about four o'clock.' After a
little pause she added, 'If I hadn't been brought to this, I never
should have accepted his grace.' Then she told of her early
orphanage in England, of her poverty, waywardness, and wan-
dering, but seemed glad to be brought back to the fold, even
through suffering."

PUTTING ON THE WHOLE ARMOR OF GOD.

" One of the patients, who is better, and again able to work,
said to-day, 'The Lord is blessing me in every way. I have
been obeying the command, "Search the Scriptures." When I
was twelve or thirteen years old, my old grandmother offered me
a prize if I would read the Bible through. I read to Second
Kings, and then left it for years. They were years of sin; so
deep and dark that I almost tremble when I think of them. The
morning after I came here, I took up the Bible and said to myself, now, though poor old grandmother is gone, I will finish up
that job. And I read forty or fifty chapters a day, just to finish
it. And after I had read it through, something still impelled me
to read the Bible. I have read the New Testament through
three times; the Psalms twice; and now I am reading it through
again.' 'When did you begin to read it because you *loved* it?'
was asked; 'Not till after we moved to the new Home; the
first Sabbath after we came here, I arose for prayers. Last
night I awoke, and the command came to me, "Put on the
whole armor of God"; and that is ringing through my mind to-
day. O, God is blessing me so much!'"

JUST AS HAPPY AS I CAN BE.

" Dear Lewis, has left us. He said he was not a Christian
when he came to the Home. The exact time of his conversion
we do not know, unless it may be seen in this. He said that at
a certain time he *felt blue*, and went away and prayed, and *Jesus
took it all away*.

" The fruits of a great change, however, were abundantly seen.
He knew he should not recover, and hoped to go quickly. Death
approached. It was remarked, 'Lewis is going soon.' He

asked Jesus to give him an easy death. But instead of that he suffered greatly. He bore it all with sweet patience, saying, ' It is all right. Jesus wants I should show the power of religion to those around me. I am willing to have a hard death if that will glorify him ' The nurse said, ' Lewis, you are never irritable or hard to please.' He answered, ' O, I know my sickness is from the Lord and is all right.' He was full of thankfulness and praise for everything, — for *that* room, and *that* bed ; for the frequent visits of his friends, and said, ' I do not dread the spasms of distress, because Jesus is nearer to me then than at any other time.' And while in one of the spasms, he said, ' Well, I can bear it. O, I could bear *more* than this.'

" I found him one night sitting up in bed, because he could not breathe while lying down. A friend was fanning him. He beckoned me near, and said, ' I am just as happy as I can be, singing to myself everything I can think of.' He enjoyed greatly our singing to him. Once, as I saw how weak he was, I thought he must be weary, and said so ; ' O, no,' he answered, ' I could listen forty years.' When asked what we should sing; whether anything in particular ? he said, ' No; sing anything about Jesus.'

" At last, quietly and sweetly one night, at half past nine, he ceased panting for breath, and went with Jesus."

The following notes of others were made by Doctor Cullis : —

HE DOES FORGIVE.

"This morning, a nurse thought a patient who was dying spoke to her. She listened, and heard him say, ' O Jesus, forgive my sins; it is my last wish; I ask it with my dying breath.' She said, ' He will forgive you,' and repeated some promises from the Bible. He replied, ' Yes, he will forgive; he *does* forgive me ; glory to his name ! ' Soon he said, ' My limbs feel strangely; is this death ? ' The nurse told him that it was. He said, ' O, death is nothing,' and soon passed from earth."

A RESTORED ONE.

The Lord converted him, and blessed the means used for healing. A letter, written the week after

leaving the Home, tells of both salvation and gratitude : —

"*Dear Doctor Cullis*, — Being unable to obtain an interview
with you last week, I write to convey to you my heartfelt thanks
for the interest and kindness shown me in the Home.

"It was a blessed day for me that I went there; it has been
the means of saving me. The matrons, nurses, and all, have
been so kind, that no words could express what I feel.

"Please accept the humble thanks of one who wishes you
every prosperity in the 'Work,' that its usefulness may be increased more and more.   "Yours sincerely,
                                                    "R. C."

PEACE IN JESUS.

"Another weary soul has found its resting-place in Jesus.
He is failing rapidly, and cannot have long to stay with us.
To-day he said, 'I have some one with me now.' The nurse
said, 'Jesus?' He answered, 'Yes; I wish I had had him be-
fore.' And afterwards whispered, 'Peace in Jesus; peace in
Jesus.'"

JESUS IS MINE.

"Praise to Jesus that another patient has been so sweetly converted! Last night a man called the night-watcher to tell her
that he had found Jesus! She said, 'No matter what comes
then, life or death, you are safe.' 'Yes,' he replied; 'I am safe,
but I want to live to *praise* him.' This morning, when I went
through the ward, I said, 'How do you do, this morning?' Said
he, 'I am *happy*.' I said, 'Now you can say, Jesus is mine.'
'Yes,' said he; 'O, how wonderful! when I had been such a
sinner al my life, that he should call after me. And he came
so suddenly; and everything seemed so bright! Now I hope
he'll *keep* me.' 'He will keep you so long as you *trust* him.'
'Well, that will be *forever*.'"

JESUS IS THINKING OF ME.

"Another sweet testimony must not be withheld. It is that
of a patient who lately died. His last day, with the exception
of a few intervals, was passed in unconsciousness. Seeing a look
of returning intelligence, one asked, 'Are you thinking of Jesus,
to-day?' His reply was, '*When I am conscious. I am thinking of
Jesus: when I am unconscious Jesus is thinking of me.*'"

Here was a man who, within a few weeks, had not only learned that he was accepted, pardoned, and saved, but that the loving Saviour was watching over him when he was not thinking of the Saviour at all ; a great and glorious reality, which, if fully understood by all Christians, would go far to free them from doubts and fears, and fill them with abiding peace and joy in the Lord.

Thus through the eighth year, and through all the years of the work, has the power of the Spirit rested upon and abode in the Home as its crowning glory.

The same is true of every branch of the work. Of no other is it more blessedly so than of that which has led to confident expectation of the opening very soon of a new and important department, namely : —

FAITH CHAPEL AND TRAINING-COLLEGE.

In the sixth year of the work, a precious witness for Jesus as a present Saviour from sin, of another city, visited Boston on business, and as one of the many wayside services given him of the Lord, met a little company of Christians, hungering and thirsting for righteousness, in Doctor Cullis's parlor. The meeting was so precious that Doctor Cullis continued it from week to week on Tuesday afternoon. It grew in numbers and power steadily until the place was overcrowded. When the Lord gave Doctor Cullis his present residence, No. 16 Somerset Street, the large double parlor, called in England the drawing-room, was given up and furnished exclusively as a chapel for the Tuesday meeting. This room, though double the size of the former one, soon filled up and overflowed, and the passageways and stairways were occupied. Many, even ladies, who could not be seated, preferred to remain, though compelled to stand through the entire time, and not a few, for want of room, went away. Strangers from far and near, visiting Boston, sought out and attended these meetings. Ministers of all denominations and from distant places, in considerable numbers frequented it.

All this, however, would have been little indeed, but for the crowning glory of the meetings, the crowning glory of the work, the power of the Spirit manifested in all. Ministers and people were blessed from week to week. Not a few of the dear chosen servants of the Lord, like the eloquent Apollos, taught in the home of Aquila and Priscilla, learned in the home of Doctor Cullis *the way of the Lord more perfectly.* Souls also were converted there. Testimonies to these facts came out frequently in the meetings, and yet more so in letters and personal conversation.

To accommodate the growing numbers, Doctor Cullis asked the Lord for a larger place, and made various efforts to secure one and failed. Gathering from this that it might be the Lord's will to give him a chapel, by purchase or building, he began asking for means for the purpose. At the same time the desire sprang up in his heart to have a Faith Training-college for Christian workers in connection with a chapel, and this was included in his prayers.

Very soon a brother gave him five dollars, and shortly after that another gave him five hundred dollars, and another also gave him five hundred, and still another twenty-five dollars.

Thus began the gifts of the Lord toward this new branch of the work, and although it is not yet opened, the contributions have reached an amount sufficient to encourage the faith of Doctor Cullis to ask for the place where it shall be, and look in confidence to find it, and to receive the necessary gifts to purchase or build, and open both chapel and college at an early day in the future.

The twofold hope is to have a place open, not only from Tuesday to Tuesday, but every day of the week, where Christians from far and near may come and be taught the way of holiness as an experimental verity for themselves. And also where men and women who desire to teach and to work for Christ in fullness of personal consecration, and experimental union with Jesus, in any and every department of Christian labor, may come and learn the way of faith for themselves, and be thoroughly taught in the word of God, and fully trained in the way of teaching others, and of doing various kinds of Christian work.

The field is the world, the harvest is great, the laborers are few, and the prayer is that the Lord of the harvest will raise up a multitude who shall enter the field as workmen, needing not to be ashamed, and gather in the golden grain which is daily falling to the ground ungathered.

The great want of the church to-day is full salvation. The great want of the world is a church filled with faith and the Holy Ghost, sending forth its men and women in the fullness of the blessings of the gospel, that by them God may work his wonderful works for the benefit and salvation of all whom the Lord our God shall call; and the fervent prayer of Doctor Cullis is that the Lord will, in addition to the work now in his hands, and with all the vantage ground it gives as a known work of faith, and all the opportunity it affords for both teaching and training, bestow whatever is necessary, and create a blessed centre of salvation, and multiply qualified Christian workers for all fields of the ripened harvest. God speed him in his prayer, and do for him exceeding abundantly above all he can ask or think according to the power that worketh in us. And now unto him be all the glory, world without end. Amen.

NEW WING TO THE CONSUMPTIVES' HOME.

As these last pages are going to press, ground has been broken for a new wing to the Consumptives' Home. It is planned to accommodate thirty more patients. The women's wards have been full some time, and many have applied and been refused for want of room. This caused Doctor Cullis to ask the Lord for means to build a new wing. The answer to this prayer was not long delayed. A friend who had incidentally heard about it, called and asked the Doctor how much it would cost? And when told said, " Well, I will give you five thousand dollars towards it." Dr. Cullis thanked God and began at once to secure plans and proposals, and the work is now in progress. At least twenty-five hundred dollars more will be required to finish it, besides the furnishing and the daily expense it will add ; but the work will go forward as far and as fast as the Lord sends the means

ND - #0034 - 210922 - C0 - 229/152/17 [19] - CB - 9780331774702 - Gloss Lamination